JAPANESE

in 10 minutes a day®

by Kristine Kershul, M.A., University of California, Santa Barbara

Consultants: Shaun and Yukari Doig
Jeffrey Sievert

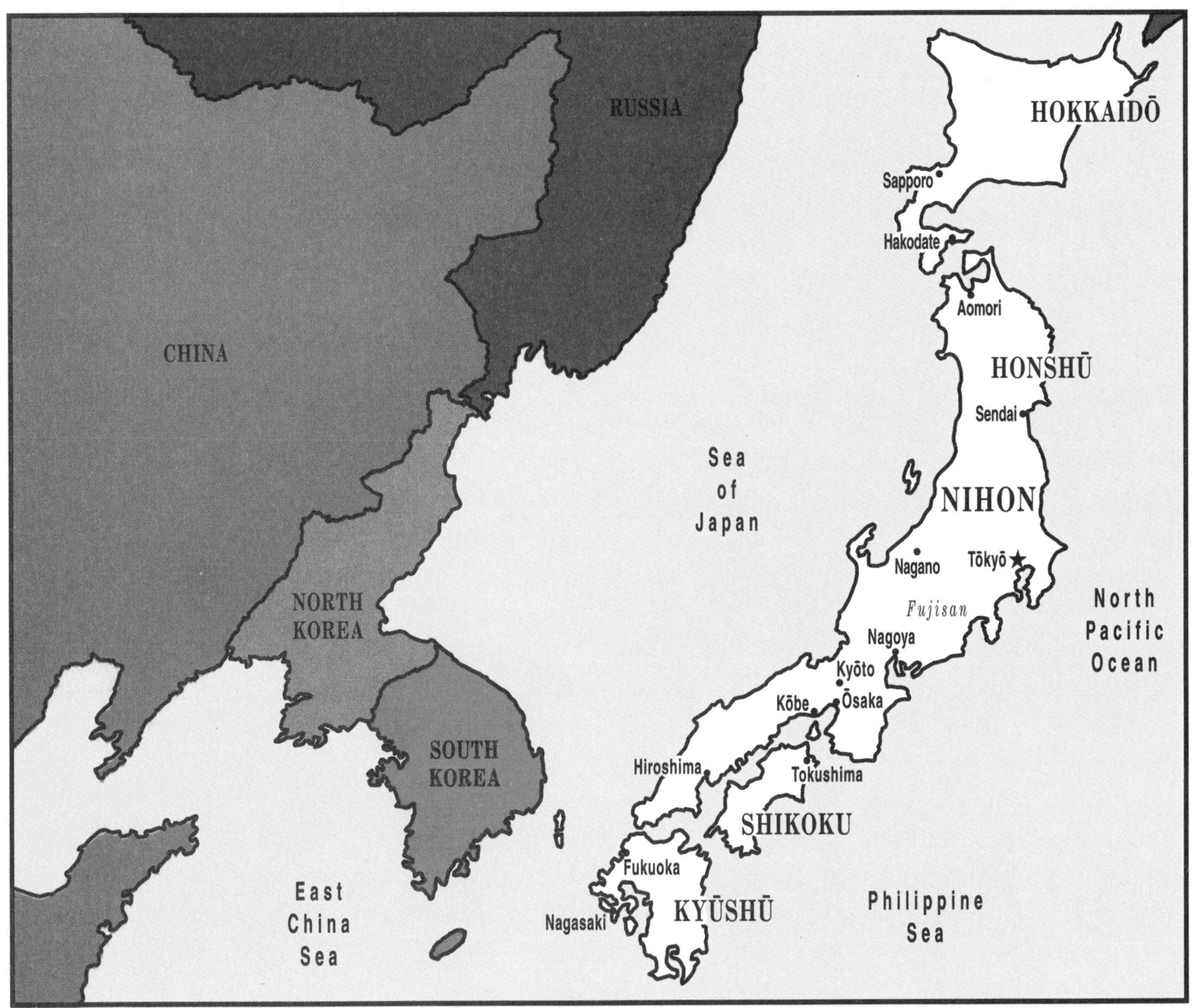

Bilingual Books, Inc.
1719 West Nickerson Street, Seattle, WA 98119
Tel: (206) 284-4211 Fax: (206) 284-3660
www.10minutesaday.com

Second printing, May 2003

 ISBN 0-944502-36-9

Can you say this?

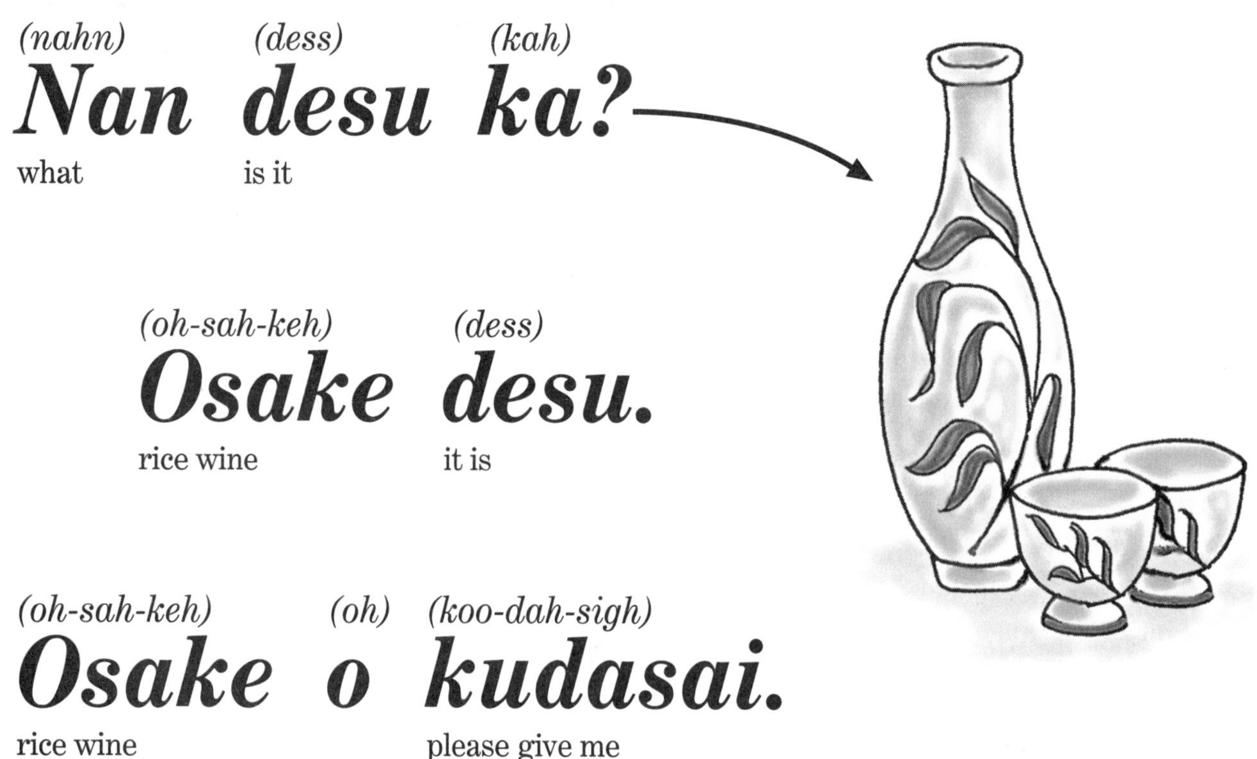

(nahn) *(dess)* *(kah)*
Nan desu ka?
what is it

(oh-sah-keh) *(dess)*
Osake desu.
rice wine it is

(oh-sah-keh) *(oh)* *(koo-dah-sigh)*
Osake o kudasai.
rice wine please give me

If you can say this, you can learn to speak Japanese. You will be able to easily order wine, lunch, theater tickets, tea, or anything else you wish. With your best Japanese accent, you simply ask **"Nan desu ka?"** *(nahn) (dess) (kah)* and, upon learning what it is, you can order it with **"Sore o kudasai,"** *(soh-reh) (oh) (koo-dah-sigh)*. Sounds easy, doesn't it?

The purpose of this book is to give you an **immediate** speaking ability in Japanese. Using the acclaimed "*10 minutes a day*®" methodology, you will acquire a large working vocabulary that will suit your needs, and you will acquire it almost automatically. To aid you, this book offers a unique and easy system of pronunciation above each word which walks you through learning Japanese.

If you are planning a trip or moving to where Japanese is spoken, you will be leaps ahead of everyone if you take just a few minutes a day to learn the easy key words that this book offers. Start with Step 1 and don't skip around. Each day work as far as you can comfortably go in those 10 minutes. Don't overdo it. Some days you might want to just review. If you forget a word, you can always look it up in the glossary. Spend your first 10 minutes studying the map on the previous page. And yes, have fun learning your new language.

As you work through the Steps, always use the special features which only this series offers. This book contains sticky labels and flash cards, free words, puzzles and quizzes. When you have completed this book, cut out the menu guide and take it along on your trip.

1 *(ah-roo-fah-bet-toh)* Arufabetto
(the) alphabet

The Japanese language consists of three different sets of characters: *kanji, katakana* and *hiragana*. Traditionally, the language was written vertically using these pictographs although today it is not uncommon to find books written horizontally as well. **JAPANESE *in 10 minutes a day*®** helps you learn Japanese by starting with **rōmaji** *(rōh-mah-jee)*. **Rōmaji** is a widely-used system of spelling Japanese using the Roman alphabet.

Throughout this book you will find an easy pronunciation guide above all new words. Japanese pronunciation is very easy for English speakers. For example, the following letters are pronounced just as they are in English so you do not need to spend any extra time on them.

(b) **b**	*(d)* **d**	*(f)* **f**	*(g)* **g**	*(k)* **k**	*(m)* **m**	*(n)* **n**	*(p)* **p**	*(s)* **s**	*(t)* **t**	*(w)* **w**	*(z)* **z**

Here is a guide to help you learn the sounds of the other Japanese letters. Practice these sounds with the examples given which are mostly areas or places you might wish to visit. Remember you can always refer back to these pages if you need a review.

Vowels which have a macron or bar over them **(ā, ē, ī, ō, ū)** are called long vowels. When pronouncing these letters draw out the sound. This contrasts with the vowels which do not have the bar and are pronounced in a rather clipped or shorter fashion.

Japanese letter	English sound	Examples	*Write it here*
a	ah	**Nagano** *(nah-gah-noh)*	
ā	āh	**Tōkyō tawā** *(tōh-kyōh)(tah-wāh)*	
ai	eye/ai/I	**Aichi** *(eye-chee)*	
ch	ch	**Chichibu** *(chee-chee-boo)*	
e	*(as in let)* eh	**Kōbe** *(kōh-beh)*	
ē	ēh	**Supēsu wārudo** *(soo-pēh-soo)(wāh-roo-doh)* Space World	
ei	*(as in day)* ay	**Meiji jingū** *(may-jee)(jeen-gōō)* shrine	
i	ee	**Hiroshima** *(hee-roh-shee-mah)*	
ii	ēē	**Niigata** *(nēē-gah-tah)*	
ī	ēē	**Tōkyō Dizunī rando** *(tōh-kyōh)(dee-zoo-nēē)(rahn-doh)* Disneyland	
j	*(as in jeep)* j	**Fujisan** *(foo-jee-sahn)* Mt. Fuji	
o	oh	**Okinawa** *(oh-kee-nah-wah)*	
ō	ōh	**Kyōto** *(kyōh-toh)*	
oi	*(as in toy)* oy	**Oiwake** *(oy-wah-keh)*	
r	*(slightly rolled)* r	**Nara** *(nah-rah)*	

Letter	Sound	Example	*Write it here*
tsu	*(t + the name Sue)* tsu	**Ōtsu** *(ōh-tsoo)* or *(ōh-tsue)*	
u	oo	**Fukuoka** *(foo-koo-oh-kah)*	
ū	o͞o	**Honshū** *(hohn-sho͞o)*	
y	*(as in you)* y	**Yokohama** *(yoh-koh-hah-mah)*	

Note:

- Japanese does not distinguish between singular and plural. You don't need to learn any complicated systems for making nouns plural. *(hohn)* **Hon** could mean "one book" or "many books." You can usually determine this from the context of the sentence.

- As Japanese is written in pictograms, there are no capitals. *(rōh-mah-jee)* **Rōmaji** will be seen both with and without capitals. Either way is correct.

- Japanese has many "particle words," such as *(wah)* **wa,** (P) *(gah)* **ga,** (P) *(oh)* **o,** (P) *(nee)* **ni** (P) and *(toh)* **to**. (P) Often, particle words cannot be translated into English. When these particle words have no English equivalents, they will simply be marked (P).

- Don't be surprised if you see words written sometimes with a hyphen, sometimes as separate words or sometimes joined together as one word. All are acceptable.

- Both "**ii**" and "**ī**" are pronounced "e͞e." The "**ī**" indicates this is a loan word in the Japanese language. For example, *(kōh-he͞e)* "**kōhī**" (coffee) and *(be͞e-roo)* "**bīru.**" (beer)

- Your *(tsoo)* "**tsu**" sound is fundamental to Japanese so practice it with words such as *(ee-tsoo)* "**itsu,**" (when) *(nah-tsoo)* "**natsu,**" (summer) *(tsoo-kee)* "**tsuki**" (month) and *(ee-koo-tsoo)* "**ikutsu.**" (how many)

- Your *(eye)* "**ai**" sound as in *(dye-doh-koh-roh)* "**daidokoro,**" (kitchen) will frequently be seen in the phonetics as the English "dye" to make it easier for you.

Japanese pronunciation is very simple. If at any time the phonetics seem to contradict your pronunciation guide, don't panic! The easiest and best phonetics have been chosen for each individual word. If there is a word in English which reflects the sound in Japanese, we will use that word to make it even easier for you to pronounce. Pronounce the phonetics just as you see them. Don't over-analyze them. Speak slowly and clearly and, above all, enjoy yourself!

2 Key Question Words

When you arrive in **Nihon** (nee-hohn) [Japan], the very first thing you will need to do is ask questions — "Where (**doko**) (doh-koh) [where] is the bus stop?" "**Doko** (doh-koh) [where] can I exchange money?" "**Doko** is the lavatory?" "**Doko** is a restaurant?" "**Doko** do I catch a taxi?" "**Doko** is a good hotel?" "**Doko** is my luggage?" — and the list will go on and on for the entire length of your visit. In Japanese, there are EIGHT KEY QUESTION WORDS to learn. For example, the eight key question words will help you find out exactly what you are ordering in a restaurant before you order it — and not after the surprise (or shock!) arrives. These **tango** (tahn-goh) [words] are extremely important, so learn them now. Take a few minutes to study and practice saying the eight key question words listed below. Then cover the Japanese with your hand and fill in each of the blanks with the matching Japanese **tango** (tahn-goh) [word].

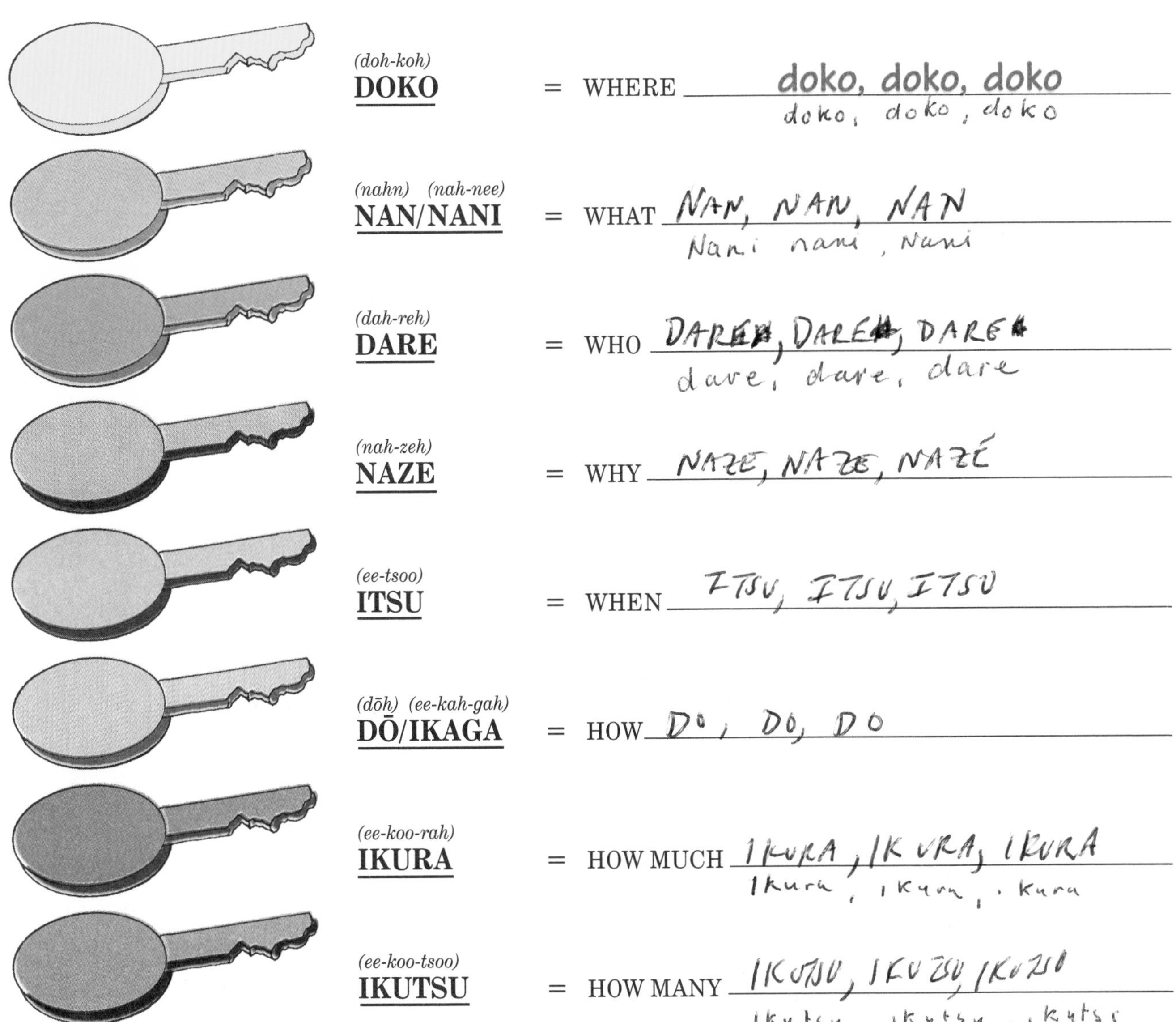

(doh-koh) **DOKO** = WHERE doko, doko, doko

(nahn) (nah-nee) **NAN/NANI** = WHAT ____________

(dah-reh) **DARE** = WHO ____________

(nah-zeh) **NAZE** = WHY ____________

(ee-tsoo) **ITSU** = WHEN ____________

(dōh) (ee-kah-gah) **DŌ/IKAGA** = HOW ____________

(ee-koo-rah) **IKURA** = HOW MUCH ____________

(ee-koo-tsoo) **IKUTSU** = HOW MANY ____________

Now test yourself to see if you really can keep these **tango** *(tahn-goh)* (words) straight in your mind. Draw lines between the Japanese **to** *(toh)* (and) English equivalents below.

Examine the following questions containing these **tango** *(tahn-goh)* (words). Practice the sentences out loud **to** *(toh)* (and) then practice by copying the Japanese in the blanks underneath each question.

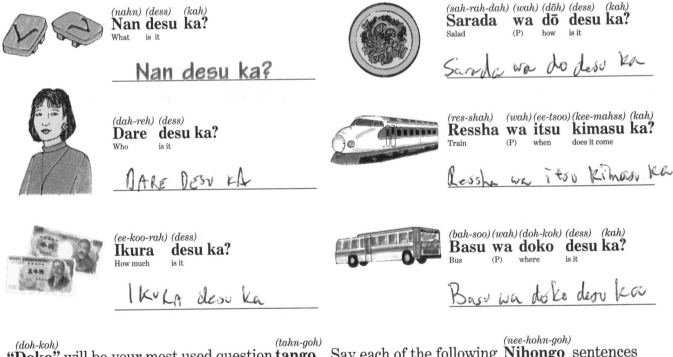

(nahn) (dess) (kah)
Nan desu ka?
What is it

(dah-reh) (dess)
Dare desu ka?
Who is it

(ee-koo-rah) (dess)
Ikura desu ka?
How much is it

(sah-rah-dah) (wah) (dōh) (dess) (kah)
Sarada wa dō desu ka?
Salad (P) how is it

(res-shah) (wah) (ee-tsoo) (kee-mahss) (kah)
Ressha wa itsu kimasu ka?
Train (P) when does it come

(bah-soo) (wah) (doh-koh) (dess) (kah)
Basu wa doko desu ka?
Bus (P) where is it

"Doko" *(doh-koh)* will be your most used question **tango** *(tahn-goh)* (word). Say each of the following **Nihongo** *(nee-hohn-goh)* (Japanese) sentences aloud. Then write out each sentence without looking at the example. If you don't succeed on the first try, don't give up. Just practice each sentence until you are able to do it easily.

Remember **"desu"** is pronounced "*dess,*" and **"i"** is always "*ee.*"

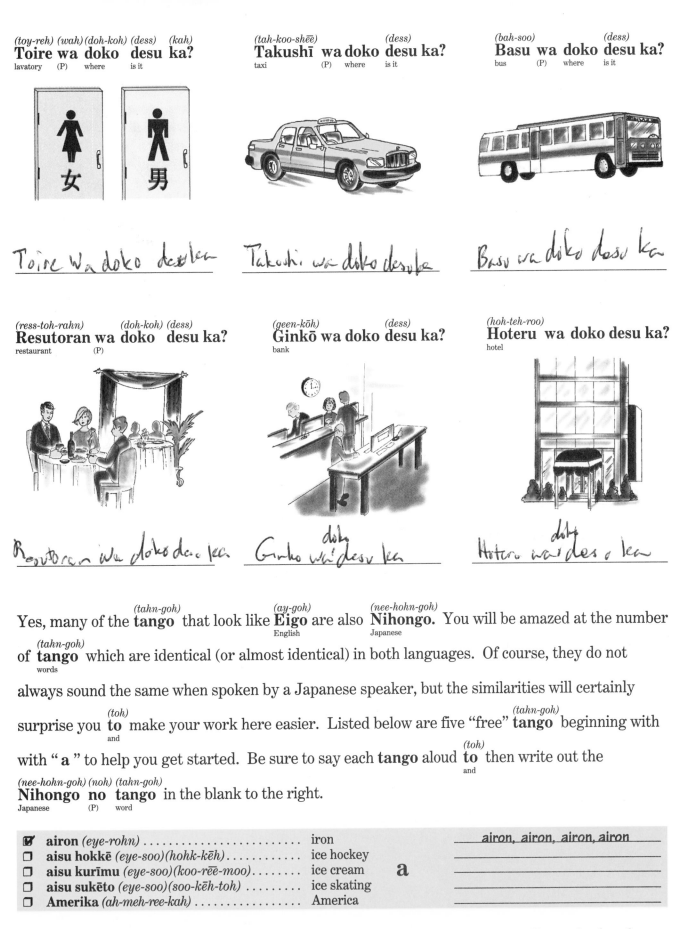

(toy-reh) (wah) (doh-koh) (dess) (kah)
Toire wa doko desu ka?
lavatory (P) where is it

Toire Wa doko desuka

(tah-koo-shēē) (dess)
Takushī wa doko desu ka?
taxi (P) where is it

Takushi wa doko desuka

(bah-soo) (dess)
Basu wa doko desu ka?
bus (P) where is it

Basu wa doko desu ka

(ress-toh-rahn) (doh-koh) (dess)
Resutoran wa doko desu ka?
restaurant (P)

Resutoran Wa doko desu ka

(geen-kōh) (dess)
Ginkō wa doko desu ka?
bank

Ginko wa doko desu ka

(hoh-teh-roo)
Hoteru wa doko desu ka?
hotel

Hoteru wa doko desu ka

Yes, many of the **tango** *(tahn-goh)* that look like **Eigo** *(ay-goh)* (English) are also **Nihongo.** *(nee-hohn-goh)* (Japanese) You will be amazed at the number of **tango** *(tahn-goh)* (words) which are identical (or almost identical) in both languages. Of course, they do not always sound the same when spoken by a Japanese speaker, but the similarities will certainly surprise you **to** *(toh)* (and) make your work here easier. Listed below are five "free" **tango** *(tahn-goh)* beginning with with " **a** " to help you get started. Be sure to say each **tango** aloud **to** *(toh)* (and) then write out the **Nihongo no tango** *(nee-hohn-goh) (noh) (tahn-goh)* (Japanese (P) word) in the blank to the right.

☑ **airon** *(eye-rohn)*	iron	**a**	airon, airon, airon, airon
❐ **aisu hokkē** *(eye-soo)(hohk-kēh)*	ice hockey		
❐ **aisu kurīmu** *(eye-soo)(koo-rēē-moo)*	ice cream		
❐ **aisu sukēto** *(eye-soo)(soo-kēh-toh)*	ice skating		
❐ **Amerika** *(ah-meh-ree-kah)*	America		

Free **tango** like these will appear at the bottom of the following pages in a yellow color band.

They are easy — enjoy them! Remember, **"oi"** is pronounced "oy."

3 Odds 'n Ends

Nihongo *(nee-hohn-goh)* [Japanese] does not have **tango** *(tahn-goh)* [words] for "the" and "a." Instead **kono,** *(koh-noh)* [this] **sono** *(soh-noh)* [that] and **ano** *(ah-noh)* [that over there] are used. These **tango** reflect the object's distance from the speaker.

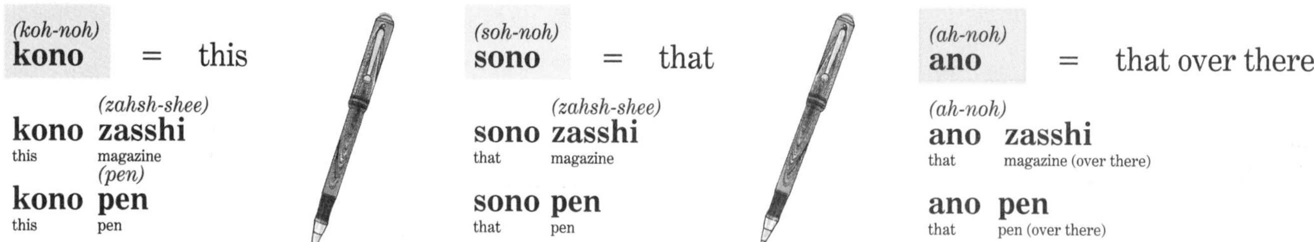

kono *(koh-noh)* = this

kono zasshi *(zahsh-shee)* — this magazine

kono pen *(pen)* — this pen

sono *(soh-noh)* = that

sono zasshi *(zahsh-shee)* — that magazine

sono pen — that pen

ano *(ah-noh)* = that over there

ano zasshi *(ah-noh)* — that magazine (over there)

ano pen — that pen (over there)

Nihongo has "measure words" for everything. **Mai** *(my)* [thin, flat] is used with words like paper and stamp. **Hon** *(hohn)* [long, cylindrical] is used with words like pen and pencil. **Satsu** *(sah-tsoo)* [bound together] is used with words like book and magazine. Throughout **kono** [this] **hon,** *(hohn)* [book] measure words will be marked (M). Here are some examples.

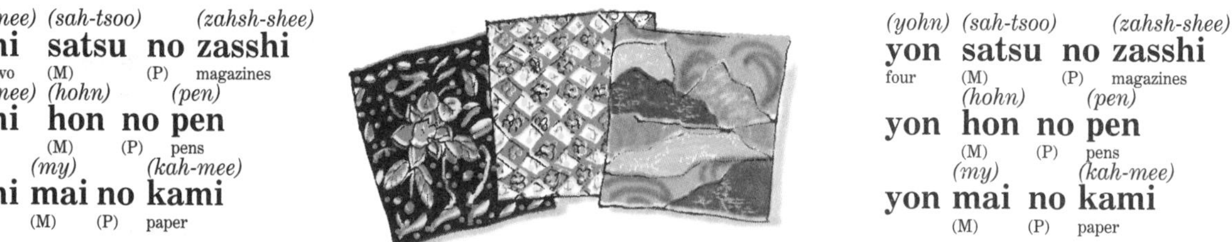

ni satsu no zasshi *(nee) (sah-tsoo) (zahsh-shee)* — two (M) (P) magazines

ni hon no pen *(nee) (hohn) (pen)* — (M) (P) pens

ni mai no kami *(my) (kah-mee)* — (M) (P) paper

yon satsu no zasshi *(yohn) (sah-tsoo) (zahsh-shee)* — four (M) (P) magazines

yon hon no pen *(hohn) (pen)* — (M) (P) pens

yon mai no kami *(my) (kah-mee)* — (M) (P) paper

All these measure words and particle words might appear difficult, but only because they are different from **Eigo.** *(ay-goh)* [English] Just remember you will be understood whether you say **"ni hon no pen"** *(nee)(hohn)* [(M) (P)] or **"ni mai no pen."** *(my)* [(M) (P)] Soon you will automatically select the right one without even thinking about it.

In Step 2 you were introduced to the Key Question Words. These words are the basics, the most essential building blocks for learning Japanese. Throughout this book you will come across keys asking you to fill in the missing question word. Use this opportunity not only to fill in the blank on that key, but to review all your question words.

a

- ❒ **anaunsā** *(ah-noun-sāh)* .... announcer ____________
- ❒ **apāto** *(ah-pāh-toh)* .... apartment ____________
- ❒ **appuru pai** *(ahp-poo-roo)(pie)* .... apple pie ____________
- ❒ **arubamu** *(ah-roo-bah-moo)* .... album ____________
- ❒ **asuparagasu** *(ah-soo-pah-rah-gah-soo)* .... asparagus ____________

4 Look Around You

Before you proceed with this Step, situate yourself comfortably in your living room. Now look around you. Can you name the **mono** *(moh-noh)* things that you see in this **heya** *(heh-yah)* room in **Nihongo** *(nee-hohn-goh)* Japanese? You can probably guess **sofā** *(soh-fāh)* sofa and maybe even **tēburu.** *(tēh-boo-roo)* table Let's learn the rest of them. After practicing these **tango** *(tahn-goh)* out loud, write them in the blanks below.

ranpu *(rahn-poo)* (the) lamp ranpu, ranpu, ranpu

sofā *(soh-fāh)* (the) sofa sofa, sofa, sofa

isu *(ee-soo)* (the) chair isu, isu, isu

kāpetto *(kāh-pet-toh)* (the) carpet kapetto, kapetto, kapetto

tēburu *(tēh-boo-roo)* (the) table teburu, teburu, teburu

doa *(doh-ah)* (the) door doa, doa, doa

tokei *(toh-kay)* (the) clock tokei, tokei, tokei

kāten *(kāh-ten)* (the) curtain katen, katen, katen

denwa *(den-wah)* (the) telephone denwa, denwa, denwa

mado *(mah-doh)* (the) window ____________

e *(eh)* (the) picture ____________

Remember **Nihongo** *(nee-hohn-goh)* Japanese does not have words for "the" and "a." Now open your **hon** *(hohn)* book to the sticky labels on page 17 and later on page 35. Peel off the first 11 labels and proceed around the **heya** *(heh-yah)* room labeling these items in your home. This will help to increase your **Nihongo** *(nee-hohn-goh)* word power easily. Don't forget to say each **tango** *(tahn-goh)* word as you attach the label.

Now ask yourself, **"Ranpu** *(rahn-poo)* lamp **wa** (P) **doko** where **desu ka?"** *(dess)* is it and point at it while you answer, **"Ranpu** *(rahn-poo)* lamp **wa** (P) **soko** *(soh-koh)* there **desu."** *(dess)* it is Continue on down the list above until you feel comfortable with these new **tango.**

❒ **badominton** *(bah-doh-meen-tohn)*	badminton	**b**	____________
❒ **banana** *(bah-nah-nah)*	banana		____________
❒ **basu** *(bah-soo)*	bus		____________
❒ **basukettobōru** *(bah-soo-ket-toh-bōh-roo)*	basketball		____________
❒ **batā** *(bah-tāh)*	butter		____________

(ee-eh)
ie = the house

(ee-eh) *(wah)* *(soh-koh)* *(dess)*
Ie wa soko desu.
house (P) there it is

(shoh-sigh)
shosai
office, study

(foo-roh-bah)(yoh-koo-shee-tsoo)
furoba / yokushitsu
bathroom

(dye-doh-koh-roh)
daidokoro
kitchen

(sheen-shee-tsoo)
shinshitsu
bedroom

(die-neen-goo)
dainingu
dining room

(ee-mah)
ima
living room

(shah-koh) *(gah-rēh-jee)*
shako / garēji
garage

(chee-kah-shee-tsoo)
chikashitsu
basement

While learning these new **tango,** *(tahn-goh)* (words) let's not forget:

(jee-dōh-shah) *(koo-roo-mah)*
jidōsha / kuruma
automobile, car

____

(ōh-toh-by)
ōtobai
motorcycle

____

(jee-ten-shah)
jitensha
bicycle

____

b

- ❒ **batterī** *(baht-teh-rēē)* .... battery ________________
- ❒ **beddo** *(bed-doh)* .... bed ________________
- ❒ **bēkon** *(bēh-kohn)* .... bacon ________________
- ❒ **bēsubōru** *(bēh-soo-bōh-roo)* .... baseball ________________
- ❒ **bīfusutēki** *(bēē-foo-stēh-kee)* .... beefsteak ________________

(neh-koh)
neko
cat

(nee-wah)
niwa
garden, yard

(hah-nah)
hana
flowers

niwa, niwa, niwa

(ee-noo)
inu
dog

(pohss-toh)
posuto
mailbox

(yōō-bean)
yūbin
mail

Peel off the next set of labels and wander through your **ie** *(ee-eh)* [house] learning these **atarashii** *(ah-tah-rah-shēē)* [new] **tango.** *(tahn-goh)* [words]

It will be somewhat difficult to label your **neko,** *(neh-koh)* [cat] **hana** *(hah-nah)* [flowers] or **inu** *(ee-noo)* [dog] but be creative. Practice by asking yourself, "**Neko** *(neh-koh)* [cat] **wa** [(P)] **doko** [where] **desu ka?**" *(dess)* [is it] and reply, "**Neko** *(neh-koh)* [cat] **wa soko** [there] **desu.**" *(dess)* [it is]

(ee-eh) *(dess)*
Ie wa doko desu ka?

❒ **bīru** *(bēē-roo)*	beer	**b**	________
❒ **bijinesuman** *(bee-jee-neh-soo-mahn)*	businessman		________
❒ **bitamin** *(bee-tah-meen)*	vitamin		________
❒ **botan** *(boh-tahn)*	button		________
❒ **burēki** *(boo-rēh-kee)*	brake		________

5 Ichi, Ni, San!

(ee-chee) (nee) (sahn)
Ichi, Ni, San!
one two three

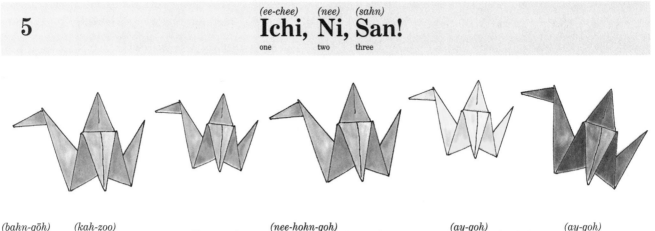

Bangō, *(bahn-gōh)* [numbers] or **kazu,** *(kah-zoo)* [numbers] are used differently in **Nihongo** *(nee-hohn-goh)* [Japanese] than they are in **Eigo.** *(ay-goh)* [English] Unlike in **Eigo,** *(ay-goh)* [English] months in **Nihongo** *(nee-hohn-goh)* [Japanese] are indicated by numbers. For example, **ichi** *(ee-chee)* [first] **gatsu** *(gah-tsoo)* [month] means January in **Nihongo.** *(nee-hohn-goh)* [Japanese] When practicing the numbers below, notice the similarities between **shi** *(shee)* (4) and **jūshi** *(jōō-shee)* (14), **shichi** *(shee-chee)* (7) and **jūshichi** *(jōō-shee-chee)* (17) and so on.

0	*(zeh-roh) (ray)* **zero / rei**	
1	*(ee-chee)* **ichi**	
2	*(nee)* **ni**	
3	*(sahn)* **san**	
4	*(yohn) (shee)* **yon / shi**	
5	*(goh)* **go**	
6	*(roh-koo)* **roku**	
7	*(nah-nah) (shee-chee)* **nana / shichi**	
8	*(hah-chee)* **hachi**	
9	*(kyōō) (koo)* **kyū / ku**	
10	*(jōō)* **jū**	

10	*(jōō)* **jū**	
11	*(jōō-ee-chee)* **jūichi**	
12	*(jōō-nee)* **jūni**	
13	*(jōō-sahn)* **jūsan**	
14	*(jōō-yohn) (jōō-shee)* **jūyon / jūshi**	
15	*(jōō-goh)* **jūgo**	
16	*(jōō-roh-koo)* **jūroku**	
17	*(jōō-nah-nah) (jōō-shee-chee)* **jūnana / jūshichi**	
18	*(jōō-hah-chee)* **jūhachi**	
19	*(jōō-kyōō) (jōō-koo)* **jūkyū / jūku**	
20	*(nee-jōō)* **nijū**	

C

- ☑ **channeru** *(chahn-neh-roo)* . . . . channel — channeru, channeru, channeru
- ☐ **chekku** *(chek-koo)* . . . . check (verify)
- ☐ **chesu** *(cheh-soo)* . . . . chess
- ☐ **chikin** *(chee-keen)* . . . . chicken
- ☐ **chīzu** *(chēē-zoo)* . . . . cheese

Use these (bahn-gōh) **bangō** (numbers) on a daily basis. Count to yourself in Japanese when you brush your teeth, exercise or commute to work. Fill in the blanks below according to the (bahn-gōh) **bangō** (numbers) given in parentheses. (bahn-gōh) **Bangō** change slightly depending on what they refer to. Always listen for the core of the word. Now is also a good time to learn the following **tango.**

(koo-dah-sigh)
kudasai kudasai, kudasai, kudasai
please/please give me

(hah-gah-kee) (oh) **Hagaki o** _______ (1) (my) (koo-dah-sigh) **mai kudasai.**		(nahn) (my) **Nan mai?** _______ (1)
postcard (P) sheets (M) please give me		how many (M)
(keet-teh) (oh) **Kitte o** _______ (7) (my) (koo-dah-sigh) **mai kudasai.**		**Nan** (my) **mai?** _______ (7)
stamp (P) (M) please give me		(M)
(keet-teh) **Kitte o** _______ (8) (my) (koo-dah-sigh) **mai kudasai.**		**Nan** (my) **mai?** _______ (8)
stamp (P) (M)		(M)
(keet-teh) **Kitte o** _______ (5) (my) **mai kudasai.**		**Nan mai?** _______ (5)
(P) (M)		(M)
(hah-gah-kee) **Hagaki o** _______ (9) (my) **mai kudasai.**		**Nan mai?** _______ (9)
postcard (P) (M)		(M)
(hah-gah-kee) **Hagaki o** _______ (10) **mai kudasai.**		**Nan mai?** _______ (10)
(P) (M)		(M)
(keep-poo) **Kippu o** _______ (1) **mai kudasai.**		**Nan mai?** _______ (1)
ticket (P) (M)		(M)
(keep-poo) **Kippu o** _______ (4) **mai kudasai.**		**Nan mai?** _______ (4)
(P) (M)		(M)
(keep-poo) **Kippu o** _______ (11) **mai kudasai.**		**Nan mai?** _______ (11)
(P) (M)		(M)
(bēē-roo) **Bīru o** _______ (3) (by) **bai kudasai.**		**Nan** (by) **bai?** _______ (3)
beer (P) glasses (M)		(M)
(bēē-roo) **Bīru o** _______ (4) (by) **bai kudasai.**		(how many) _______ (4)
(P) (M)		

- ❒ **daiyamondo** *(die-yah-mohn-doh)* .... diamond
- ❒ **dekorēshon** *(deh-koh-rēh-shohn)* .... decoration
- ❒ **demo** *(deh-moh)* .... demonstration
- ❒ **depāto** *(deh-pāh-toh)* .... department store
- ❒ **dezain** *(deh-zine)* .... design

d

Now see if you can translate the following thoughts into **Nihongo.** *(nee-hohn-goh)* Japanese **Kotae** *(koh-tah-eh)* (the) answers are provided upside down at the bottom of the **pēji.** *(pēh-jee)* page Do your best.

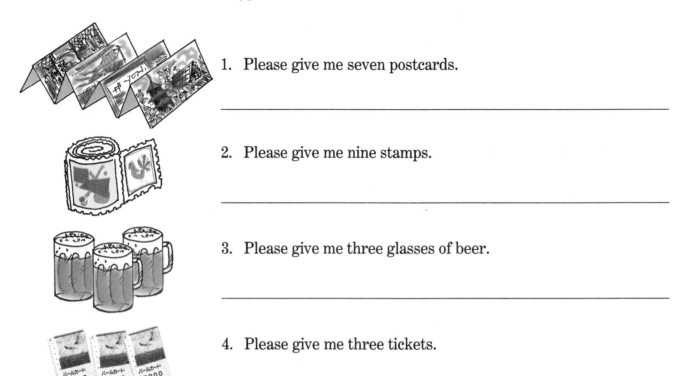

1. Please give me seven postcards.

____

2. Please give me nine stamps.

____

3. Please give me three glasses of beer.

____

4. Please give me three tickets.

____

Review **bangō** *(bahn-gōh)* 1 through 20. Write out your telephone number, fax number, and cellular number. Then write out a friend's telephone number and a relative's telephone number.

(2 0 6) 3 4 0 — 4 4 2 2

ni zero roku ______________________________

(_ _) _ _ _ — _ _ _ _

____

(_ _) _ _ _ — _ _ _ _

____

KOTAE

1. Hagaki o nana mai kudasai.
2. Kitte o kyū mai kudasai.
3. Bīru o san bai kudasai.
4. Kippu o san mai kudasai.

6 *(ee-roh)* Iro colors

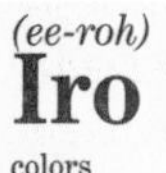

(ee-roh) **Iro** (colors) are the same in *(nee-hohn)* **Nihon** (Japan) as they are in the United States — they just have different *(nah-mah-eh)* **namae.** (names) You can easily recognize *(oh-ren-jee)* **orenji** as orange and *(peen-koo)* **pinku** as pink. Let's learn the basic *(ee-roh)* **iro** (colors) so when you are invited to someone's *(ee-eh)* **ie** (house) and you want to bring flowers, you will be able to order the color you want. Once you've learned the *(ee-roh)* **iro,** quiz yourself. What color are your shoes? Your eyes? Your hair? Your house?

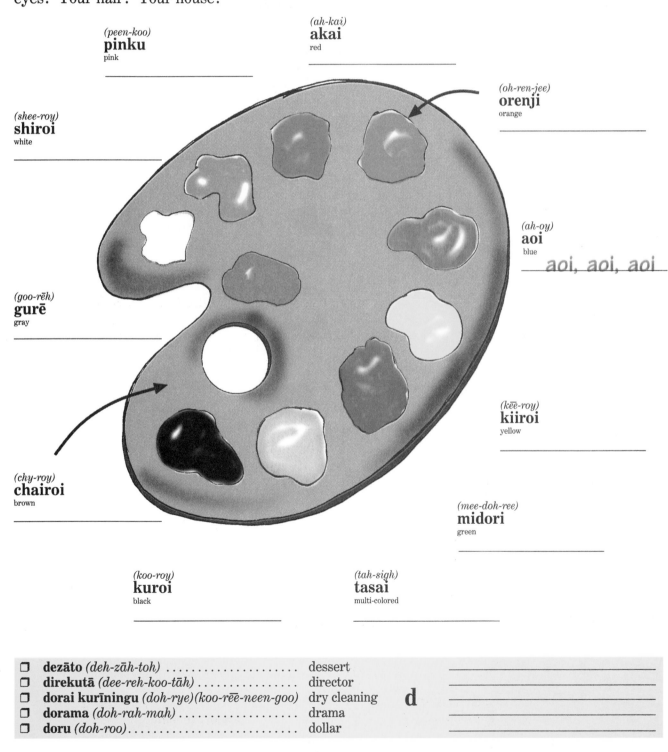

(peen-koo) **pinku** pink ____________

(ah-kai) **akai** red ____________

(oh-ren-jee) **orenji** orange ____________

(shee-roy) **shiroi** white ____________

(ah-oy) **aoi** blue aoi, aoi, aoi

(goo-rēh) **gurē** gray ____________

(kēē-roy) **kiiroi** yellow ____________

(chy-roy) **chairoi** brown ____________

(mee-doh-ree) **midori** green ____________

(koo-roy) **kuroi** black ____________

(tah-sigh) **tasai** multi-colored ____________

- ❒ **dezāto** *(deh-zāh-toh)* . . . . dessert ____________
- ❒ **direkutā** *(dee-reh-koo-tāh)* . . . . director ____________
- ❒ **dorai kurīningu** *(doh-rye)(koo-rēē-neen-goo)* dry cleaning **d** ____________
- ❒ **dorama** *(doh-rah-mah)* . . . . drama ____________
- ❒ **doru** *(doh-roo)* . . . . dollar ____________

Peel off the next group of labels and proceed to label these (ee-roh) **iro** in your (ee-eh) **ie.** (house) Identify the two or three dominant colors in the flags below.

Japan ____________________

Thailand ____________________

Malaysia ____________________

Canada ____________________

South Korea ____________________

Philippines ____________________

People's Republic of China ____________________

Russia ____________________

New Zealand ____________________

United States ____________________

Australia ____________________

Vietnam ____________________

United Kingdom ____________________

Singapore ____________________

Laos ____________________

Indonesia ____________________

____ (where) (bah-soo) **Basu wa** ____ (where) (dess) **desu ka?**

____ (what) ____ (what) (dess) **desu ka?** (is it)

e

- ❒ **echiketto** *(eh-chee-ket-toh)* . . . . etiquette ____________________
- ❒ **ekisu** *(eh-kee-soo)* . . . . extract ____________________
- ❒ **ekurea** *(eh-koo-reh-ah)* . . . . eclair ____________________
- ❒ **enameru** *(eh-nah-meh-roo)* . . . . enamel ____________________
- ❒ **etchingu** *(et-cheen-goo)* . . . . etching ____________________

(rahn-poo)
ranpu

(soh-fāh)
sofā

(ee-soo)
isu

(kāh-pet-toh)
kāpetto

(tēh-boo-roo)
tēburu

(doh-ah)
doa

(toh-kay)
tokei

(kāh-ten)
kāten

(den-wah)
denwa

(mah-doh)
mado

(eh)
e

(ee-eh)
ie

(shoh-sigh)
shosai

(foo-roh-bah)
furoba

(dye-doh-koh-roh)
daidokoro

(sheen-shee-tsoo)
shinshitsu

(die-neen-goo)
dainingu

(ee-mah)
ima

(shah-koh)
shako

(chee-kah-shee-tsoo)
chikashitsu

(jee-dōh-shah)
jidōsha

(ōh-toh-by)
ōtobai

(jee-ten-shah)
jitensha

(neh-koh)
neko

(nee-wah)
niwa

(hah-nah)
hana

(yōō-bean)
yūbin

(ee-noo)
inu

(pohss-toh)
posuto

(zeh-roh)
0 zero

(ee-chee)
1 ichi

(nee)
2 ni

(sahn)
3 san

(yohn)
4 yon

(goh)
5 go

(roh-koo)
6 roku

(nah-nah)
7 nana

(hah-chee)
8 hachi

(kyōō)
9 kyū

(jōō)
10 jū

(shee-roy)
shiroi

(koo-roy)
kuroi

(kēē-roy)
kiiroi

(ah-kai)
akai

(ah-oy)
aoi

(goo-rēh)
gurē

(chy-roy)
chairoi

(mee-doh-ree)
midori

(peen-koo)
pinku

(oh-ren-jee)
orenji

(tah-sigh)
tasai

(oh-hah-yōh) (goh-zye-mahss)
ohayō gozaimasu

(kohn-nee-chee-wah)
konnichiwa

(kohn-bahn-wah)
konbanwa

(oh-yah-soo-mee) (nah-sigh)
oyasumi nasai

(sah-yōh-nah-rah)
sayōnara

(oh-gen-kee) (dess) (kah)
Ogenki desu ka?

(ray-zōh-koh)
reizōko

(gah-soo) (ren-jee)
gasu renji

(wine)
wain

(bēē-roo)
bīru

(mee-roo-koo)
miruku

(bah-tāh)
batā

(oh-sah-rah)
osara

(shee-oh)
shio

(koh-shōh)
koshō

(wine) (goo-rah-soo)
wain gurasu

(nye-foo)
naifu

(kohp-poo)
koppu

(oh-hah-shee)
ohashi

(fōh-koo)
fōku

(goo-rah-soo)
gurasu

(nah-poo-keen)
napukin

(soo-pōōn)
supūn

(shohk-kee-dah-nah)
shokkidana

(pahn)
pan

(oh-chah)
ocha

(kōh-chah)
kōcha

(kōh-hēē)
kōhī

(koo-dah-sigh)
kudasai

STICKY LABELS

This book has over 150 special sticky labels for you to use as you learn new words. When you are introduced to one of these words, remove the corresponding label from these pages. Be sure to use each of these unique self-adhesive labels by adhering them to a picture, window, lamp, or whatever object it refers to. And yes, they are removable! The sticky labels make learning to speak Japanese much more fun and a lot easier than you ever expected. For example, when you look in the mirror and see the label, say

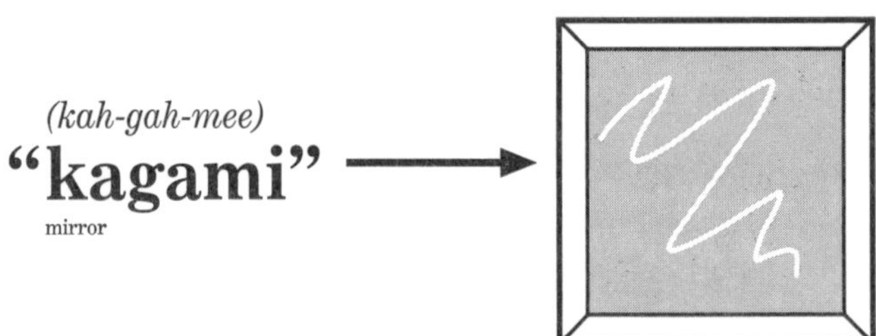

Don't just say it once, say it again and again. And once you label the refrigerator, you should never again open that door without saying

By using the sticky labels, you not only learn new words, but friends and family learn along with you! The sooner you start, the sooner you can use these labels at home or work.

7 Okane

(oh-kah-neh) **Okane** money

Before starting this Step, go back and review Step 5. It is important that you can count to **nijū** (nee-jōō) twenty without looking at **kono** (koh-noh) this **hon.** (hohn) book Let's learn the larger **bangō** (bahn-gōh) numbers now. After practicing aloud the **Nihongo** (nee-hohn-goh) Japanese **no** (P) **bangō** (bahn-gōh) numbers 10 through 5,000 below, write these **bangō** in the blanks provided. Again, notice the similarities (underlined) between numbers such as **roku** (roh-koo) (6), **jūroku** (jōō-roh-koo) (16), and **rokujū** (roo-koo-jōō) (60).

10	(jōō) **jū**	________
20	(nee-jōō) **nijū**	________
30	(sahn-jōō) **sanjū**	________
40	(yohn-jōō) **yonjū**	________
50	(goh-jōō) **gojū**	gojū, gojū, gojū, gojū, gojū, gojū
60	(roh-koo-jōō) **rokujū**	________
70	(nah-nah-jōō) **nanajū**	________
80	(hah-chee-jōō) **hachijū**	________
90	(kyōō-jōō) **kyūjū**	________
100	(hyah-koo) **hyaku**	________
500	(goh-hyah-koo) **gohyaku**	________
1,000	(sen) **sen**	________
5,000	(goh-sen) **gosen**	________

Here is an important phrase to go with all these **bangō.** (bahn-gōh) Say it out loud over and over and then write it out twice as many times.

(moht-teh) (ee-mahss) **motte imasu** (I) have ________

- ❒ **enerugī** *(eh-neh-roo-gēē)* .... energy ________
- ❒ **enjin** *(ehn-jeen)* .... engine ________
- ❒ **epuron** *(eh-poo-rohn)* .... apron **e** ________
- ❒ **erebētā** *(eh-reh-bēh-tāh)* .... elevator ________
- ❒ **esukarētā** *(ess-kah-rēh-tāh)* .... escalator ________

The unit of currency in **Nihon** (nee-hohn) [Japan] is the **en,** (en) [yen] abbreviated "¥." Let's learn the various kinds of **kōka** (kōh-kah) [coins] (or **dama** (dah-mah) [coins]) and **satsu.** (sah-tsoo) [bills] Always be sure to practice each **tango** out loud. You might want to exchange some money now so you can familiarize yourself with the various types of **okane.** (oh-kah-neh) [money]

(sah-tsoo)
Satsu
bills

(kōh-kah)
Kōka
coins

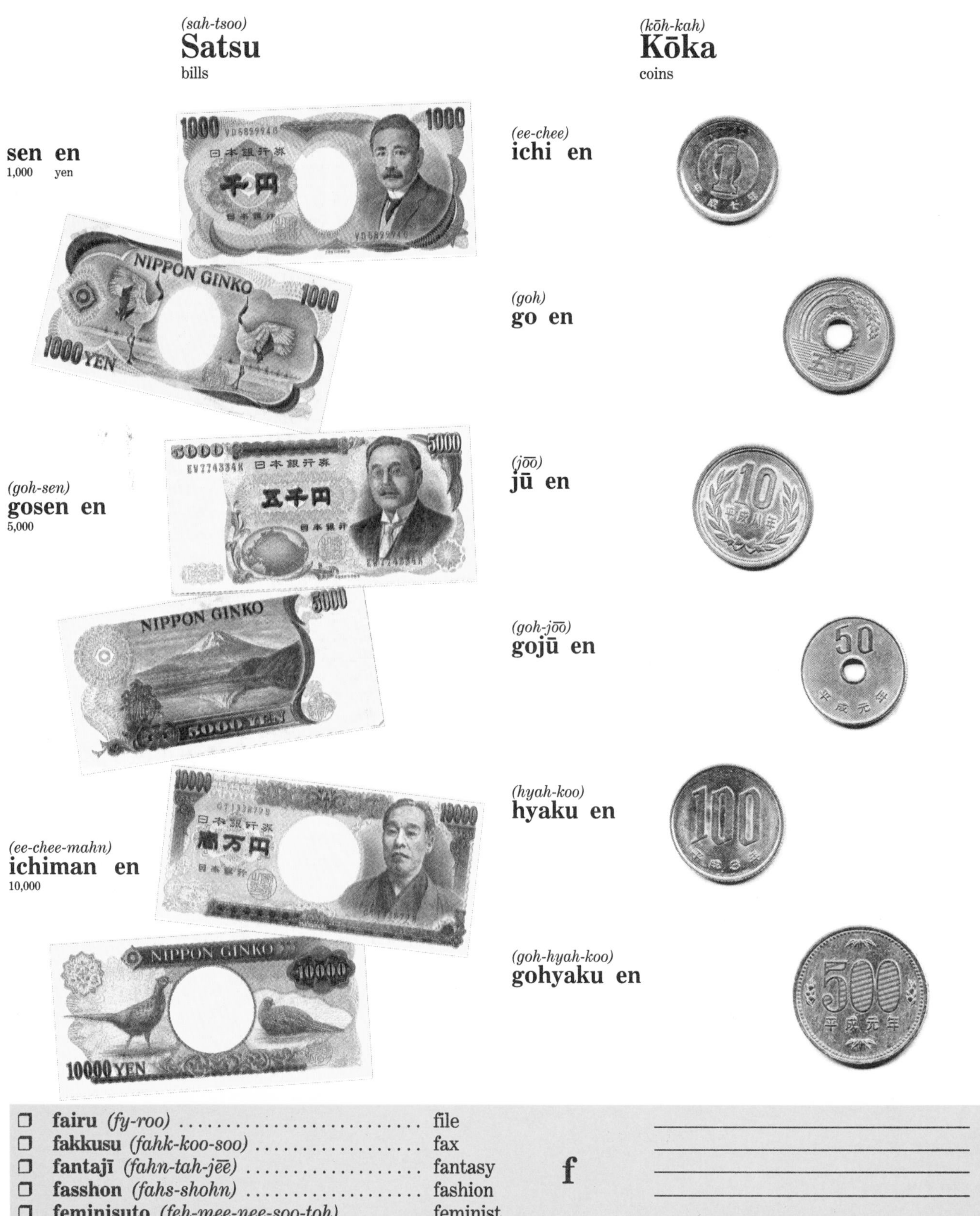

sen en — 1,000 yen

(goh-sen) **gosen en** — 5,000

(ee-chee-mahn) **ichiman en** — 10,000

(ee-chee) **ichi en**

(goh) **go en**

(jōō) **jū en**

(goh-jōō) **gojū en**

(hyah-koo) **hyaku en**

(goh-hyah-koo) **gohyaku en**

f

- ❒ **fairu** *(fy-roo)* . . . . file
- ❒ **fakkusu** *(fahk-koo-soo)* . . . . fax
- ❒ **fantajī** *(fahn-tah-jēē)* . . . . fantasy
- ❒ **fasshon** *(fahs-shohn)* . . . . fashion
- ❒ **feminisuto** *(feh-mee-nee-soo-toh)* . . . . . feminist

Review the *(bahn-gōh)* **bangō** (numbers) *(jōō)* **jū** (10) through *(goh-sen)* **gosen** (5,000) again. Now, how do you say "twenty-two" or "fifty-three" in *(nee-hohn-goh)* **Nihongo?** (Japanese) You actually do a bit of arithmetic: **5** *(goh)* **(go)** times **10** *(jōō)* **(jū)** plus **3** *(sahn)* **(san)** equals **53 (gojūsan).** See if you can say and write out the **bangō** on *(koh-noh)* **kono** (this) *(pēh-jee)* **pēji.** (page) *(koh-tah-eh)* **Kotae** ((the) answers) are at the bottom of the *(pēh-jee)* **pēji.** (page)

1. ____________________ (25 = 2 x 10 + 5)

2. ____________________ (84 = 8 x 10 + 4)

3. ____________________ (47 = 4 x 10 + 7)

4. kyūjūsan, kyūjūsan (93 = 9 x 10 + 3)

Now, how would you say the following in *(nee-hohn-goh)* **Nihongo?**

5. ____________________ (I have 80 yen.)

6. ____________________ (I have 750 yen.)

To ask how much something costs in *(nee-hohn-goh)* **Nihongo,** one asks — *(ee-koo-rah)* **Ikura** (how much) *(dess)* **desu** (is it) *(kah)* **ka?**

Now you try it. ____________________ (How much is it?)

Answer the following questions based on the numbers in parentheses.

7. *(koh-reh)* **Kore** (this) *(wah)* **wa** (P) *(ee-koo-rah)* **ikura** (how much) *(dess)* **desu** (is it) *(kah)* **ka?** __________ (20) *(en)* **en** (yen) *(dess)* **desu.**

8. *(soh-reh)* **Sore** (that) **wa** (P) *(ee-koo-rah)* **ikura** (how much) *(dess)* **desu ka?** __________ (100) **en** *(dess)* **desu.**

9. *(hohn)* **Hon** (book) **wa** (P) **ikura desu ka?** __________ (250) **en** *(dess)* **desu.**

7. *(fee-roo-moo)* **Firumu** (film) **wa ikura desu ka?** __________ (1,000) **en desu.**

KOTAE

1. nijūgo
2. hachijūyon
3. yonjūnana
4. kyūjūsan
5. Hachijū en o motte imasu.
6. Nanahyakugojū en o motte imasu.
7. nijū
8. hyaku
9. nihyakugojū
10. sen

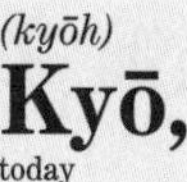

8 *(kyōh)* Kyō, *(ahsh-tah)* Ashita, *(kee-nōh)* Kinō
today, tomorrow, yesterday

(kah-ren-dāh)
Karendā
(the) calendar

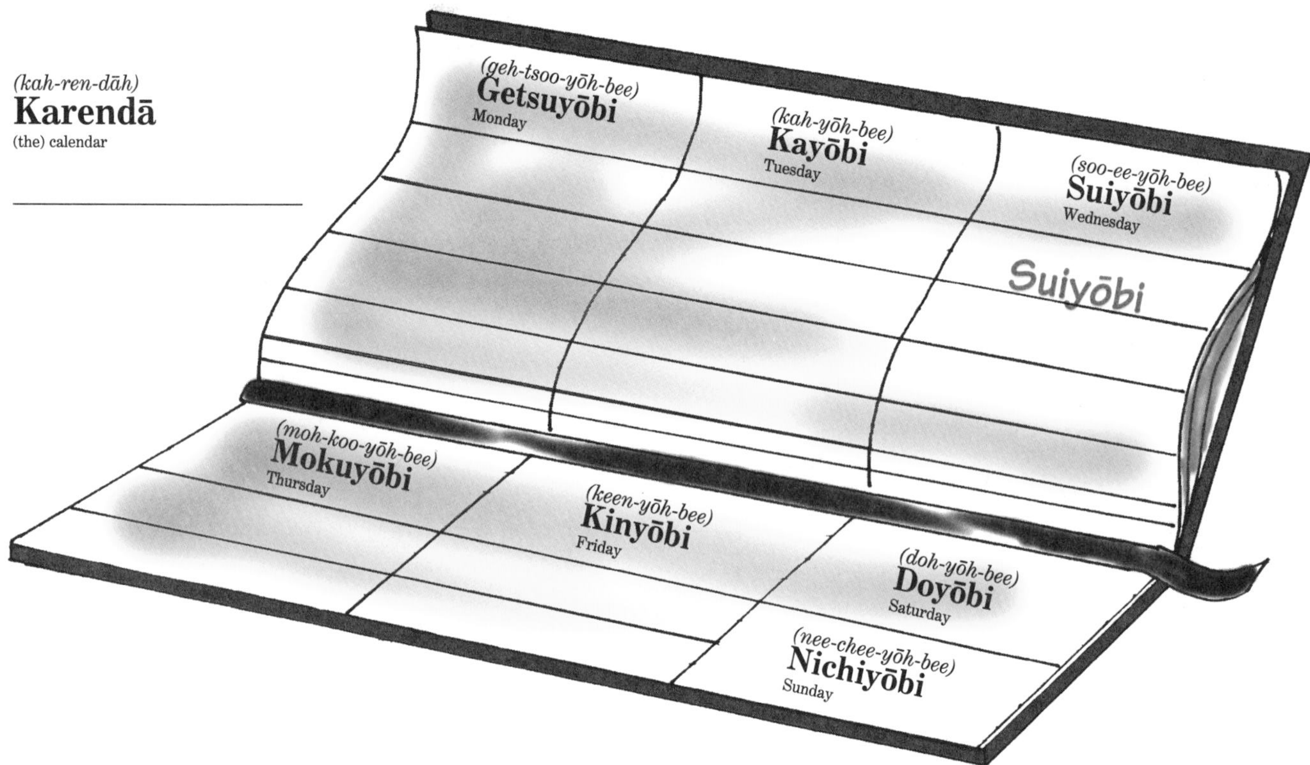

Learn the days of the week by writing them in the **karendā** *(kah-ren-dah)* [calendar] above and then move on to the **yon** *(yohn)* [four] parts to each **hi.** *(hee)* [day]

(ah-sah) (goh-zen)
asa / gozen
morning

(goh-goh)
gogo
afternoon

(bahn)
ban
evening

(yoh-roo)
yoru
night

f

- ❒ **fenshingu** *(fen-sheen-goo)* .... fencing
- ❒ **firumu** *(fee-roo-moo)* .... film
- ❒ **fōku** *(fōh-koo)* .... fork
- ❒ **Furansu** *(foo-rahn-soo)* .... France
- ❒ **futtobōru** *(foot-toh-bōh-roo)* .... football

(hee-jōh) (nee) (tye-seh-tsoo)
It is **hijō ni taisetsu** to know the days of the week and the various parts of the day as well as
very (P) important
(sahn) (koh) (tahn-goh)
these **san ko no tango.**
three (M) (P)

(kee-nōh) **kinō** — (kyōh) **kyō** — (ahsh-tah) **ashita**

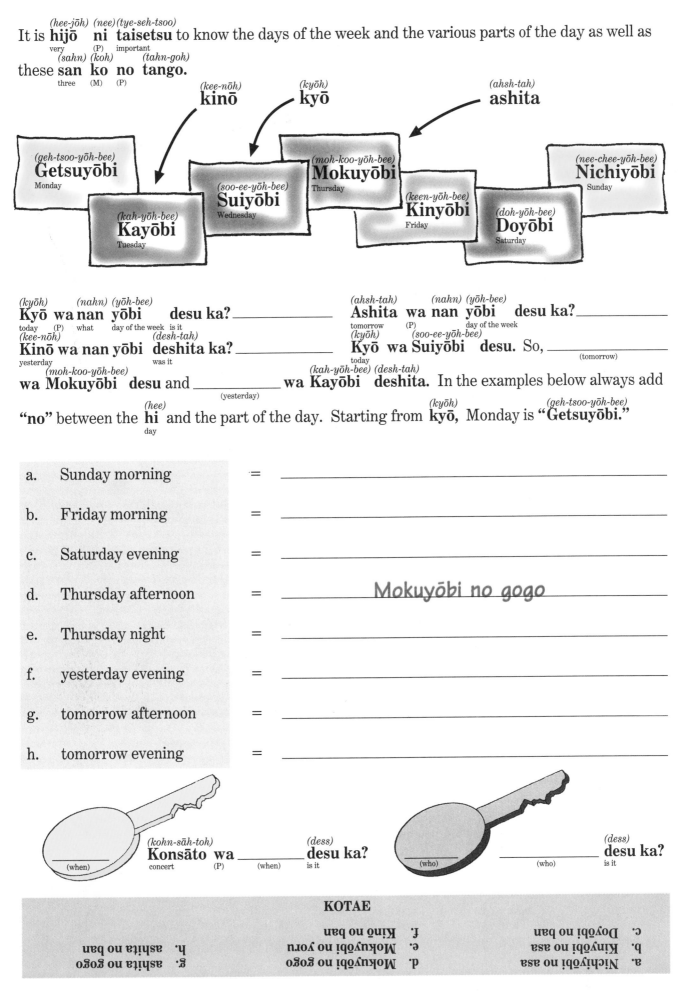

(geh-tsoo-yōh-bee) **Getsuyōbi**	Monday
(kah-yōh-bee) **Kayōbi**	Tuesday
(soo-ee-yōh-bee) **Suiyōbi**	Wednesday
(moh-koo-yōh-bee) **Mokuyōbi**	Thursday
(keen-yōh-bee) **Kinyōbi**	Friday
(doh-yōh-bee) **Doyōbi**	Saturday
(nee-chee-yōh-bee) **Nichiyōbi**	Sunday

(kyōh) (nahn) (yōh-bee)
Kyō wa nan yōbi desu ka? ______________
today (P) what day of the week is it

(kee-nōh) (desh-tah)
Kinō wa nan yōbi deshita ka? ______________
yesterday was it

(ahsh-tah) (nahn) (yōh-bee)
Ashita wa nan yōbi desu ka? ______________
tomorrow (P) day of the week

(kyōh) (soo-ee-yōh-bee) (moh-koo-yōh-bee) (kah-yōh-bee) (desh-tah)
Kyō wa Suiyōbi desu. So, ______________ (tomorrow) **wa Mokuyōbi desu** and ______________ (yesterday) **wa Kayōbi deshita.** In the examples below always add "**no**" between the (hee) **hi** (day) and the part of the day. Starting from (kyōh) **kyō,** Monday is (geh-tsoo-yōh-bee) "**Getsuyōbi.**"

a. Sunday morning = ______________

b. Friday morning = ______________

c. Saturday evening = ______________

d. Thursday afternoon = Mokuyōbi no gogo

e. Thursday night = ______________

f. yesterday evening = ______________

g. tomorrow afternoon = ______________

h. tomorrow evening = ______________

______ (when)

(kohn-sāh-toh) (dess)
Konsāto wa ______ **desu ka?**
concert (P) (when) is it

______ (who)

(dess)
______ (who) **desu ka?**
is it

KOTAE

a. Nichiyōbi no asa
b. Kinyōbi no asa
c. Doyōbi no ban
d. Mokuyōbi no gogo
e. Mokuyōbi no yoru
f. Kinō no ban
g. ashita no gogo
h. ashita no ban

Knowing the parts of the *(hee)* **hi** (day) will help you to learn the various *(nee-hohn-goh)* **Nihongo** greetings below.

Practice these every day until your trip.

(oh-hah-yōh) (goh-zye-mahss)
ohayō gozaimasu ____________________
good morning

(kohn-nee-chee-wah)
konnichiwa ____________________
good day/hello

(kohn-bahn-wah)
konbanwa ____________________
good evening

(oh-yah-soo-mee) (nah-sigh)
oyasumi nasai ____________________
good night

(sah-yōh-nah-rah)
sayōnara ____________________
good-bye

Take the next *(goh)* **go** (five) *(my)* **mai** (M) labels and stick them on the appropriate *(moh-noh)* **mono** (things) in your *(ee-eh)* **ie.** (house) Make sure you attach them to the correct items, as they are only in **Nihongo.** How about the bathroom mirror for "*(oh-hah-yōh)* **ohayō** *(goh-zye-mahss)* **gozaimasu**"? Or your alarm clock for "*(oh-yah-soo-mee)* **oyasumi** *(nah-sigh)* **nasai**"? Let's not forget,

(oh-gen-kee) (dess)
Ogenki desu ka? ____________________
how are you

Now for some "*(hi)* **hai** (yes)" or "*(ēē-eh)* **iie** (no)" questions –

Are your eyes *(ah-oy)* **aoi?** ____________

Is your car *(ah-kai)* **akai?** ____________

Do you own an *(ee-noo)* **inu?** ____________

Are your shoes *(chy-roh)* **chairo?** ____________

Is today *(doh-yōh-bee)* **Doyōbi?** ____________

Do you own a *(neh-koh)* **neko?** ____________

You are about one-fourth of your way through **kono** (this) *(hohn)* **hon** (book) and it is a good time to quickly review the *(tahn-goh)* **tango** you have learned before doing the crossword puzzle on the next *(pēh-jee)* **pēji.**

(tah-noh-sheen-deh) (koo-dah-sigh)
Tanoshinde kudasai!
have fun

KUROSUWĀDO NO KOTAE

ACROSS
1. kāten
7. tokei
8. kuroi
9. jūshichi
11. niwa
13. kinōi
14. shichi
15. shako
17. bangō
18. jidōsha
21. sarada
24. ressha
26. isu
27. mado
28. nijū
31. nan
32. furoba
35. aoi
36. oyasumi nasai
38. shosai
39. asa
41. bīru
42. Nihongo
44. ie
45. doa
46. gurē
47. dezāto
48. ie

DOWN
2. Nichiyōbi
3. denwa
4. okane
5. Mokuyōbi
6. ginkō
10. shinshitsu
12. ashita
13. kotae
14. satsu
16. basu
19. ban
20. kippu
22. resutoran
23. hagaki
24. roku
25. san
29. jūgo
30. takushī
33. banana
34. kiiroi
37. hoteru
40. yoru
41. batā
43. neko

(koo-roh-soo-wāh-doh)
CROSSWORD PUZZLE (KUROSUWĀDO)

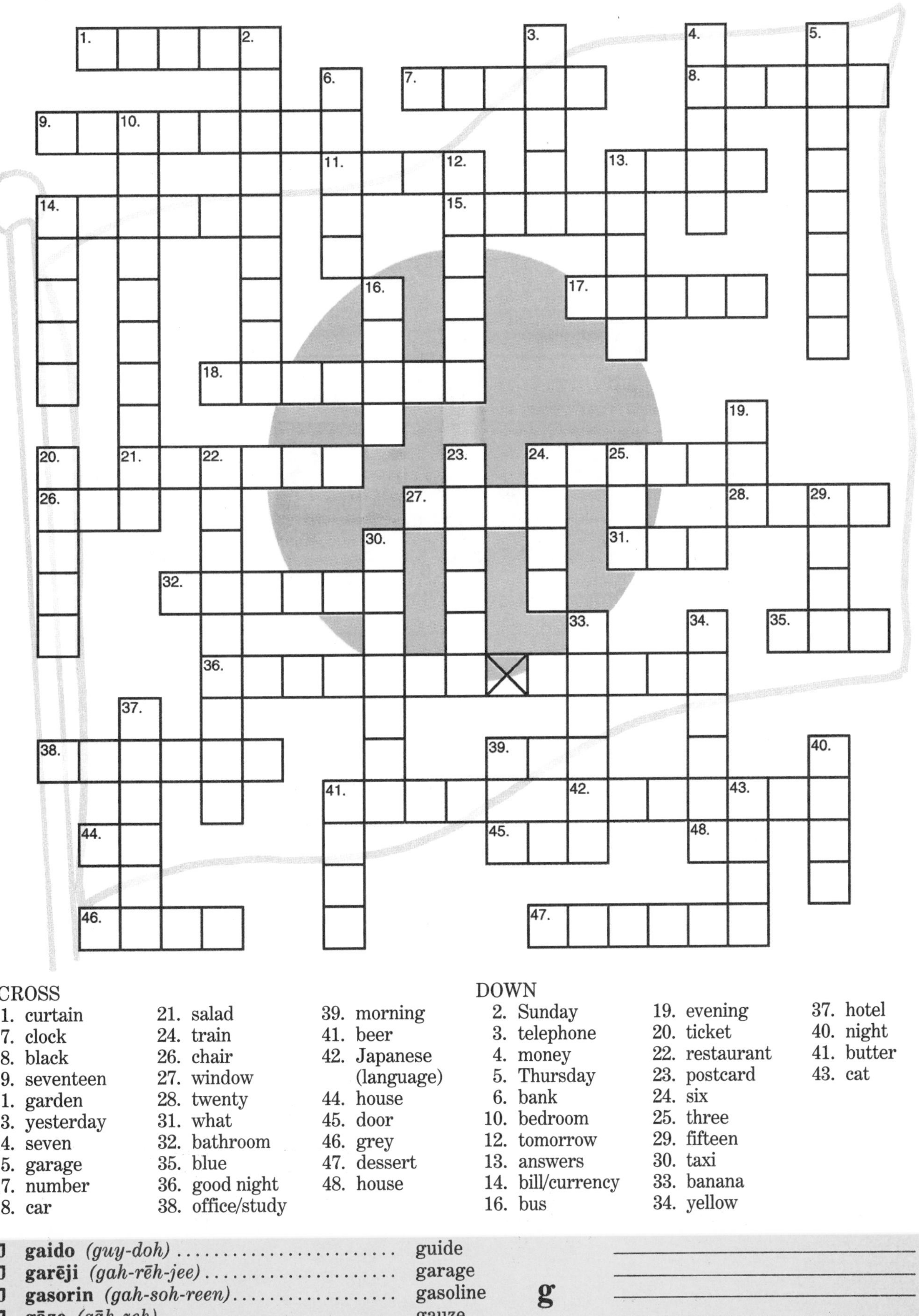

ACROSS
1. curtain
7. clock
8. black
9. seventeen
11. garden
13. yesterday
14. seven
15. garage
17. number
18. car
21. salad
24. train
26. chair
27. window
28. twenty
31. what
32. bathroom
35. blue
36. good night
38. office/study
39. morning
41. beer
42. Japanese (language)
44. house
45. door
46. grey
47. dessert
48. house

DOWN
2. Sunday
3. telephone
4. money
5. Thursday
6. bank
10. bedroom
12. tomorrow
13. answers
14. bill/currency
16. bus
19. evening
20. ticket
22. restaurant
23. postcard
24. six
25. three
29. fifteen
30. taxi
33. banana
34. yellow
37. hotel
40. night
41. butter
43. cat

- ❒ **gaido** *(guy-doh)* . . . . guide
- ❒ **garēji** *(gah-rēh-jee)* . . . . garage
- ❒ **gasorin** *(gah-soh-reen)* . . . . gasoline
- ❒ **gāze** *(gāh-zeh)* . . . . gauze
- ❒ **gēmu** *(gēh-moo)* . . . . game

g

9 Ue, Shita, Tonari

(oo-eh) (shtah) (toh-nah-ree)
Ue, Shita, Tonari
above under next to

Japanese prepositions (words like "in," "on," "through" and "next to") will allow you to be precise with a minimum of effort. Instead of having to point **roku** *(roh-koo)* (six) times at a piece of yummy pastry you would like, you can explain precisely which one you want by saying it is behind, in front of, next to or under the piece of pastry that the salesperson is starting to pick up. Let's learn some of these little **tango.** *(tahn-goh)*

(shtah) **shita** ____________ under / below

(oo-eh) **ue** ____________ above / over / on top

(eye-dah) **aida** ____________ between

(toh-nah-ree) **tonari** ____________ next to

(nee) **ni** ____________ on / at

(nee) **ni** ____________ into / in

(mah-eh) **mae** ____________ in front of

(oo-shee-roh) **ushiro** ____________ behind

(kah-rah) **kara** ____________ from

(kēh-kee) **kēki** ____________ cake

Note that prepositions in **Nihongo** follow the noun and with the exception of "**ni**" and "**kara**" are preceded by "**no.**" (P) Fill in the blanks on the next **pēji** *(pēh-jee)* with the correct prepositions.

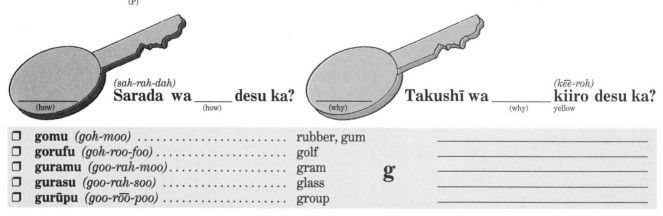

______ (how) *(sah-rah-dah)* **Sarada wa** ______ (how) **desu ka?**

______ (why) **Takushī wa** ______ (why) *(kēē-roh)* **kiiro** (yellow) **desu ka?**

- ❒ **gomu** *(goh-moo)* .... rubber, gum ____________
- ❒ **gorufu** *(goh-roo-foo)* .... golf ____________
- ❒ **guramu** *(goo-rah-moo)* .... gram **g** ____________
- ❒ **gurasu** *(goo-rah-soo)* .... glass ____________
- ❒ **gurūpu** *(goo-rōō-poo)* .... group ____________

(kēh-kee) (tēh-boo-roo) (dess)
Kēki wa tēburu no ______________ **desu.**
cake table (P) (on top of)

(kēh-kee)
Kēki wa doko desu ka? ______________
cake

(ee-shah) (sahn) (hoh-teh-roo) (ee-mahss)
Isha san wa hoteru ______________ **imasu.**
doctor (P) (in) is

(ee-shah) (ee-mahss)
Isha san wa doko ni imasu ka? ______________
doctor (P) is

(oh-toh-koh) (hee-toh)
Otoko no hito wa hoteru no __________ **desu.**
man (P) person (P) (in front of)

(oh-toh-koh) (hee-toh)
Otoko no hito wa doko desu ka? ______________
man

(ohn-nah) (hee-toh) (foo-rohn-toh)
Onna no hito wa furonto no __________ **desu.**
woman (P) person front desk (P) (behind)

(ohn-nah) (hee-toh)
Onna no hito wa doko desu ka? ______________
woman

(ee-mah)
Ima, fill in each blank on the picture below with the best possible one of these little **tango.**
now

Hopefully you will visit many beautiful castles like the one below.

❒ **haikingu** *(hi-keen-goo)*..................	hiking		______________
❒ **hanbāgā** *(hahn-bāh-gāh)*..................	hamburger		______________
❒ **handobaggu** *(hahn-doh-bahg-goo)*.........	handbag	**h**	______________
❒ **handobōru** *(hahn-doh-bōh-roo)*...........	handball		______________
❒ **hankachi** *(hahn-kah-chee)*................	handkerchief		______________

10 Ichigatsu, Nigatsu, Sangatsu

(ee-chee-gah-tsoo) **Ichigatsu,** January · *(nee-gah-tsoo)* **Nigatsu,** February · *(sahn-gah-tsoo)* **Sangatsu** March

You have learned the **hi** *(hee)* [days] of **isshūkan** *(eesh-shōō-kahn)* [(one) week] so now it is time to learn the **tsuki** *(tsoo-kee)* [months] of the **toshi** *(toh-shee)* [year] and all the different kinds of **tenki.** *(ten-kee)* [weather] Do you recognize your numbers in these new **tango?**

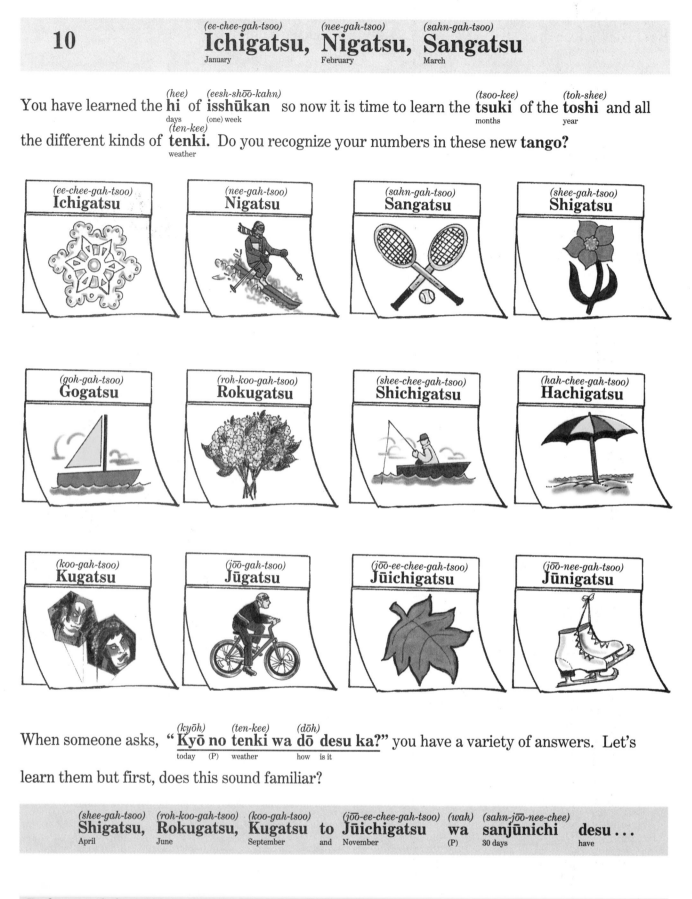

(ee-chee-gah-tsoo) **Ichigatsu**

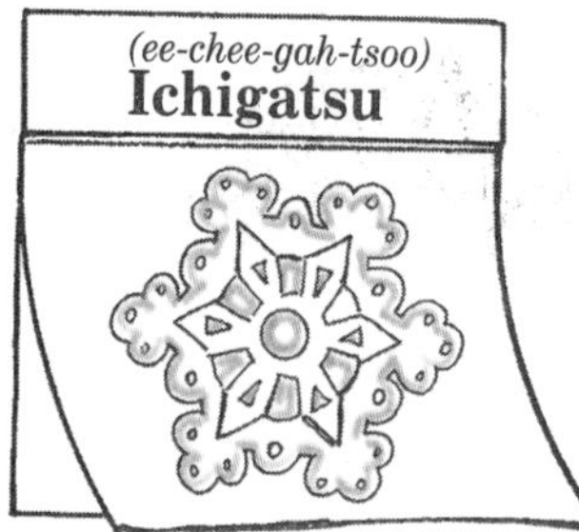

(nee-gah-tsoo) **Nigatsu**

(sahn-gah-tsoo) **Sangatsu**

(shee-gah-tsoo) **Shigatsu**

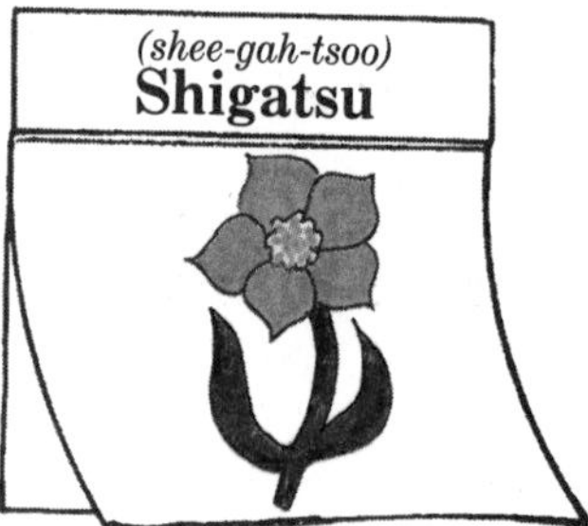

(goh-gah-tsoo) **Gogatsu**

(roh-koo-gah-tsoo) **Rokugatsu**

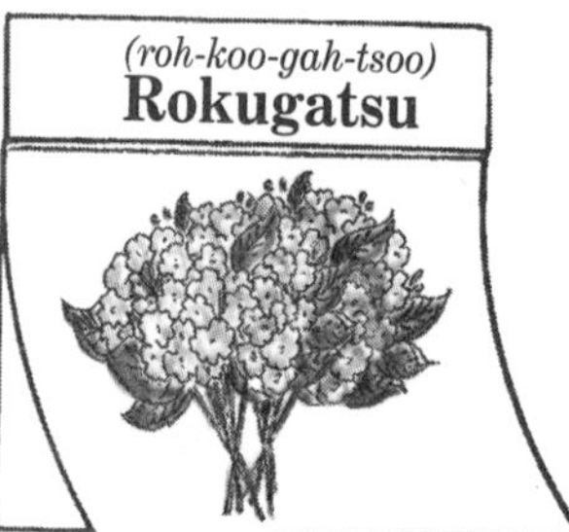

(shee-chee-gah-tsoo) **Shichigatsu**

(hah-chee-gah-tsoo) **Hachigatsu**

(koo-gah-tsoo) **Kugatsu**

(jōō-gah-tsoo) **Jūgatsu**

(jōō-ee-chee-gah-tsoo) **Jūichigatsu**

(jōō-nee-gah-tsoo) **Jūnigatsu**

When someone asks, "**Kyō** *(kyōh)* [today] **no** [(P)] **tenki** *(ten-kee)* [weather] **wa dō** *(dōh)* [how] **desu ka?**" [is it] you have a variety of answers. Let's learn them but first, does this sound familiar?

Shigatsu, *(shee-gah-tsoo)* [April] **Rokugatsu,** *(roh-koo-gah-tsoo)* [June] **Kugatsu** *(koo-gah-tsoo)* [September] **to** [and] **Jūichigatsu** *(jōō-ee-chee-gah-tsoo)* [November] **wa** *(wah)* [(P)] **sanjūnichi** *(sahn-jōō-nee-chee)* [30 days] **desu . . .** [have]

- ❒ **hanmā** *(hahn-māh)*. . . . . hammer
- ❒ **herikoputā** *(heh-ree-koh-poo-tāh)* . . . . helicopter
- ❒ **hītā** *(hēē-tāh)* . . . . heater
- ❒ **hitto** *(heet-toh)*. . . . . hit
- ❒ **hokkē** *(hohk-kēh)* . . . . hockey

h

____
____
____
____
____

(kyōh) (ten-kee) (doh) (dess)
Kyō no tenki wa dō desu ka? ____________
today (P) weather how

(yoo-kee) (foo-ree-mahss)
Ichigatsu ni wa yuki ga furimasu. ____________
in (P) snow (P) falls

(moh) (foo-ree-mahss)
Nigatsu ni mo yuki ga furimasu. ____________
in also (P)

(kah-zeh) (foo-kee-mahss)
Sangatsu ni wa kaze ga fukimasu. ____________
(P) wind blows

(moh) (kah-zeh) (foo-kee-mahss)
Shigatsu ni mo kaze ga fukimasu. ____________
also wind

(ah-meh) (foo-ree-mahss)
Gogatsu ni wa ame ga furimasu. ____________
rain (P) falls

(ah-meh)
Rokugatsu ni mo ame ga furimasu. ____________
rain

(ah-tsoo-ee)
Shichigatsu wa atsui desu. ____________
hot is

(ah-tsoo-ee)
Hachigatsu mo atsui desu. ____________
also hot is

(ten-kee) (ēē)
Kugatsu wa tenki ga ii desu. ____________
weather good

(kee-ree) (kah-kah-ree-mahss)
Jūgatsu ni wa kiri ga kakarimasu. ____________
fog hangs

(sah-moo-ee)
Jūichigatsu wa samui desu. ____________
cold

(ten-kee) (wah-roo-ee)
Jūnigatsu wa tenki ga warui desu. ____________
bad

(nee-gah-tsoo) (dess)
Nigatsu no tenki wa dō desu ka? ____________
(P) weather how is it

(shee-gah-tsoo)
Shigatsu no tenki wa dō desu ka? ____________
(P)

(goh-gah-tsoo)
Gogatsu no tenki wa dō desu ka? ____________
(P)

Hachigatsu no tenki wa dō desu ka? ____________
(P)

h

- ❒ **hosuteru** *(hoh-soo-teh-roo)* . . . . hostel ____________
- ❒ **hoteru** *(hoh-teh-roo)* . . . . hotel ____________
- ❒ **hotto doggu** *(hoht-toh)(dohg-goo)* . . . . hot dog ____________
- ❒ **hotto kēki** *(hoht-toh)(kēh-kee)* . . . . hotcake (pancake) ____________
- ❒ **howaito sōsu** *(hoh-why-toh)(sōh-soo)* . . . . . . white sauce ____________

Ima for the seasons of the **toshi** *(toh-shee)* [year] . . .

(foo-yoo) **fuyu** [winter]

(nah-tsoo) **natsu** [summer]

(ah-kee) **aki** [autumn]

(hah-roo) **haru** [spring]

______ ______ ______ ______

(sehs-shee) **sesshi** [Centigrade]

(kah-shee) **kashi** [Fahrenheit]

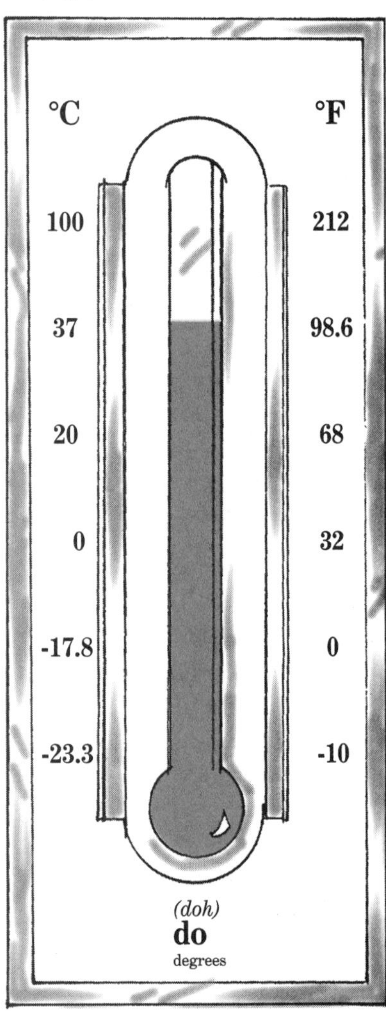

At this point, it is a good time to familiarize yourself with **Nihon** *(nee-hohn)* [Japan] **no** [(P)] **kion.** *(kee-ohn)* [temperatures] Carefully study the thermometer because temperatures in **Nihon** are calculated on the basis of Centigrade (not Fahrenheit).

To convert °F to °C, subtract 32 and multiply by 0.55.

98.6 °F - 32 = 66.6 x 0.55 = 37 °C

To convert °C to °F, multiply by 1.8 and add 32.

37 °C x 1.8 = 66.6 + 32 = 98.6 °F

What is normal body temperature in **sesshi?** *(sehs-shee)*

What is the freezing point in **sesshi?**

- ❒ **imēji** *(ee-mēh-jee)* . . . . image ______
- ❒ **imitēshon** *(ee-mee-tēh-shohn)* . . . . imitation ______
- ❒ **inchi** *(een-chee)* . . . . inch **i** ______
- ❒ **inku** *(een-koo)* . . . . ink ______
- ❒ **intabyū** *(een-tah-byōō)* . . . . interview ______

11 Wagaya — Kazoku

(wah-gah-yah) **Wagaya** — *(kah-zoh-koo)* **Kazoku**
our home — family

Study the family tree below. In **Nihongo,** the family *(nah-mah-eh)* **namae** (name) comes first, and the given or first *(nah-mah-eh)* **namae** follows. *(sahn)* **"San"** is often used with the **namae** of relatives. It is a term of respect, meaning "honorable." The words in parentheses are the names used when the individual is a member of one's immediate family just as English speakers might use "daddy" or "mommy."

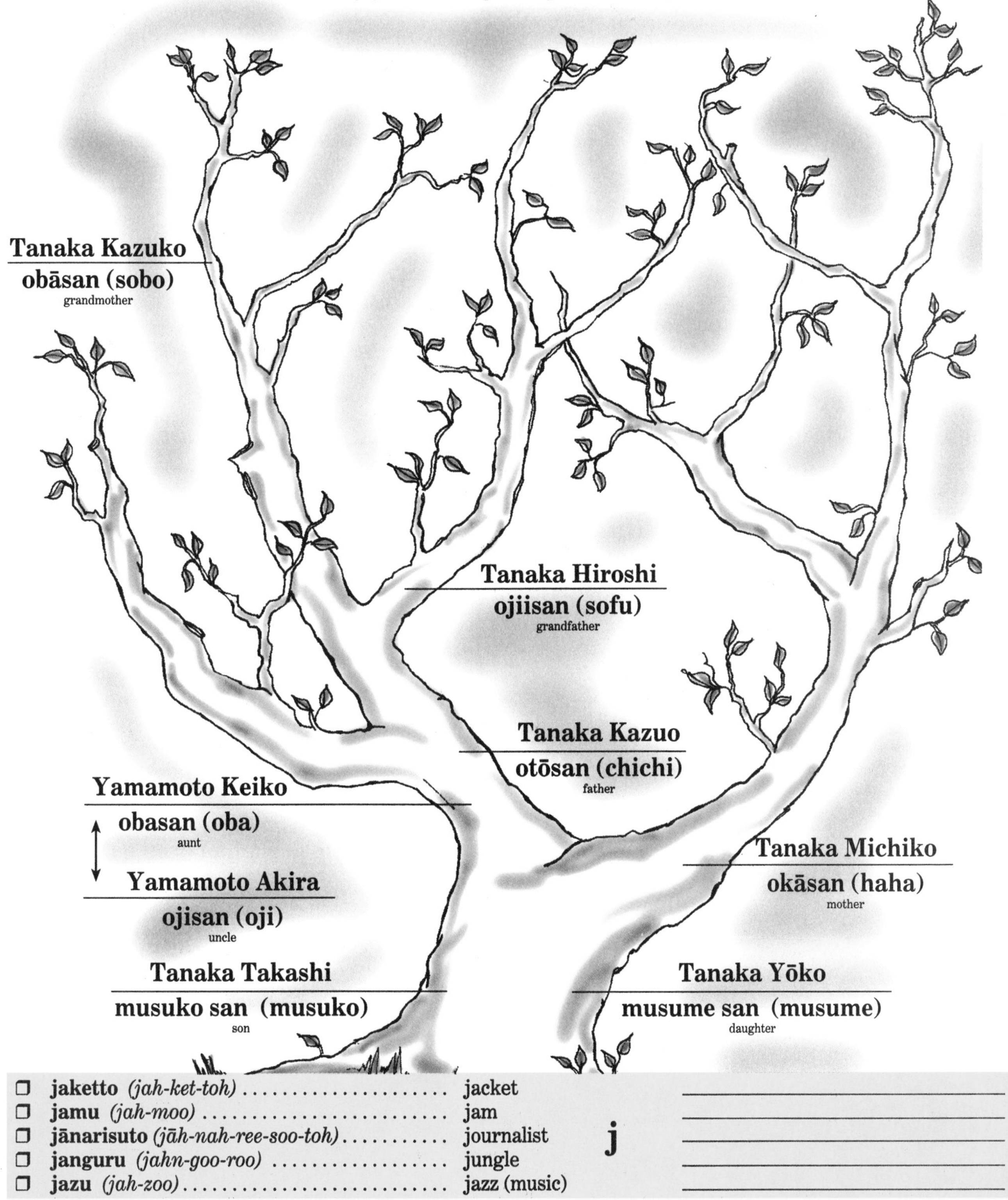

j

- ❐ **jaketto** *(jah-ket-toh)* .... jacket ________________
- ❐ **jamu** *(jah-moo)* .... jam ________________
- ❐ **jānarisuto** *(jāh-nah-ree-soo-toh)* .... journalist ________________
- ❐ **janguru** *(jahn-goo-roo)* .... jungle ________________
- ❐ **jazu** *(jah-zoo)* .... jazz (music) ________________

Let's learn how to identify family members by **namae** *(nah-mah-eh)* [name]. Study the following examples carefully.

(oh-nah-mah-eh) (nahn)
Onamae wa nan desu ka? __________
your name — what — is it

(wah-tah-shee) (nah-mah-eh)
Watashi no namae wa __________ desu.
I — (P) — name — (P) — (your name) — is

(ryōh-sheen)
ryōshin
parents

(oh-tōh-sahn)
otōsan (chichi) __________
father

(oh-tōh-sahn) (nah-mah-eh) (nahn)
Otōsan no namae wa nan desu ka?
father — (P) — name — what — is it

(oh-kāh-sahn)
okāsan (haha) __________
mother

(oh-kāh-sahn) (nah-mah-eh) (nahn)
Okāsan no namae wa nan desu ka?
(P) — what

(koh-doh-moh) (tah-chee) (koh-doh-moh-tah-chee)
kodomo + tachi = kodomotachi
child — children

(moo-soo-koh) (toh) (moo-soo-meh) (oh-toh-koh) (toh) (ohn-nah) (kyōh-dye)
musuko to musume = otoko to onna no kyōdai
son — and — daughter — brother — and — sister — (P) — sibling

(moo-soo-koh) (sahn)
musuko san (musuko) __________
son

(moo-soo-koh) (sahn) (nah-mah-eh) (nahn)
Musuko san no namae wa nan desu ka?
son — (P) — name — what

(moo-soo-meh)(sahn)
musume san (musume) __________
daughter

(moo-soo-meh) (sahn)
Musume san no namae wa nan desu ka?
daughter — (P)

(soh-foo-boh)
sofubo
grandparents

(oh-jēe-sahn)
ojiisan (sofu) __________
grandfather

(oh-jēe-sahn) (nah-mah-eh) (nahn)
Ojiisan no namae wa nan desu ka?
grandfather — (P)

(oh-bāh-sahn)
obāsan (sobo) __________
grandmother

(oh-bāh-sahn)
Obāsan no namae wa nan desu ka?
grandmother

Now you ask —

____
(How are you called?/What is your name?)

And answer —

____
(My name is . . .)

j

- ❒ **jerī** *(jeh-rēe)* .... jelly __________
- ❒ **jettoki** *(jet-toh-kee)* .... jet airplane __________
- ❒ **jinjāēru** *(jeen-jāh-ēh-roo)* .... ginger ale __________
- ❒ **jīppu** *(jēe-poo)* .... jeep __________
- ❒ **jōku** *(jōh-koo)* .... joke __________

(dye-doh-koh-roh)
Daidokoro
kitchen

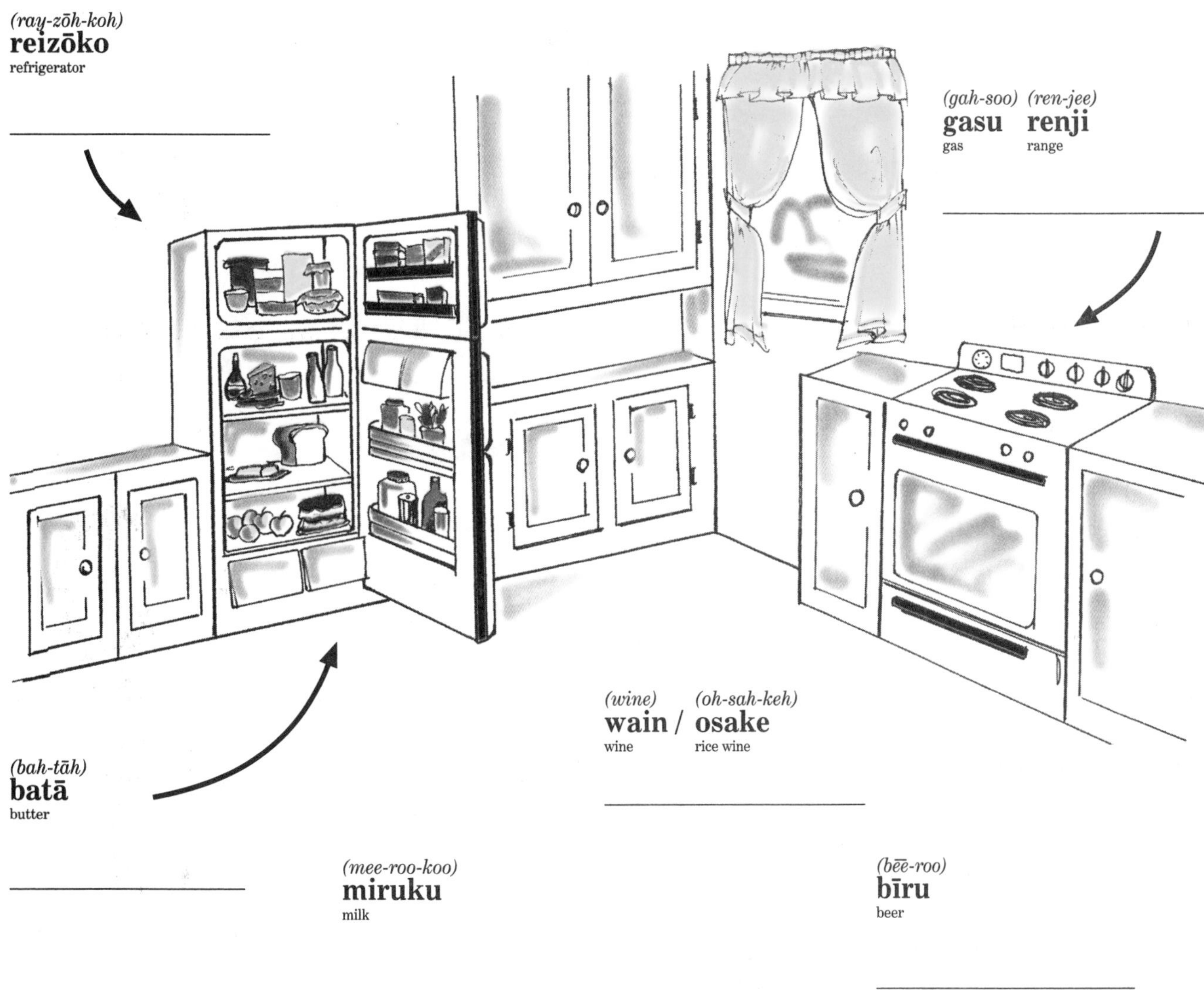

(ray-zōh-koh)
reizōko
refrigerator

(gah-soo) (ren-jee)
gasu renji
gas range

(wine) (oh-sah-keh)
wain / osake
wine / rice wine

(bah-tāh)
batā
butter

(mee-roo-koo)
miruku
milk

(bēē-roo)
bīru
beer

Answer these questions aloud.

Bīru *(bēē-roo)* beer **wa** (P) **doko** where **desu ka?** *(dess)* is it . . . . **Bīru** *(bēē-roo)* **wa reizōko** *(ray-zōh-koh)* **no** (P) **naka** *(nah-kah)* inside **desu.** is

Miruku *(mee-roo-koo)* milk **wa doko desu ka?** **Osake** *(oh-sah-keh)* rice wine **wa doko desu ka?** **Batā** *(bah-tāh)* **wa doko desu ka?**

Ima open your **hon** *(hohn)* book to the **pēji** *(pēh-jee)* with the labels and remove the next group of labels and proceed to label all these **mono** *(moh-noh)* things in your **daikokoro.** *(dye-doh-koh-roh)* kitchen

k

❒	**kābu** *(kāh-boo)*	curve	______
❒	**kādigan** *(kāh-dee-gahn)*	cardigan	______
❒	**kādo** *(kāh-doh)*	card	______
❒	**kafe** *(kah-feh)*	café, coffeehouse	______
❒	**kafeteria** *(kah-feh-teh-ree-ah)*	cafeteria	______

(shee-oh)
shio
salt

(koh-shōh)
koshō
pepper

(wine) *(goo-rah-soo)*
wain gurasu
wine glass

(goo-rah-soo) *(kohp-poo)*
gurasu / koppu
glass

(oh-hah-shee)
ohashi
chopsticks

(kahp-poo)
kappu
cup

(sheen-boon)
shinbun
newspaper

(soo-pōōn)
supūn
spoon

(nah-poo-keen)
napukin
napkin

(fōh-koo)
fōku
fork

(oh-sah-rah)
osara
plate

(nye-foo)
naifu
knife

And more . . .

(shohk-kee-dah-nah)
shokkidana ______________________
cupboard

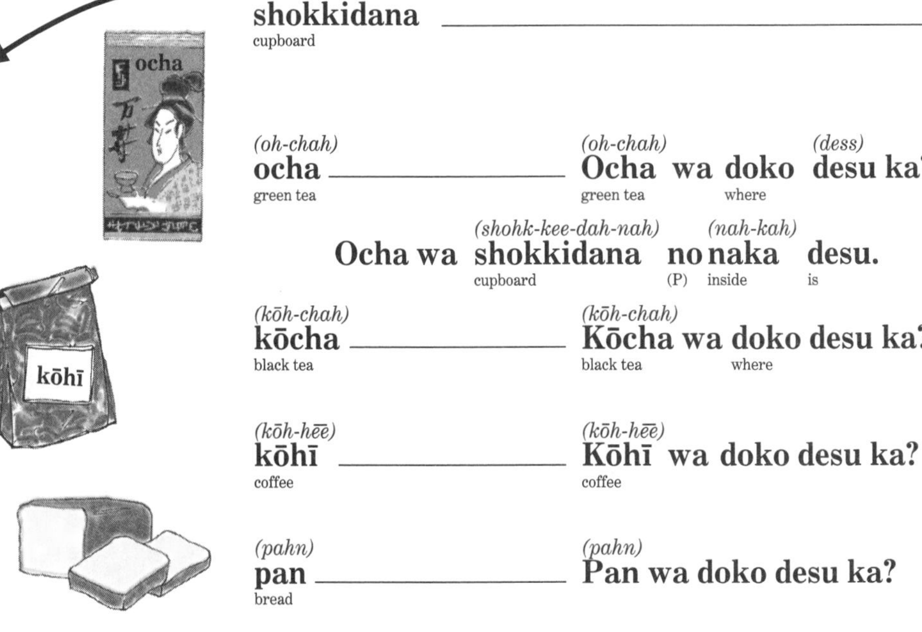

(oh-chah)
ocha ______________
green tea

(oh-chah) *(dess)*
Ocha wa doko desu ka?
green tea where

(shohk-kee-dah-nah) *(nah-kah)*
Ocha wa shokkidana no naka desu.
cupboard (P) inside is

(kōh-chah)
kōcha ______________
black tea

(kōh-chah)
Kōcha wa doko desu ka?
black tea where

(kōh-hēē)
kōhī ______________
coffee

(kōh-hēē)
Kōhī wa doko desu ka?
coffee

(pahn)
pan ______________
bread

(pahn)
Pan wa doko desu ka?

Don't forget to label all these things and do not forget to use every opportunity to say these **tango** out loud.

(koh-reh) *(hee-jōh)* *(tye-seh-tsoo)(dess)*
Kore wa hijō ni taisetsu desu.
this very (P) important

❒ **kākī** *(kāh-kēē)*	khaki	**k**	______________
❒ **kamera** *(kah-meh-rah)*	camera		______________
❒ **kanbasu** *(kahn-bah-soo)*	canvas		______________
❒ **kānēshon** *(kāh-nēh-shohn)*	carnation		______________
❒ **kangarū** *(kahn-gah-rōō)*	kangaroo		______________

-ree-gah-tōh) (goh-zye-mahss)
rigatō gozaimasu

(soo-mee-mah-sen)
sumimasen

ōh) (ee-tah-shee-mahsh-teh)
ō itashimashite

ōh-foo-koo) (dahn-soo)
ōfuku dansu

(bed-doh)
beddo

(mah-koo-rah)
makura

(kah-keh-boo-tohn)
kakebuton

eh-zah-mah-shee) (doh-kay)
ezamashi dokei

(kah-gah-mee)
kagami

(sen-men-dye)
senmendai

(tah-oh-roo)
taoru

(toy-reh)
toire

(shah-wāh)
shawā

(en-pee-tsoo)
enpitsu

(teh-reh-bee)
terebi

(pen)
pen

(kohn-pyōō-tāh)
konpyūtā

(meh-gah-neh)
megane

(kah-mee)
kami

(zahsh-shee)
zasshi

(sheen-boon)
shinbun

(goh-mee-bah-koh)
gomibako

(hohn)
hon

(teh-gah-mee)
tegami

(keet-teh)
kitte

(hah-gah-kee)
hagaki

(pah-soo-pōh-toh)
pasupōto

(keep-poo)
kippu

(sōō-tsoo-kēh-soo)
sūtsukēsu

(hahn-doh-bahg-goo)
handobaggu

(sigh-foo)
saifu

(oh-kah-neh)
okane

(koo-reh-jeet-toh) (kāh-doh)
kurejitto kādo

(toh-rah-beh-rāh-zoo) (chek-koo)
toraberāzu chekku

(kah-meh-rah)
kamera

(fee-roo-moo)
firumu

(mee-zoo-gee)
mizugi

(sahn-dah-roo)
sandaru

(sahn-goo-rah-soo)
sangurasu

(hah-boo-rah-shee)
haburashi

(hah-mee-gah-kee)
hamigaki

(sek-ken)
sekken

(kah-mee-soh-ree)
kamisori

(deh-oh-doh-rahn-toh)
deodoranto

(koo-shee)
kushi

(rain-kōh-toh)
reinkōto

(kah-sah)
kasa

(ōh-bāh)
ōbā

(teh-boo-koo-roh)
tebukuro

(bōh-shee)
bōshi

(nah-gah-goo-tsoo)
nagagutsu

(koo-tsoo)
kutsu

(teh-nee-soo) (shōō-zoo)
tenisu shūzu

(sōō-tsoo)
sūtsu

(neh-koo-tie)
nekutai

(shah-tsoo)
shatsu

(jah-ket-toh)
jaketto

(zoo-bohn)
zubon

(jēēn-zoo)
jīnzu

(shōh-toh) (pahn-tsoo)
shōto pantsu

(tēē) (shah-tsoo)
tī shatsu

(pahn-tsoo)
pantsu

(hah-dah-gee)
hadagi

(wahn-pēē-soo)
wanpīsu

(boo-rah-oo-soo)
burausu

(soo-kāh-toh)
sukāto

(sēh-tāh)
sētā

(boo-rah-jāh)
burajā

(pahn-tēē)
pantī

(nye-toh-gown)
naitogaun

(koo-tsoo-shtah)
kutsushita

(bah-soo-rōh-boo)
basurōbu

(pah-jah-mah)
pajama

(soo-reep-pah)
surippa

(wah-tah-shee) (wah) (ah-meh-ree-kah) (kah-rah) (kee-mahsh-tah)
Watashi wa Amerika kara kimashita.

(nee-hohn-goh) (oh) (nah-rye-mahss)
Nihongo o naraimasu.

(wah-tah-shee) (wah) (toh) (yoh-bah-reh-teh) (ee-mahss)
Watashi wa ________ to yobarete imasu.

PLUS . . .

This book includes a number of other innovative features unique to the ***"10 minutes a day®"*** series. At the back of this book, you will find twelve pages of flash cards. Cut them out and flip through them at least once a day.

On pages 116, 117 and 118 you will find a beverage guide and a menu guide. Don't wait until your trip to use them. Clip out the menu guide and use it tonight at the dinner table. Take them both with you the next time you dine at your favorite Japanese restaurant.

By using the special features in this book, you will be speaking Japanese before you know it.

(tah-noh-sheen-deh) *(koo-dah-sigh)*
Tanoshinde kudasai!
have fun

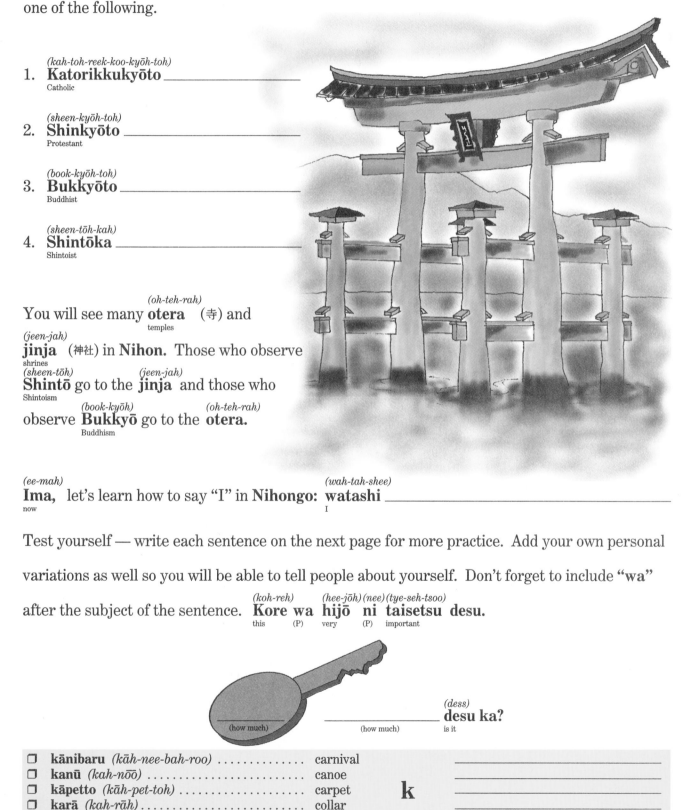

(shōō-kyōh)
Shūkyō
religion

In **Nihon,** there is not the wide variety of (shōō-kyōh) **shūkyō** (religions) that we find in **Amerika.** A person is usually one of the following.

1. (kah-toh-reek-koo-kyōh-toh) **Katorikkukyōto** (Catholic) ____________________
2. (sheen-kyōh-toh) **Shinkyōto** (Protestant) ____________________
3. (book-kyōh-toh) **Bukkyōto** (Buddhist) ____________________
4. (sheen-tōh-kah) **Shintōka** (Shintoist) ____________________

You will see many (oh-teh-rah) **otera** (temples) (寺) and (jeen-jah) **jinja** (shrines) (神社) in **Nihon.** Those who observe (sheen-tōh) **Shintō** (Shintoism) go to the (jeen-jah) **jinja** and those who observe (book-kyōh) **Bukkyō** (Buddhism) go to the (oh-teh-rah) **otera.**

(ee-mah) **Ima,** (now) let's learn how to say "I" in **Nihongo:** (wah-tah-shee) **watashi** (I) ____________________

Test yourself — write each sentence on the next page for more practice. Add your own personal variations as well so you will be able to tell people about yourself. Don't forget to include **"wa"** after the subject of the sentence. (koh-reh) **Kore** (this) **wa** (P) (hee-jōh) **hijō** (very) (nee) **ni** (P) (tye-seh-tsoo) **taisetsu** (important) **desu.**

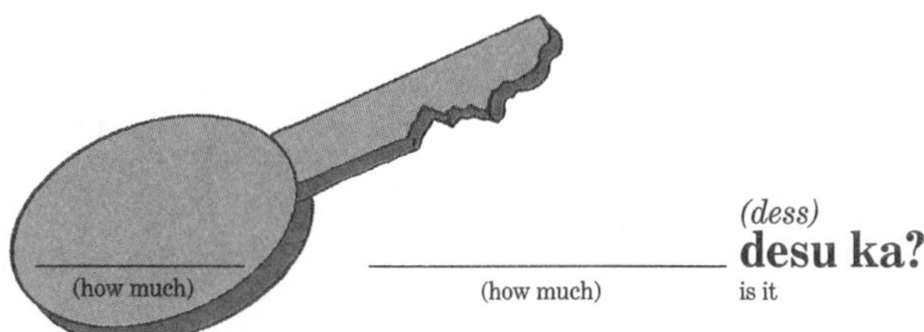

____________________ (how much) (dess) **desu ka?** (is it)

❒ **kānibaru** *(kāh-nee-bah-roo)*	carnival	**k**	____________________
❒ **kanū** *(kah-nōō)*	canoe		____________________
❒ **kāpetto** *(kāh-pet-toh)*	carpet		____________________
❒ **karā** *(kah-rāh)*	collar		____________________
❒ **karatto** *(kah-raht-toh)*	carat		____________________

(wah-tah-shee)(wah) (kah-toh-reek-koo-kyōh-toh) (dess)
Watashi wa Katorikkukyōto desu. ____________
I (P) Catholic am

(wah-tah-shee) (sheen-kyōh-toh)
Watashi wa Shinkyōto desu. ____________
I (P) Protestant am

(book-kyōh-toh)
Watashi wa Bukkyōto desu. ____________
Buddhist

(hah-hah)
Watashi wa haha desu. ____________
mother

(chee-chee)
Watashi wa chichi desu. ____________
father

(kah-nah-dah-jeen)
Watashi wa Kanadajin desu. ____________
Canadian

(hoh-teh-roo) (nee) (ee-mahss)
Watashi wa hoteru ni imasu. ____________
in am

(nee-hohn-jeen)
Watashi wa Nihonjin desu. ____________
Japanese

(ress-toh-rahn) (ee-mahss)
Wastshi wa resutoran ni imasu. ____________
restaurant in am

(sheen-tōh-kah)
Watashi wa Shintōka desu. ____________
Shintoist

(ah-meh-ree-kah-jeen)
Watashi wa Amerikajin desu. ____________
American

(kyōh-kai) (ee-mahss)
Watashi wa kyōkai ni imasu. ____________
church in am

(oh-teh-rah) (ee-mahss)
Watashi wa otera ni imasu. ____________
temple in

(jeen-jah) (ee-mahss)
Watashi wa jinja ni imasu. ____________
shrine in am

To negate statements, the verb's ending *generally* changes from "**u**" to "**en**."

(ee-mah-sen)
Watashi wa hoteru ni imasen.
I in am not

(ress-toh-rahn) (ee-mah-sen)
Watashi wa resutoran ni imasen.
I in am not

(dess) (deh-wah) (ah-ree-mah-sen)
However, "**desu**" changes to "**dewa arimasen.**"

(chee-chee) (deh-wah)
Watashi wa chichi dewa arimasen.
father am not

(hah-hah) (ah-ree-mah-sen)
Watashi wa haha dewa arimasen.
mother am not

Drill all of the above sentences again, but in the negative this time. **Ima,** take a piece of paper.

(kah-zoh-koo) *(tah-dah-shēē)*
Our **kazoku** (family) from earlier had a reunion. Identify everyone below by writing the **tadashii** (correct)

(hee-toh) *(ee-noo)*
Nihongo no tango ((P) word) for each **hito** (person) — **haha, ojisan** and so on. Don't forget the **inu!**

- ❒ **karē** *(kah-rēh)* .... curry ____________
- ❒ **karendā** *(kah-ren-dāh)*.................. calendar ____________
- ❒ **karifurawā** *(kah-ree-foo-rah-wāh)*.......... cauliflower **k** ____________
- ❒ **karorī** *(kah-roh-rēē)* .... calorie ____________
- ❒ **kashimia** *(kah-shee-mee-ah)*.............. cashmere ____________

Naraimasu

(nah-rye-mahss) learn

You have already used **ni** (nee) two very important phrases: **kudasai** (koo-dah-sigh) please give me and **motte imasu** (moht-teh) (ee-mahss) have. Although you might be able to get by with only these, let's assume you want to do better. First, a quick review.

How do you say **"I"** in **Nihongo?** ____________

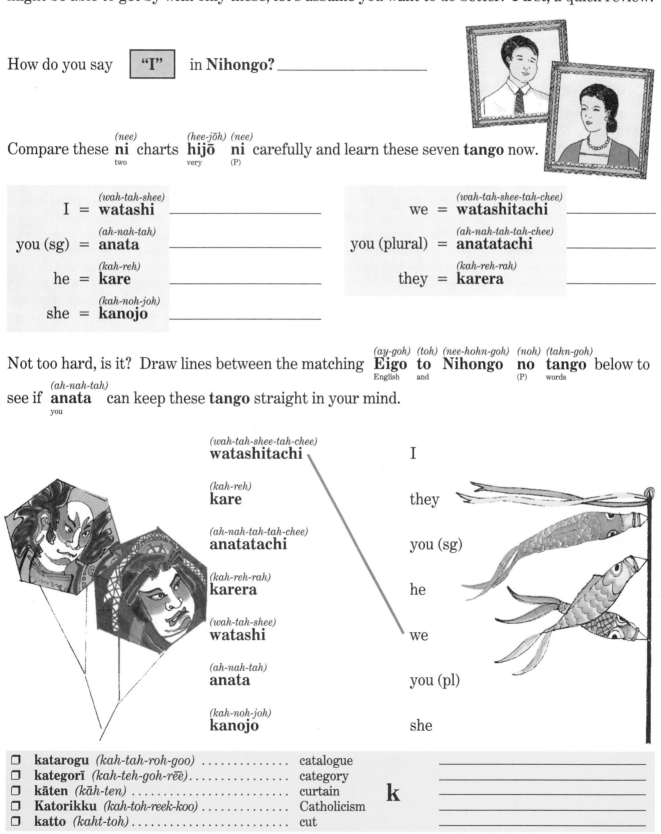

Compare these **ni** (nee) two charts **hijō** (hee-jōh) very **ni** (nee) (P) carefully and learn these seven **tango** now.

I =	**watashi** (wah-tah-shee)	____________
you (sg) =	**anata** (ah-nah-tah)	____________
he =	**kare** (kah-reh)	____________
she =	**kanojo** (kah-noh-joh)	____________

we =	**watashitachi** (wah-tah-shee-tah-chee)	____________
you (plural) =	**anatatachi** (ah-nah-tah-tah-chee)	____________
they =	**karera** (kah-reh-rah)	____________

Not too hard, is it? Draw lines between the matching **Eigo** (ay-goh) English **to** (toh) and **Nihongo** (nee-hohn-goh) **no** (noh) (P) **tango** (tahn-goh) words below to see if **anata** (ah-nah-tah) you can keep these **tango** straight in your mind.

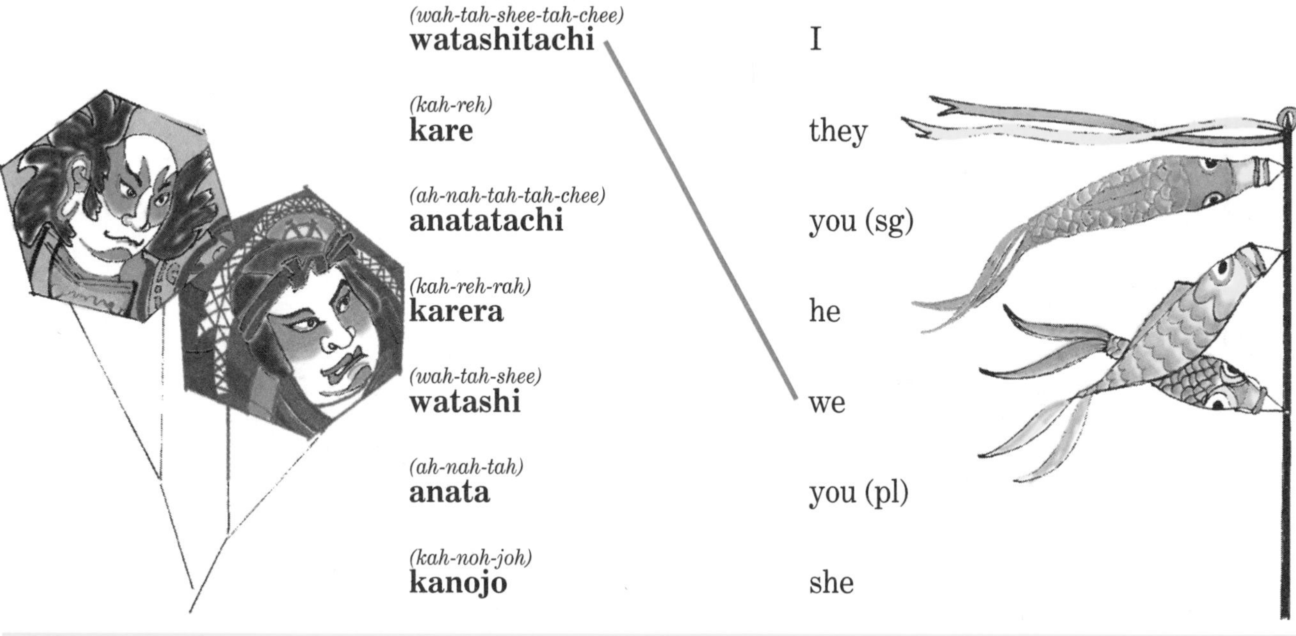

watashitachi (wah-tah-shee-tah-chee)	I
kare (kah-reh)	they
anatatachi (ah-nah-tah-tah-chee)	you (sg)
karera (kah-reh-rah)	he
watashi (wah-tah-shee)	we
anata (ah-nah-tah)	you (pl)
kanojo (kah-noh-joh)	she

k

- ❒ **katarogu** *(kah-tah-roh-goo)* .... catalogue ____________
- ❒ **kategorī** *(kah-teh-goh-rēē)*.............. category ____________
- ❒ **kāten** *(kāh-ten)* .... curtain ____________
- ❒ **Katorikku** *(kah-toh-reek-koo)* .... Catholicism ____________
- ❒ **katto** *(kaht-toh)*........................ cut ____________

Ima close **kono** *(hohn)* **hon** and write out both columns of this *(ren-shōō)* **renshū** on a piece of *(kah-mee)* **kami.** *(dōh)* **Dō** did **anata** do? *(ēē)* **Ii** or *(wah-roo-ee)* **warui?** **Ima** that *(ah-nah-tah)* **anata** know these **tango, anata** can say almost anything in **Nihongo** with one basic formula, as long as you know the correct verb to use.

(kono = this, hon = book, renshū = practice, kami = paper, Dō = how, Ii = well, warui = poorly, anata = you)

To demonstrate, let's take six basic and practical verbs and see how the "plug-in" formula works. Write the verbs in the blanks after **anata** have practiced saying them out loud many times.

(hah-nah-shee-mahss) **hanashimasu** speak	____________	*(tye-zye) (shee-mahss)* **taizai shimasu** remain, stay	____________
(soon-deh) (ee-mahss) **sunde imasu** live, reside	____________	*(chōō-mohn) (shee-mahss)* **chūmon shimasu** order	____________
(kye-mahss) **kaimasu** buy	kaimasu, kaimasu	*(yoh-bah-reh-teh) (ee-mahss)* **yobarete imasu** be called	____________

Besides the familiar words already circled, can **anata wa** find three of the above verbs in the puzzle below? When **anata** find them, write them in the blanks to the right.

S	U	N	D	E	I	M	A	S	U	K
A	N	A	T	A	Ē	N	A	N	K	A
R	I	D	O	Y	H	K	J	J	A	I
Ū	K	R	S	D	E	Ē	B	O	R	M
E	U	M	E	T	Ō	Ū	U	Y	E	A
R	R	W	A	T	A	S	H	I	R	S
K	A	N	O	J	O	K	D	E	A	U
H	A	N	A	S	H	I	M	A	S	U

1. ____________

2. ____________

3. ____________

k

- ❒ **kēburu** *(kēh-boo-roo)* .... cable ____________
- ❒ **kēburukā** *(kēh-boo-roo-kāh)* .... cable car ____________
- ❒ **kechappu** *(keh-chahp-poo)* .... ketchup ____________
- ❒ **kēki** *(kēh-kee)* .... cake ____________
- ❒ **kī** *(kēē)* .... key ____________

Notice that each verb contains the component *(mahss)* **"-masu"** which is an auxiliary component indicating the present tense. The past tense is generally signaled by the ending **"-ta." Nihongo** has numerous levels of a verb. You are learning the **"-masu"** form which is the polite form.

Note:
- Japanese has two ways of saying "you" whereas in English we only use one word.
- *(ah-nah-tah)* **"Anata"** (you (singular)) refers to one person.
- *(ah-nah-tah-tah-chee)* **"Anatatachi"** (you (plural)) refers to more than one person, as we might say "you all." In this book we will focus on *(ah-nah-tah)* **"anata."** (you (singular))
- *(tah-chee)* **"Tachi"** is sometimes added to a word to indicate more than one person. *(tah-toh-eh-bah)* **Tatoeba,** (for example)

  (wah-tah-shee) **watashi** (I) + **tachi** ⟶ *(wah-tah-shee-tah-chee)* **watashitachi** (we)

  (ah-nah-tah) **anata** (you (singular)) + **tachi** ⟶ *(ah-nah-tah-tah-chee)* **anatatachi** (you (plural))

- Unlike **Eigo,** verbs are placed at the end of sentences in **Nihongo.**
- The same verb form is used in **Nihongo** for all subjects. It's that easy!
- In **Nihongo,** "particle words," such as **wa,** (P) are often placed after the subject.
- Pronouns, words like "I," "he," "she," "we" or "they," are frequently omitted.

Subject	Verb		Meaning
(wah-tah-shee) **watashi** (I) **wa** (P) *(kah-reh)* **kare** (he) **wa** (P) *(kah-noh-joh)* **kanojo** (she) **wa** (P)	*(hah-nah-shee-mahss)* **hanashimasu**	=	I *speak* ______ he/she *speaks*
	(kye-mahss) **kaimasu**	=	I *buy* ______ he/she *buys*
	(tye-zye) (shee-mahss) **taizai shimasu**	=	I *stay* ______ he/she *stays*
	(chōō-mohn) (shee-mahss) **chūmon shimasu**	=	I *order* ______ he/she *orders*
	(soon-deh) (ee-mahss) **sunde imasu**	=	I *live* ______ he/she *lives*
	(yoh-bah-reh-teh) (ee-mahss) **yobarete imasu**	=	I *am called* ______ he/she *is called*

Speak slowly and clearly, and you will be perfectly understood whether you say **"watashi wa kaimasu"** or **"watashi kaimasu."** Japanese speakers will be delighted that you have taken the time to learn their language.

❐ **kiro** *(kee-roh)*	kilo, kilogram		______
❐ **kōhī** *(kōh-hēe)*	coffee		______
❐ **Koka Kōra** *(koh-kah)(kōh-rah)*	Coca-Cola	**k**	______
❐ **kokku** *(kohk-koo)*	cook		______
❐ **kokoa** *(koh-koh-ah)*	cocoa		______

(wah-tah-shee-tah-chee) (ah-nah-tah) (ah-nah-tah-tah-chee) (kah-reh-rah)
Again, notice that **watashitachi,** **anata,** **anatatachi** and **karera** use the same verb form
we / you / you / they

(wah-tah-shee) (kah-reh) (kah-noh-joh)
as **watashi,** **kare** and **kanojo.**
I / he / she

<table>
<tr>
<td rowspan="6">

(wah-tah-shee-tah-chee)
watashitachi wa
we (P)

(ah-nah-tah)
anata wa
you (P)

(ah-nah-tah-tah-chee)
anatatachi wa
you (P)

(kah-reh-rah)
karera wa
they (P)

</td>
<td>(hah-nah-shee-mahss)
hanashimasu</td><td>=</td><td>we/you/they speak ______</td>
</tr>
<tr><td>(kye-mahss)
kaimasu</td><td>=</td><td>we/you/they buy ______</td></tr>
<tr><td>(tye-zye) (shee-mahss)
taizai shimasu</td><td>=</td><td>we/you/they stay ______</td></tr>
<tr><td>(chōō-mohn) (shee-mahss)
chūmon shimasu</td><td>=</td><td>we/you/they order ______</td></tr>
<tr><td>(soon-deh) (ee-mahss)
sunde imasu</td><td>=</td><td>we/you/they live ______</td></tr>
<tr><td>(yoh-bah-reh-teh) (ee-mahss)
yobarete imasu</td><td>=</td><td>we/you/they are called ______</td></tr>
</table>

Fill in the following blanks with the verb shown. Each time you write out the verb, be sure to say it aloud several times. **Kono renshū** *(ren-shōō)* [practice] **wa hijō ni taisetsu** *(tye-seh-tsoo)* [important] **desu.**

Here are six more **dōshi** *(dōh-shee)* [verbs].

(kee-mahss) **kimasu** come	______	*(ee-kee-mahss)* **ikimasu** go	______
(nah-rye-mahss) **naraimasu** learn	______	*(moht-teh) (ee-mahss)* **motte imasu** have	motte imasu
(hoh-shēē) (dess) **hoshii desu** would like	______	*(ee-ree-mahss)* **irimasu** need	______

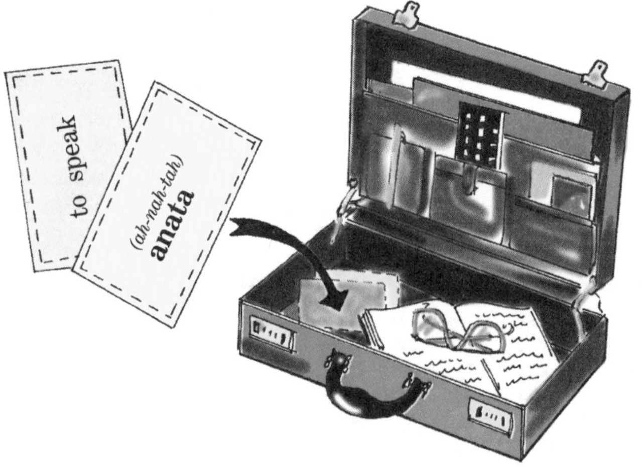

At the back of **kono hon, anata wa** will find twelve **pēji** *(pēh-jee)* [pages] of flash cards to help **anata** learn these **atarashii** *(ah-tah-rah-shēē)* [new] **tango.** Cut them out; carry them in your briefcase, purse, pocket or knapsack; review them whenever **anata** have a free moment.

❐ **komedian** *(koh-meh-dee-ahn)*	comedian		______
❐ **konma** *(kohn-mah)*	comma		______
❐ **konbīfu** *(kohn-bēē-foo)*	corned beef	**k**	______
❐ **konbinēshon** *(kohn-bee-nēh-shohn)*	combination		______
❐ **kondakutā** *(kohn-dah-koo-tāh)*	conductor		______

Ima, it is your turn to practice what **anata** *(ah-nah-tah)* (you) have learned. Fill in the following blanks with the correct form of the verb. Remember, in **Nihongo** the verb comes at the end of the sentence.

(hah-nah-shee-mahss)
hanashimasu
speak

Ogenki desu ka?

Watashi wa Nihongo o ______________.
(P) (P)

Kare / Kanojo wa Eigo o hanashimasu.
(ay-goh) (P) English (P)

Anata wa Furansugo o ______________.
(foo-rahn-soo-goh) French

Watashitachi wa Chūgokugo o ______________.
(chōō-goh-koo-goh) Chinese

Karera wa Itariago o ______________.
(ee-tah-ree-ah-goh) Italian

(tye-zye) (shee-mahss)
taizai shimasu
stay

Watashi wa Nihon ni ______________.
(P) *(nee)* in

Kare / Kanojo wa Amerika ni ______________.
(ah-meh-ree-kah) (nee) in

Anata wa hoteru ni ______________.
(hoh-teh-roo) hotel

Watashitachi wa Ajia ni ______________.
(ah-jee-ah) Asia

Karera wa Kanada ni taizai shimasu.
(kah-nah-dah) Canada

(soon-deh) (ee-mahss)
sunde imasu
live

Watashi wa Nihon ni ______________.
(P) *(nee)* in

Kare / Kanojo wa Amerika ni ______________.

Anata wa Furansu ni ______________.
(foo-rahn-soo) France

Watashitachi wa Supein ni ______________.
(soo-pain) Spain

Karera wa Doitsu ni ______________.
(doy-tsoo) Germany

(chōō-mohn) (shee-mahss)
chūmon shimasu
order

Watashi wa ippai no mizu o ______________.
(eep-pie) one glass (P) *(mee-zoo)* water (P)

Kare / Kanojo wa ippai no wain o ______________.
(eep-pie) one glass (P) *(wine)* wine

Anata wa ippai no ocha o ______________.
(P) *(oh-chah)* tea

Watashitachi wa ippai no bīru o ______________.
(P) *(bēē-roo)* beer

Karera wa ippai no miruku o ______________.
(P) *(mee-roo-koo)* milk

(kye-mahss)
kaimasu
buy

Watashi wa hon o kaimasu.
(hohn) book

Kare / Kanojo wa sarada o ______________.
(sah-rah-dah) salad

Anata wa jidōsha o ______________.
(jee-dōh-shah) car

Watashitachi wa tokei o ______________.
(toh-kay) clock

Karera wa ranpu o ______________.
(rahn-poo) lamp

(yoh-bah-reh-teh) (ee-mahss)
yobarete imasu
be called

Watashi wa Yōko to ______________.
(yōh-koh) (toh) (P)

Kare / Kanojo wa Suzuki san to ______________.
(soo-zoo-kee) (sahn) (P)

Anata wa Akira to ______________.
(ah-kee-rah)

Watashitachi wa Itō san to ______________.
(ee-tōh) (sahn)

Karera wa Yamamoto san to ______________.
(yah-mah-moh-toh) (sahn)

❒ **kone** *(koh-neh)*	connection	**k**	______________
❒ **konkurīto** *(kohn-koo-rēē-toh)*	concrete		______________
❒ **konpakuto kā** *(kohn-pah-koo-toh)(kāh)*	compact car		______________
❒ **konpasu** *(kohn-pah-soo)*	compass		______________
❒ **konsāto** *(kohn-sāh-toh)*	concert		______________

Now take a break, walk around the room, take a deep breath and do the next six *(dōh-shee)* **dōshi** (verbs). Did you notice on the previous page how *(sahn)* **"san"** was combined with last names to show respect?

(kee-mahss)
kimasu
come

Watashi wa Amerika *(kah-rah)* **kara** (from) ______________.

Kare / Kanojo wa Nihon *(kah-rah)* **kara** (from) ___kimasu___.

Anata wa *(doy-tsoo)* **Doitsu** (Germany) **kara** ______________.

Watashitachi wa *(ee-gee-ree-soo)* **Igirisu** (England) **kara** ______________.

Karera wa *(foo-rahn-soo)* **Furansu** (France) **kara** ______________.

(ee-kee-mahss)
ikimasu
go

Watashi wa Nihon *(eh)* **e** (to) ______________.

Kare / Kanojo wa Amerika *(eh)* **e** (to) ______________.

Anata wa *(soo-pain)* **Supein** (Spain) **e** ___ikimasu___.

Watashitachi wa *(yōh-rohp-pah)* **Yōroppa** (Europe) **e** ______________.

Karera wa *(ee-gee-ree-soo)* **Igirisu** (England) **e** ______________.

(nah-rye-mahss)
naraimasu
learn

Watashi wa Nihongo o (P) ______________.

Kare / Kanojo wa Eigo o ______________.

Anata wa *(ee-tah-ree-ah-goh)* **Itariago** (Italian) **o** ______________.

Watashitachi wa *(foo-rahn-soo-goh)* **Furansugo** (French) **o** ______________.

Karera wa *(chōō-goh-koo-goh)* **Chūgokugo** (Chinese) **o** ______________.

(moht-teh) (ee-mahss)
motte imasu
have

Watashi wa *(hyah-koo)* **hyaku** (100) *(en)* **en** (yen) **o** (P) ______________.

Kare / Kanojo wa *(goh-hyah-koo)* **gohyaku** (500) **en o** (P) ______________.

Anata wa sen (1,000) **en o** ______________.

Watashitachi wa *(goh-sen)* **gosen en o** ______________.

Karera wa *(ee-chee-mahn)* **ichiman** (10,000) **en o** ______________.

(hoh-shēē) (dess)
hoshii desu
would like

Watashi wa *(eep-pie)* **ippai** (one glass) **no** (P) *(wine)* **wain** (wine) *(gah)* **ga** (P) ______________.

Kare / Kanojo wa *(eep-pie)* **ippai** (one glass) **no** (P) *(mee-zoo)* **mizu** (water) **ga** (P) ______________.

Anata wa ippai no (P) *(mee-roo-koo)* **miruku ga** ______________.

Watashitachi wa ippai no (P) *(kōh-hēē)* **kōhī** (coffee) **ga** ______________.

Karera wa ippai no (P) *(oh-chah)* **ocha** (tea) **ga** ______________.

(ee-ree-mahss)
irimasu
need

Watashi wa *(eep-pie)* **ippai** (one glass) **no** (P) *(wine)* **wain ga** (P) ______________.

Kare / Kanojo wa *(eep-pie)* **ippai** (one cup) **no** (P) *(oh-chah)* **ocha** (tea) **ga** ______________.

Anata wa ippai no (P) *(mee-zoo)* **mizu** (water) **ga** ______________.

Watashitachi wa ippai no *(kōh-hēē)* **kōhī ga** ______________.

Karera wa ippai no *(mee-roo-koo)* **miruku ga** ______________.

❐ **konsome** *(kohn-soh-meh)*	consommé	**k**	______________
❐ **kōnsutāchi** *(kōhn-soo-tāh-chee)*	cornstarch		______________
❐ **kontakuto renzu** *(kohn-tah-koo-toh)(ren-zoo)*	contact lens		______________
❐ **kontena** *(kohn-teh-nah)*	container		______________
❐ **kontorasuto** *(kohn-toh-rah-soo-toh))*	contrast		______________

(hi) **Hai,** (yes) it is hard to get used to all those new words, particularly the little particle words. Just keep practicing and before *(ah-nah-tah)* **anata** (you) know it, you will be using them naturally. **Ima** is a perfect time to turn to the back of **kono** (this) *(hohn)* **hon,** (book) clip out your verb flash cards and start flashing. Don't skip over your free **tango** either. Check them off in the box provided as **anata** learn each one. See if **anata** can fill in the blanks below. **Kotae** are at the bottom of the *(pēh-jee)* **pēji.**

1. ______________________________
(I speak Japanese.)

2. ______________________________
(We learn Japanese.)

3. ______________________________
(She needs 5,000 yen.)

4. ______________________________
(He comes from Canada.)

5. ______________________________
(They live in America.)

6. ______________________________
(She buys a book.)

In the following Steps, **anata wa** will be introduced to more **dōshi** and **anata wa** should drill them in exactly the same way as **anata** did in this section. Look up the *(ah-tah-rah-shēē)* **atarashii** (new) **tango** in your *(jee-shoh)* **jisho** (dictionary) and make up your own sentences. Try out your *(ah-tah-rah-shēē)* **atarashii** **tango** for that's how you make them yours to use on your holiday. Remember, the more **anata** practice, the more enjoyable your trip will be.

(gahn-baht-teh) **Ganbatte!** (go for it)

KOTAE

1. **Watashi wa Nihongo o hanashimasu.**
2. **Watashitachi wa Nihongo o naraimasu.**
3. **Kanojo wa gosen en ga irimasu.**
4. **Kare wa Kanada kara kimasu.**
5. **Karera wa Amerika ni sunde imasu.**
6. **Kanojo wa hon o kaimasu.**

13 Nanji desu ka?

(nahn-jee) (dess)
Nanji desu ka?
what time / is it

Anata wa know how to tell the **hi** (hee) (days) of **isshūkan** (eesh-shōō-kahn) (one week) **to** (toh) (and) the **tsuki** (tsoo-kee) (months) of the **toshi,** (toh-shee) (year) so now let's learn to tell time. As a traveler, **anata wa** need to be able to tell time in order to make **yoyaku** (yoh-yah-koo) (reservations) and to catch **ressha.** (res-shah) (trains (long-distance)) Here are the "basics."

What time is it?	=	(nahn-jee) (dess) **Nanji desu ka?** ______
hour/time	=	(jee-kahn) **jikan** ______
noon	=	(shōh-goh) **shōgo** ______
half	=	(hahn) (sahn-jeep-poon) **han / sanjippun** ______
before	=	(mah-eh) **mae** ______
after	=	(soo-gee) **sugi** ______
a quarter (15 minutes)	=	(jōō-goh-foon) **jūgofun** ______
a quarter to	=	(jōō-goh-foon) (mah-eh) **jūgofun mae** ______
a quarter after	=	(jōō-goh-foon) (soo-gee) **jūgofun (sugi)** ______

Ima quiz yourself. Fill in the missing letters below.

noon = **s h ō _ o**

after = **_ u g i**

a quarter to = **j ū _ o f u _ ✕ _ a e**

half = **h _ n**

hour = **j i k _ _**

And finally, when = **_ t s u**

- ❒ **kontorōru** *(kohn-toh-rōh-roo)*............ control ______
- ❒ **kopī** *(koh-pēē)* .... copy ______
- ❒ **koppu** *(kohp-poo)* .... cup, glass **k** ______
- ❒ **kōrasu** *(kōh-rah-soo)* .... chorus ______
- ❒ **korekushon** *(koh-reh-koo-shohn)*.......... collection ______

Ima, how are these **tango** used? Study the examples below. When **anata** think it through, it really is not too difficult. Just notice that the pattern changes after the halfway mark. **"Sugi"** (after) is frequently dropped when the meaning is clearly understood.

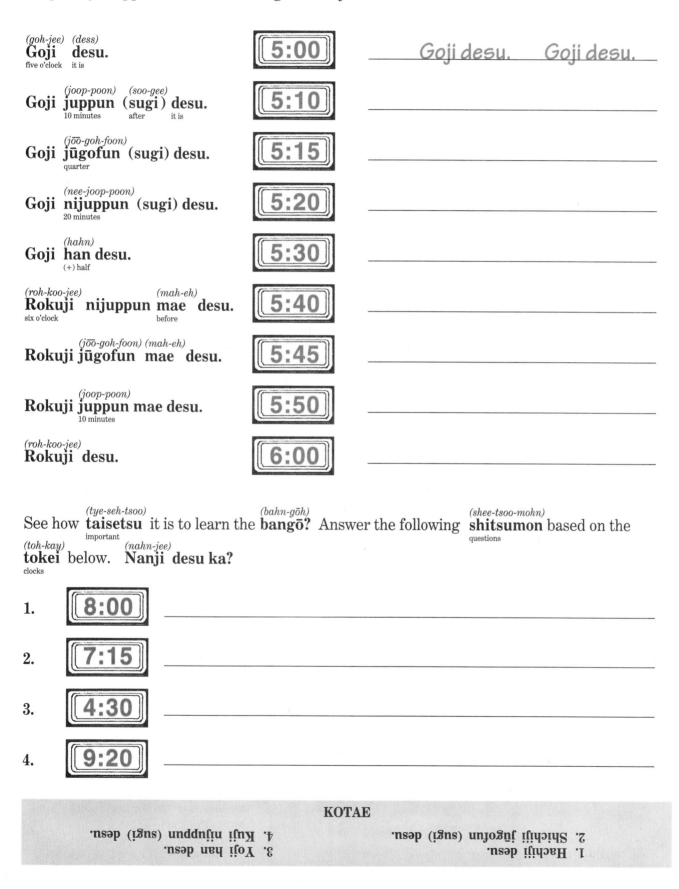

(goh-jee) (dess) **Goji desu.** five o'clock it is	5:00	Goji desu. Goji desu.
(joop-poon) (soo-gee) **Goji juppun (sugi) desu.** 10 minutes after it is	5:10	
(jōō-goh-foon) **Goji jūgofun (sugi) desu.** quarter	5:15	
(nee-joop-poon) **Goji nijuppun (sugi) desu.** 20 minutes	5:20	
(hahn) **Goji han desu.** (+) half	5:30	
(roh-koo-jee) (mah-eh) **Rokuji nijuppun mae desu.** six o'clock before	5:40	
(jōō-goh-foon) (mah-eh) **Rokuji jūgofun mae desu.**	5:45	
(joop-poon) **Rokuji juppun mae desu.** 10 minutes	5:50	
(roh-koo-jee) **Rokuji desu.**	6:00	

See how *(tye-seh-tsoo)* **taisetsu** (important) it is to learn the *(bahn-gōh)* **bangō?** Answer the following *(shee-tsoo-mohn)* **shitsumon** (questions) based on the *(toh-kay)* **tokei** (clocks) below. *(nahn-jee)* **Nanji desu ka?**

1. 8:00 __________
2. 7:15 __________
3. 4:30 __________
4. 9:20 __________

KOTAE

1. **Hachiji** desu.
2. **Shichiji jūgofun** (sugi) desu.
3. **Yoji han** desu.
4. **Kuji nijuppun** (sugi) desu.

When **anata** answer an "**itsu?**" *(ee-tsoo)* (when) question, say "**ni**" *(nee)* (at) after you give the time.

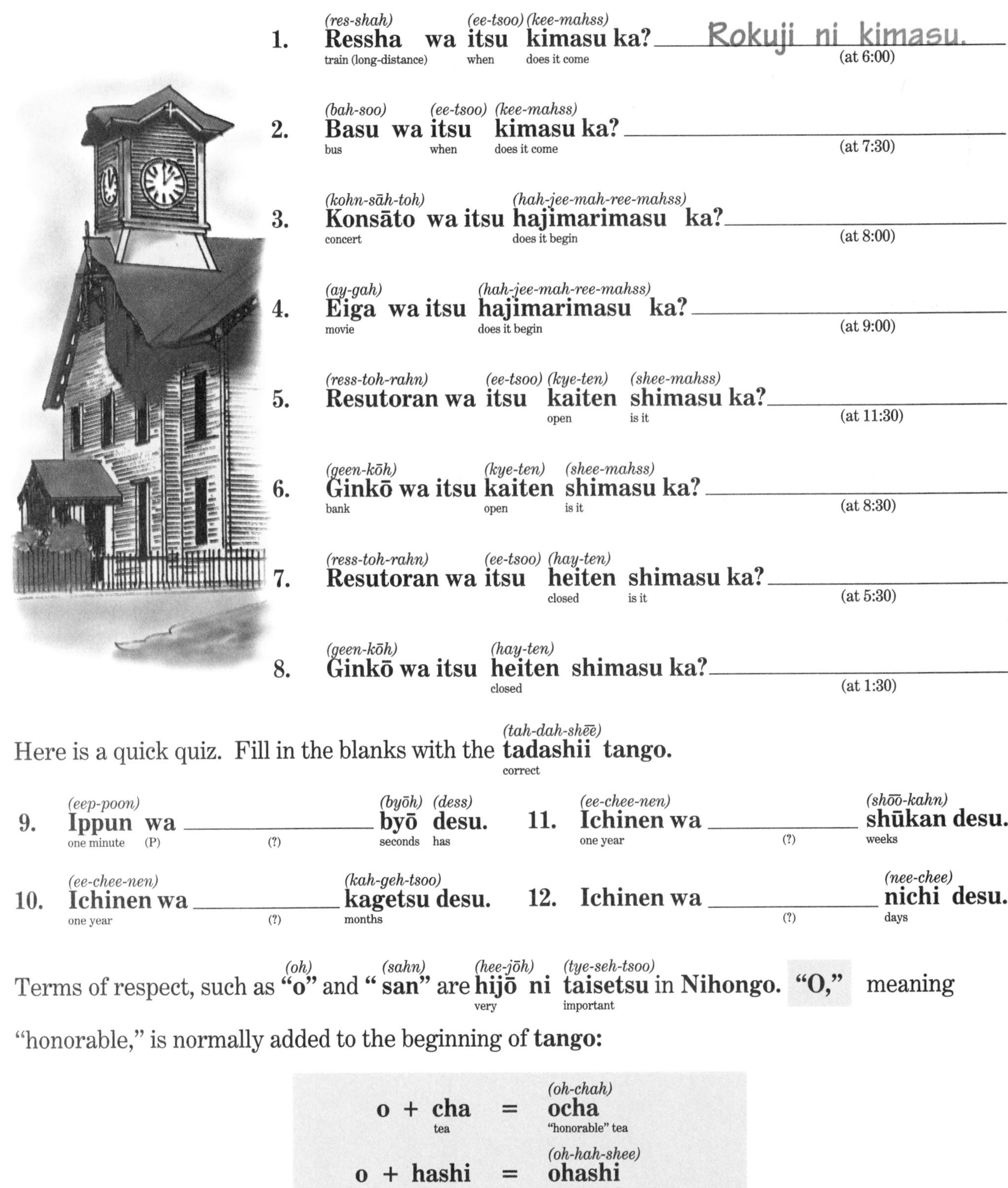

1. *(res-shah)* **Ressha** (train (long-distance)) **wa** *(ee-tsoo)* **itsu** (when) *(kee-mahss)* **kimasu** (does it come) **ka?** Rokuji ni kimasu. (at 6:00)

2. *(bah-soo)* **Basu** (bus) **wa** *(ee-tsoo)* **itsu** (when) *(kee-mahss)* **kimasu** (does it come) **ka?** ______ (at 7:30)

3. *(kohn-sāh-toh)* **Konsāto** (concert) **wa itsu** *(hah-jee-mah-ree-mahss)* **hajimarimasu** (does it begin) **ka?** ______ (at 8:00)

4. *(ay-gah)* **Eiga** (movie) **wa itsu** *(hah-jee-mah-ree-mahss)* **hajimarimasu** (does it begin) **ka?** ______ (at 9:00)

5. *(ress-toh-rahn)* **Resutoran wa** *(ee-tsoo)* **itsu** *(kye-ten)* **kaiten** (open) *(shee-mahss)* **shimasu** (is it) **ka?** ______ (at 11:30)

6. *(geen-kōh)* **Ginkō** (bank) **wa itsu** *(kye-ten)* **kaiten** (open) *(shee-mahss)* **shimasu** (is it) **ka?** ______ (at 8:30)

7. *(ress-toh-rahn)* **Resutoran wa** *(ee-tsoo)* **itsu** *(hay-ten)* **heiten** (closed) **shimasu** (is it) **ka?** ______ (at 5:30)

8. *(geen-kōh)* **Ginkō wa itsu** *(hay-ten)* **heiten** (closed) **shimasu ka?** ______ (at 1:30)

Here is a quick quiz. Fill in the blanks with the *(tah-dah-shēē)* **tadashii** (correct) **tango.**

9. *(eep-poon)* **Ippun** (one minute) **wa** (P) ______ (?) *(byōh)* **byō** (seconds) *(dess)* **desu.** (has)

10. *(ee-chee-nen)* **Ichinen wa** (one year) ______ (?) *(kah-geh-tsoo)* **kagetsu desu.** (months)

11. *(ee-chee-nen)* **Ichinen wa** (one year) ______ (?) *(shōō-kahn)* **shūkan desu.** (weeks)

12. **Ichinen wa** ______ (?) *(nee-chee)* **nichi desu.** (days)

Terms of respect, such as "**o**" *(oh)* and "**san**" *(sahn)* are *(hee-jōh)* **hijō** (very) **ni** *(tye-seh-tsoo)* **taisetsu** (important) in **Nihongo.** "**O,**" meaning "honorable," is normally added to the beginning of **tango:**

o + cha (tea) = *(oh-chah)* **ocha** ("honorable" tea)

o + hashi (chopsticks) = *(oh-hah-shee)* **ohashi** ("honorable" chopsticks)

KOTAE

1. Rokuji ni kimasu.
2. Shichiji han ni kimasu.
3. Hachiji ni hajimarimasu.
4. Kuji ni hajimarimasu.
5. Jūichiji han ni akimasu.
6. Hachiji han ni akimasu.
7. Goji han ni shimarimasu.
8. Ichiji han ni shimarimasu.
9. rokujū
10. jūni
11. gojūni
12. sanbyaku rokujū go

Do **anata** remember your greetings from earlier? It is a good time to review them as they will always be **hijō** *(hee-jōh)* very **ni taisetsu** *(tye-seh-tsoo)* important.

Asa *(ah-sah)* morning **no** (P) **hachiji** *(hah-chee-jee)* eight o'clock **ni wa**, at **"Ohayō** *(oh-hah-yōh)* good morning **gozaimasu"** *(goh-zye-mahss)* **to** *(toh)* (P) **iimasu.** *(ē-mahss)* one says

Nan *(nahn)* what **to iimasu ka?** *(ē-mahss)* does one say ______________________

Gogo *(goh-goh)* afternoon **no** (P) **ichiji** *(ee-chee-jee)* **ni wa, "Konnichiwa"** *(kohn-nee-chee-wah)* good afternoon **to** *(toh)* (P) **iimasu.** *(ē-mahss)* one says

Nan to iimasu ka? *(ē-mahss)* ______________________

Ban *(bahn)* evening **no** (P) **shichiji** *(shee-chee-jee)* **ni wa**, at **"Konbanwa"** *(kohn-bahn-wah)* good evening **to** *(toh)* **iimasu.** *(ē-mahss)*

Nan to iimasu ka? *(ē-mahss)* ______________________

Yoru *(yoh-roo)* night **no jūji** *(jōō-jee)* **ni wa**, at **"Oyasumi** *(oh-yah-soo-mee)* **nasai"** *(nah-sigh)* good night **to** *(toh)* **iimasu.**

Nan to iimasu ka? ______________________

"San," which means "Mr.," "Mrs.," "Miss" or "honorable," is added to the end of **tango** or to **hito** *(hee-toh)* person **no** (P) **namae:**

oba aunt	+	**san**	=	**obasan** *(oh-bah-sahn)* "honorable" aunt
Tanaka	+	**san**	=	**Tanaka san** *(tah-nah-kah) (sahn)* Mr. Tanaka

San is added to both men's and women's first and last names. For a boy one adds **kun** *(koon)* and for a girl one can add **chan** *(chahn)* to her first name. Let's practice using our **kazoku** from page 31.

Yōko chan	can also be	**Tanaka san** Miss Tanaka
Takashi kun *(koon)*	can also be	**Tanaka kun**

Michiko san	can also be	**Tanaka san** Mrs. Tanaka
Kazuo san	can also be	**Tanaka san** Mr. Tanaka

k

- ❑ **koruku** *(koh-roo-koo)*.................. cork ______________
- ❑ **kōsu** *(kōh-soo)*......................... course (class) ______________
- ❑ **kosuto** *(koh-soo-toh)*.................. cost ______________
- ❑ **kōto** *(kōh-toh)*......................... coat ______________
- ❑ **kukkī** *(kook-kēē)*....................... cookie ______________

Here are two *(ah-tah-rah-shēē)* **atarashii** (new) *(dōh-shee)* **dōshi** (verbs) for Step 13.

(tah-beh-mahss) **tabemasu** (eat) ______________________

(noh-mee-mahss) **nomimasu** (drink) ______________________

(tah-beh-mahss)
tabemasu
eat

Watashi wa *(yah-sigh)* **yasai** (vegetables) **o** (P) ______________________.

Kare / Kanojo wa *(soo-tēh-kee)* **sutēki** (steak) **o** ______________________.

Anata wa *(sah-kah-nah)* **sakana** (fish) **o** tabemasu.

Watashitachi wa *(pahn)* **pan** (bread) **o** ______________________.

Karera wa *(eye-soo)* **aisu** (ice) *(koo-rēē-moo)* **kurīmu** (cream) **o** ______________________.

(noh-mee-mahss)
nomimasu
drink

Watashi wa miruku o ______________________.

Kare / Kanojo wa *(shee-roh-wine)* **shirowain** (white wine) **o** ______________________.

Anata wa *(oh-sah-keh)* **osake** (rice wine) **o** ______________________.

Watashitachi wa bīru o ______________________.

Karera wa ocha o nomimasu.

Remember, to negate a statement you *generally* change the final **"-masu"** to **"-masen."**

Anata wa *(oh-sah-keh)* **osake o** *(noh-mee-mahss)* **nomimasu.** (drink)
Watashi wa Amerika kara (from) *(kee-mahss)* **kimasu.** (come)
(kah-reh) **Kare wa** *(ay-goh)* **Eigo o** *(hah-nah-shee-mahss)* **hanashimasu.** (speaks)

Anata wa osake o *(noh-mee-mah-sen)* **nomimasen.** (do not drink)
Watashi wa Amerika kara *(kee-mah-sen)* **kimasen.** (do not come)
Kare wa Eigo o *(hah-nah-shee-mah-sen)* **hanashimasen.** (does not speak)

❒ **māchi** *(māh-chee)*	march	**m**	______________________
❒ **machinē** *(mah-chee-nēh)*	matinée		______________________
❒ **madamu** *(mah-dah-moo)*	madam		______________________
❒ **magajin** *(mah-gah-jeen)*	magazine		______________________
❒ **māgarin** *(māh-gah-reen)*	margarine		______________________

(ah-nah-tah)
Anata wa have learned a lot of material in the last few steps and that means it is time to quiz yourself. Don't panic, this is just for you and no one else needs to know how **anata** did. Remember, this is a chance to review, find out what **anata** remember and what **anata** need to spend more time on. After **anata** have finished, check your **kotae** *(koh-tah-eh)* in the glossary at the back of this book. Circle the correct answers.

kōhī	tea	coffee
(ē-eh) **iie**	yes	no
obasan	aunt	uncle
to	and	or
(nah-rye-mahss) **naraimasu**	drink	learn
asa	morning	night
Kayōbi	Friday	Tuesday
hanashimasu	live	speak
natsu	summer	winter
okane	money	page
kyū	nine	ten
pan	a lot	bread

kazoku	seven	family
kodomo	child	grandfather
miruku	butter	milk
shio	pepper	salt
ue	under	over
isha san	man	doctor
Rokugatsu	June	July
daidokoro	kitchen	religions
motte imasu	would like	have
kaimasu	order	buy
kinō	yesterday	tomorrow
kiiroi	good	yellow

(oh-gen-kee) (dess)
Ogenki desu ka? What time is it? How are you? Well, how are you after this quiz?

- ❐ **maikurohon** *(my-koo-roh-hohn)* .... microphone ____________
- ❐ **mainasu** *(my-nah-soo)* .... minus ____________
- ❐ **mairu** *(my-roo)* .... mile ____________
- ❐ **majikku** *(mah-jeek-koo)* .... magic ____________
- ❐ **makaroni** *(mah-kah-roh-nee)* .... macaroni ____________

m

14 Kita - Minami, Higashi - Nishi

(kee-tah) **Kita** (north) - (mee-nah-mee) **Minami,** (south) (hee-gah-shee) **Higashi** (east) - (nee-shee) **Nishi** (west)

While in **Nihon, anata wa** (P) will probably use a **chizu** (chee-zoo) (map) to find your way around. Study the direction **tango** until **anata** are familiar with them and can recognize them on your **chizu** (chee-zoo) (map) of **Nihon.**

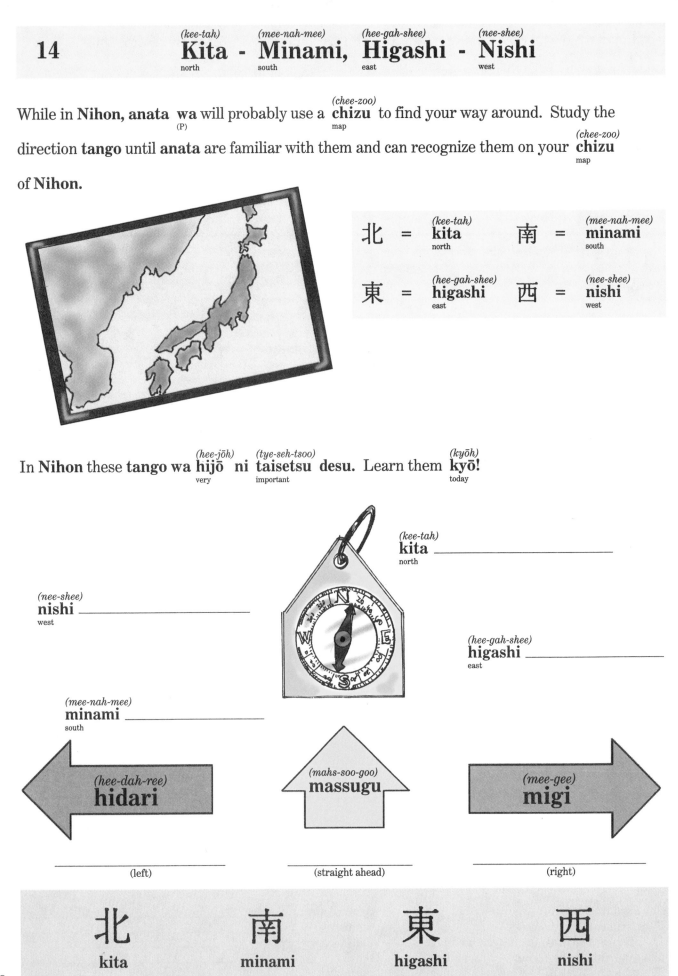

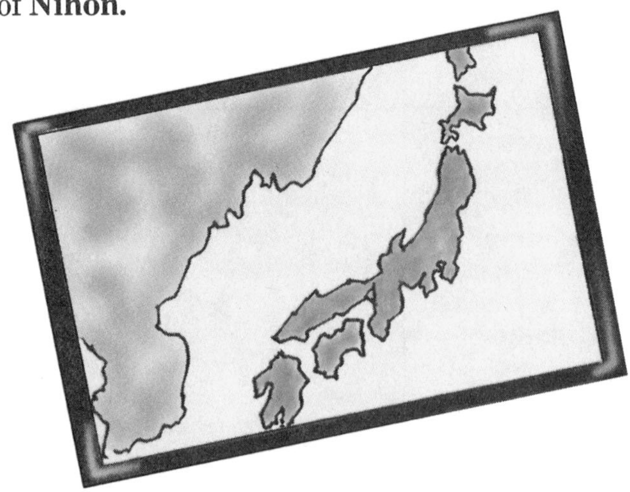

北	=	(kee-tah) **kita** north	南	=	(mee-nah-mee) **minami** south
東	=	(hee-gah-shee) **higashi** east	西	=	(nee-shee) **nishi** west

In **Nihon** these **tango wa** **hijō** (hee-jōh) (very) **ni taisetsu** (tye-seh-tsoo) (important) **desu.** Learn them **kyō!** (kyōh) (today)

(kee-tah) **kita** ________________ north

(nee-shee) **nishi** ________________ west

(hee-gah-shee) **higashi** ________________ east

(mee-nah-mee) **minami** ________________ south

(hee-dah-ree) **hidari**

(mahs-soo-goo) **massugu**

(mee-gee) **migi**

________________ (left)

________________ (straight ahead)

________________ (right)

北	南	東	西
kita	**minami**	**higashi**	**nishi**

These **tango** can go a long way. Say them aloud each time you write them in the blanks below.

(koo-dah-sigh)
kudasai ______________________________
please / please give me

(dōh-zoh)
dōzo ______________________________
please

(soo-mee-mah-sen)
sumimasen ______________________________
excuse me / sorry to bother you

(shee-tsoo-ray)
shitsurei ______________________________
excuse me

(dōh-moh)
dōmo ______________________________
very much / thank you very much / I'm very sorry

(ah-ree-gah-tōh) (goh-zye-mahss)
arigatō gozaimasu ______________________________
thank you

(ee-rahs-shy-mah-seh)
irasshaimase ______________________________
welcome

(dōh) (ee-tah-shee-mahsh-teh)
dō itashimashite ______________________________
you're welcome

(koh-koh) (nee) **Koko** (here) **ni** (P) two typical *(kye-wah)* **kaiwa** (connversations) for someone who is trying to find something **ga** *(ah-ree-mahss)* **arimasu** (are). Write them out in the blanks below.

Suzuki san: *(soo-mee-mah-sen)* **Sumimasen ga** (but) *(tay-koh-koo)* **Teikoku** ((the) Imperial) **Hoteru wa doko desu ka?**

Sumimasen ga Teikoku Hoteru wa doko desu ka?

Itō san: *(nee-bahn-meh)* **Nibanme** (second) **no** (P) *(mee-chee)* **michi** (street) **de** *(hee-dah-ree)* **hidari ni** (to the left) *(mah-gah-ree-mahss)* **magarimasu.** (turn)

____

(tay-koh-koo) **Teikoku Hoteru wa** *(soo-goo)* **sugu** (just) *(soh-koh)* **soko** (over there) **desu.** (is)

____

Akira: **Sumimasen ga** *(oo-eh-noh)* **Ueno** (Ueno) *(bee-joo-tsoo-kahn)* **Bijutsukan** (art museum) **wa doko desu ka?**

____

Yukio: *(koh-koh)* **Koko** (here) **o** (P) *(mee-gee)* **migi ni** (to the right) *(mah-gah-ree-mahss)* **magarimasu.** (turn) **Go** (five) *(mēh-toh-roo)* **mētoru** (meters) *(mahs-soo-goo)* **massugu** (straight ahead) *(ee-kee-mahss)* **ikimasu.** (go) *(kah-doh)* **Kado** (corner)

____

ni (on) *(oo-eh-noh)* **Ueno** *(bee-joo-tsoo-kahn)* **Bijutsukan** (art museum) **ga** *(ah-ree-mahss)* **arimasu.** (is)

____

m

- ❐ **māketto** *(māh-ket-toh)*. . . . . market ______________
- ❐ **māku** *(māh-koo)* . . . . mark, label ______________
- ❐ **māmarēdo** *(māh-mah-rēh-doh)* . . . . marmalade ______________
- ❐ **mandorin** *(mahn-doh-reen)* . . . . mandolin ______________
- ❐ **manējā** *(mah-nēh-jāh)*. . . . . manager ______________

Are you lost? There is no need to be lost if **anata** have learned the basic **hōkō** *(hōh-kōh)* direction **no** (P) **tango.** Do not try to memorize these **kaiwa** *(kye-wah)* conversations because you will never be looking for precisely these places. One day, you might need to ask for **hōkō** *(hōh-kōh)* directions to "**Ginza** *(geen-zah)* **Resutoran**" or **Kyōto** *(kyōh-toh)* **Bijutsukan** *(bee-joo-tsoo-kahn)* art museum." Learn the key **hōkō** *(hōh-kōh)* direction **no** (P) **tango** words and be sure **anata wa** can find your **yukisaki** *(yoo-kee-sah-kee)* destination. **Anata wa** may want to buy a guidebook to start planning which places **anata** would like to visit. Practice asking **shitsumon** *(shee-tsoo-mohn)* questions to these special places. What if the person responding to your **shitsumon** *(shee-tsoo-mohn)* answers too quickly for you to understand the entire reply? Practice saying,

Sumimasen *(soo-mee-mah-sen)* **ga** but **yoku** *(yoh-koo)* well **wakarimasen.** *(wah-kah-ree-mah-sen)* I do not understand **Mō** *(mōh)* once more **ichido** *(ee-chee-doh)* **hanashite** *(hah-nahsh-teh)* speak **kudasai.** *(koo-dah-sigh)* please

Ima, say it again and then write it out below.

____
(Excuse me but I do not understand well. Please say/speak once more.)

Hai, *(hi)* yes it is difficult at first but don't give up! When the directions are repeated, **anata wa** will be able to understand if **anata** have learned the key **tango.** Let's review by writing them in the blanks below.

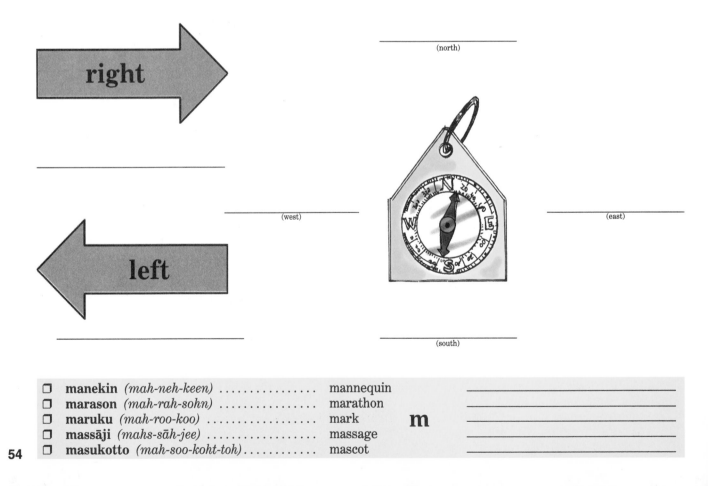

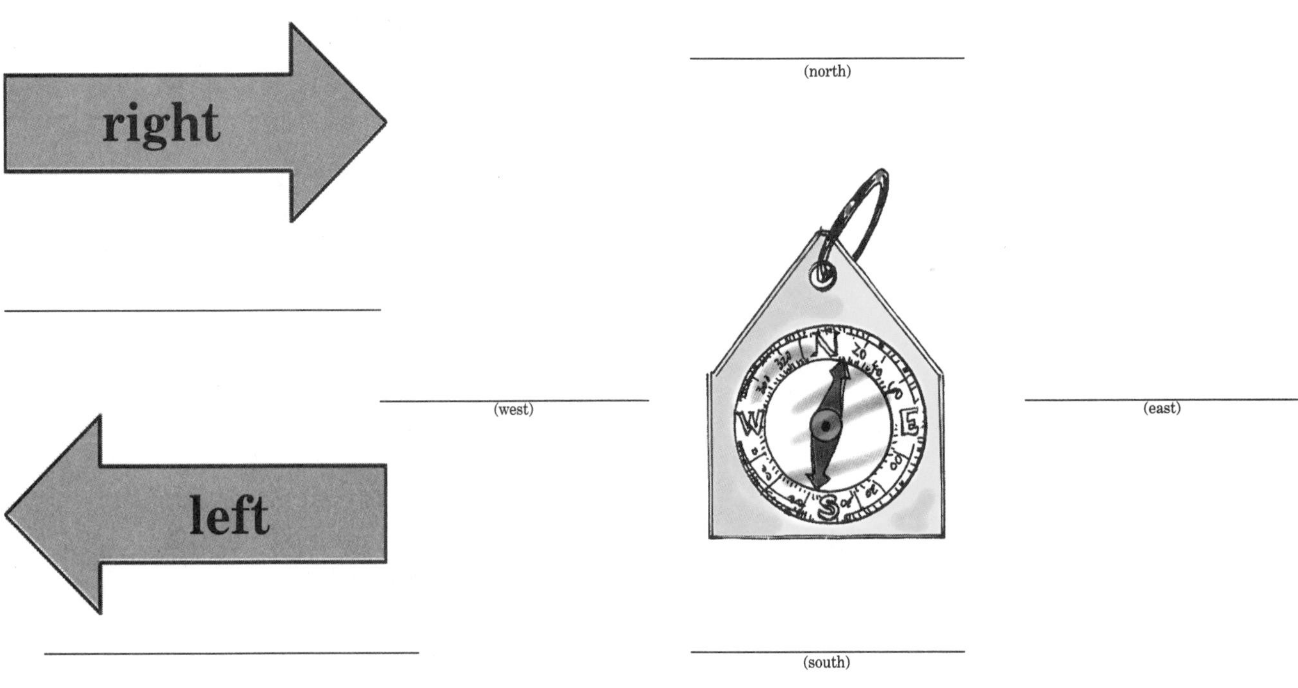

(north)

(west)

(east)

(south)

- ❒ **manekin** *(mah-neh-keen)* .... mannequin
- ❒ **marason** *(mah-rah-sohn)* .... marathon
- ❒ **maruku** *(mah-roo-koo)* .... mark
- ❒ **massāji** *(mahs-sāh-jee)* .... massage
- ❒ **masukotto** *(mah-soo-koht-toh)* .... mascot

m

(moht-toh) (ah-tah-rah-shēē) (dōh-shee)
Koko ni motto atarashii dōshi ga arimasu.
here more new are

(ēē-mahss) **iimasu** say	______	(wah-kah-ree-mahss) **wakarimasu** understand	______
(oo-ree-mahss) **urimasu** sell	______	(koo-ree-kah-eh-shee-mahss) **kurikaeshimasu** repeat	______

As always, say each sentence out loud. Say each and every **tango** carefully, pronouncing each **Nihongo** sound as well as **anata** can.

(ēē-mahss)
iimasu
say

Konnichiwa!

Watashi wa "Ōkē" to ______.
(ōh-kēh) okay; (toh) (P)

Kare / Kanojo wa "Konnichiwa" to ______.

Anata wa "Oyasumi nasai" to ______.
(oh-yah-soo-mee) (nah-sigh) good night

Watashitachi wa "Iie" to ______.
(ēē-eh) no

Karera wa "Hai" to ______.
(hi) yes

(wah-kah-ree-mahss)
wakarimasu
understand

Watashi wa Eigo ga ______.
(ay-goh) English; (P)

Kare / Kanojo wa Nihongo ga ______.
(nee-hohn-goh)

Anata wa Furansugo ga ______.
(foo-rahn-soo-goh) French

Watashitachi wa menyū ga ______.
(meh-nyōō) menu

Karera wa Roshiago ga ______.
(roh-shee-ah-goh) Russian

(oo-ree-mahss)
urimasu
sell

Watashi wa hana o ______.
(hah-nah) flowers; (P)

Kare / Kanojo wa kudamono o ______.
(koo-dah-moh-noh) fruit

Anata wa jaketto o ______.
(jah-ket-toh)

Watashitachi wa banana o ______.
(bah-nah-nah)

Karera wa kippu o ______.
(keep-poo) tickets

(koo-ree-kah-eh-shee-mahss)
kurikaeshimasu
repeat

Nani? Nani?

Watashi wa tango o ______.
(P)

Kare / Kanojo wa kotae o ______.
(koh-tah-eh) answer

Anata wa namae o ______.
(nah-mah-eh) names

Watashitachi wa hōkō o ______.
(hōh-kōh) directions

Karera wa bangō o ______.

m

- ❒ **masuku** *(mah-soo-koo)* .... mask ______
- ❒ **masuto** *(mah-soo-toh)* .... mast ______
- ❒ **matchi** *(maht-chee)* .... match, box of matches ______
- ❒ **mattoresu** *(maht-toh-reh-soo)* .... mattress ______
- ❒ **mayonēzu** *(mah-yoh-nēh-zoo)* .... mayonnaise ______

15 Ue – Shita

(oo-eh) **Ue** (above) – *(shtah)* **Shita** (below)

(ee-mah) **Ima** (now) **watashitachi wa** *(more)* **motto** *(ah-tah-rah-shēē)* **atarashii** (new) **tango o** (P) *(nah-rye-mahss)* **naraimasu.** (learn) *(koh-reh)* **Kore** (this) **ga** (P) **Nihon no** (P) *(ee-eh)* **ie** (house) *(dess)* **desu.**

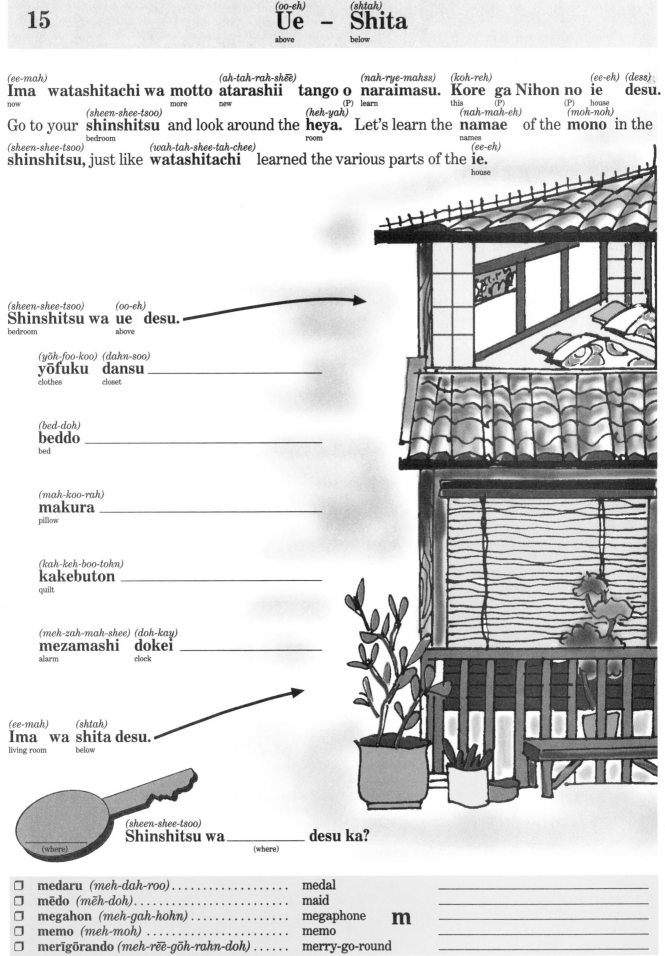

Go to your *(sheen-shee-tsoo)* **shinshitsu** (bedroom) and look around the *(heh-yah)* **heya.** (room) Let's learn the *(nah-mah-eh)* **namae** (names) of the *(moh-noh)* **mono** in the *(sheen-shee-tsoo)* **shinshitsu,** just like *(wah-tah-shee-tah-chee)* **watashitachi** learned the various parts of the *(ee-eh)* **ie.** (house)

(sheen-shee-tsoo) **Shinshitsu** (bedroom) **wa** *(oo-eh)* **ue** (above) **desu.**

(yōh-foo-koo) **yōfuku** (clothes) *(dahn-soo)* **dansu** (closet) ______________________

(bed-doh) **beddo** (bed) ______________________

(mah-koo-rah) **makura** (pillow) ______________________

(kah-keh-boo-tohn) **kakebuton** (quilt) ______________________

(meh-zah-mah-shee) **mezamashi** (alarm) *(doh-kay)* **dokei** (clock) ______________________

(ee-mah) **Ima** (living room) **wa** *(shtah)* **shita** (below) **desu.**

______ (where)

(sheen-shee-tsoo) **Shinshitsu wa** ______ (where) **desu ka?**

- ❐ **medaru** *(meh-dah-roo)* .... medal ______________
- ❐ **mēdo** *(mēh-doh)* .... maid ______________
- ❐ **megahon** *(meh-gah-hohn)* .... megaphone **m** ______________
- ❐ **memo** *(meh-moh)* .... memo ______________
- ❐ **merīgōrando** *(meh-rēē-gōh-rahn-doh)* ...... merry-go-round ______________

(ee-mah) (my) (moh-noh) (sheen-shee-tsoo)
Ima, remove the next **go** **mai** **no** stickers and label these **mono** in your **shinshitsu.** Let's move
now five (M) (P)

(foo-roh-bah) (foo-roh-bah)
into the **furoba** and do the same thing. Remember, **furoba** means a room to bathe in. If
bathroom bathroom

(ress-toh-rahn)
anata wa are in a **resutoran** and **anata wa** need to use the lavatory, **anata wa** want to ask for

(toy-reh) (foo-roh-bah) (hoh-teh-roo) (toh) (ryoh-kahn) (deh)
the **toire** and not for the **furoba. Nihon no hoteru to ryokan de, anata wa** will be
toilet (P) and inns at

(yoo-kah-tah) (oh-foo-roh)
given a special **yukata** to wear after your **ofuro.**
cotton robe bath

女

男

(ohn-nah) (hee-toh-tah-chee) (oh-toh-koh)
onna no hitotachi **otoko no hitotachi**
women (P) men (P)

(shoh-sigh)
Shosai mo ue desu.
study also

(kah-gah-mee)
kagami ______________________
mirror

(sen-men-dye)
senmendai ______________________
washstand

(tah-oh-roo)
taoru ______________________
towels

(toy-reh)
toire ______________________
toilet

(shah-wāh)
shawā ______________________
shower

(foo-roh-bah) (shtah)
Furoba mo shita desu.
also below

❒ **meron** *(meh-rohn)*.	melon		______________
❒ **messēji** *(mes-sēh-jee)*	message		______________
❒ **mētoru** *(mēh-toh-roo)*.	meter	**m**	______________
❒ **miruku** *(mee-roo-koo)*	milk		______________
❒ **mishin** *(mee-sheen)*.	sewing machine		______________

Do not forget to remove the next group of stickers and label these **mono** *(moh-noh)* in your **ie.** *(ee-eh)* Okay, it is time to review. Here's a quick quiz to see what you remember.

❒	**modan** *(moh-dahn)*	modern		________________
❒	**moderu** *(moh-deh-roo)*	model		________________
❒	**monorēru** *(moh-noh-rēh-roo)*	monorail	**m**	________________
❒	**mōtā** *(mōh-tāh)*	motor		________________
❒	**mottō** *(moht-tōh)*	motto		________________

Next stop — the **shosai** *(shoh-sigh)* (office), specifically the **tsukue** *(tsoo-koo-eh)* (desk) in the **shosai** *(shoh-sigh)*. **Tsukue** *(tsoo-koo-eh)* (desk) **no** (P) **ue** *(oo-eh)* (top) **ni** (on) **nani** *(nah-nee)* (what) **ga arimasu** (is) **ka?** Let's identify the **mono** which one normally finds on the **tsukue** *(tsoo-koo-eh)* or strewn about the **ie** *(ee-eh)*.

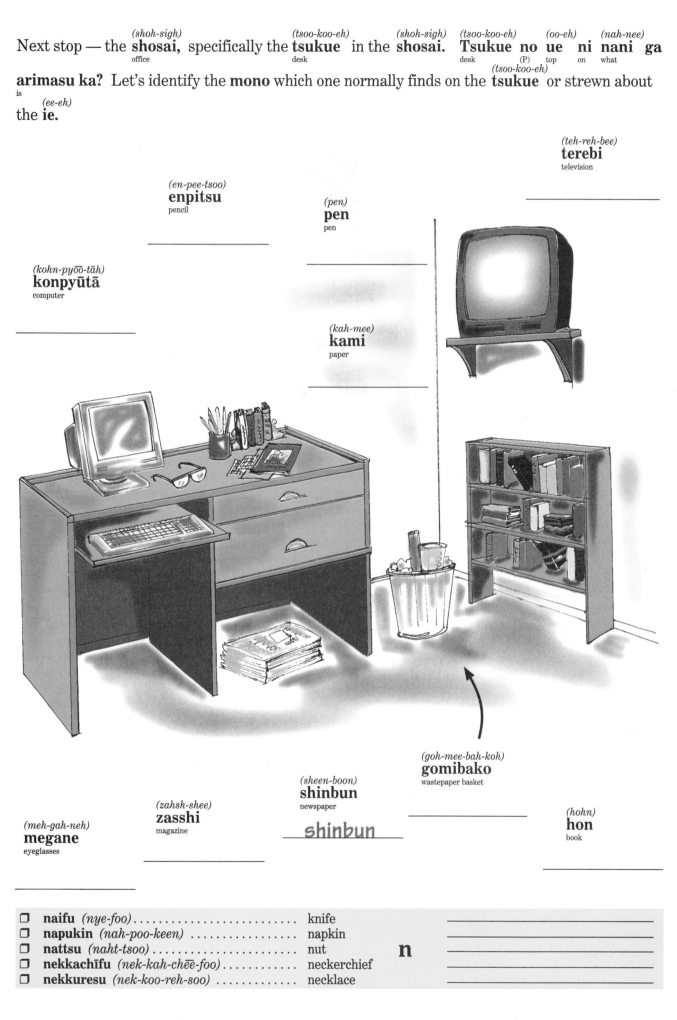

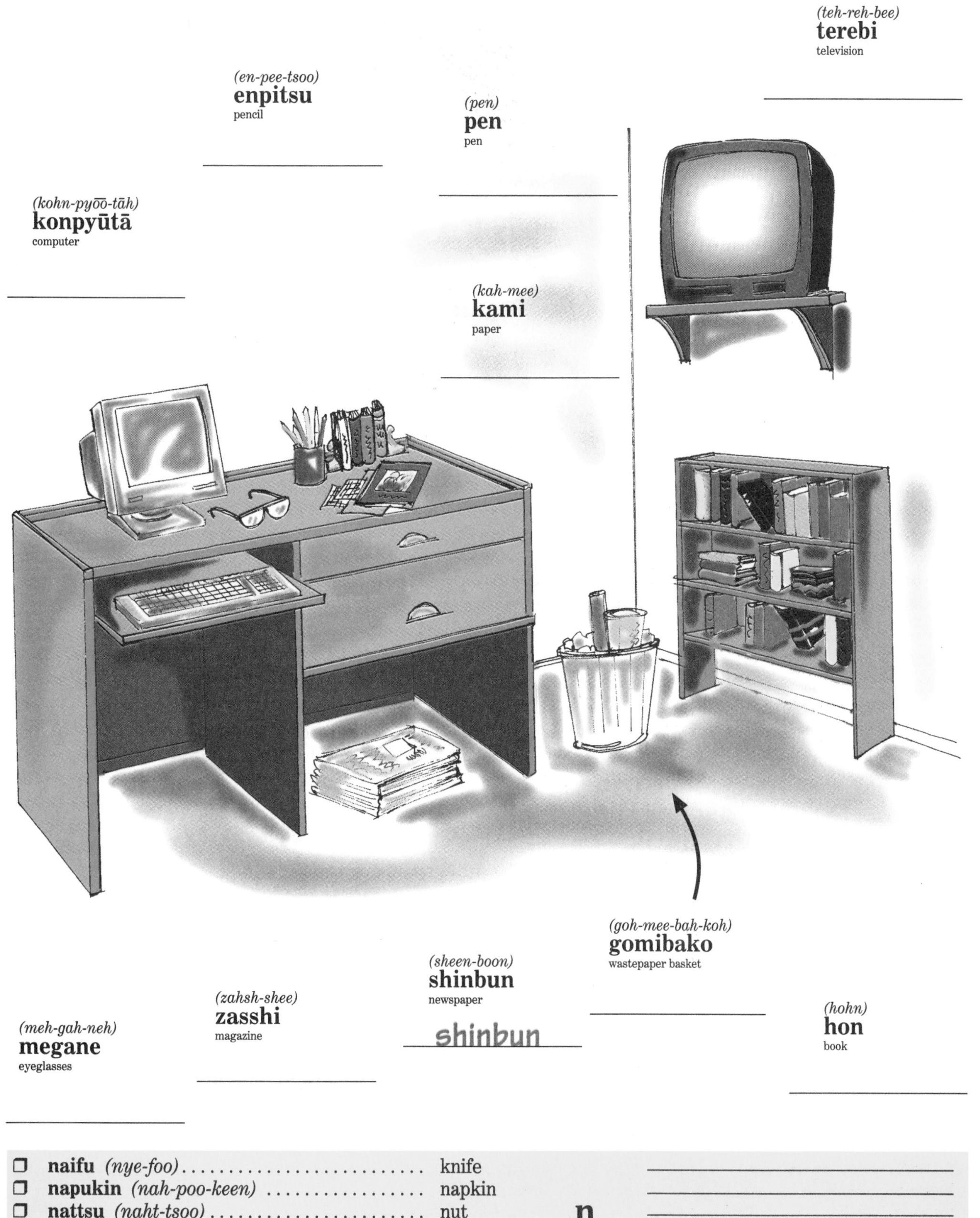

❒ **naifu** *(nye-foo)*	knife		______
❒ **napukin** *(nah-poo-keen)*	napkin		______
❒ **nattsu** *(naht-tsoo)*	nut	**n**	______
❒ **nekkachīfu** *(nek-kah-chēē-foo)*	neckerchief		______
❒ **nekkuresu** *(nek-koo-reh-soo)*	necklace		______

Don't forget these essentials!

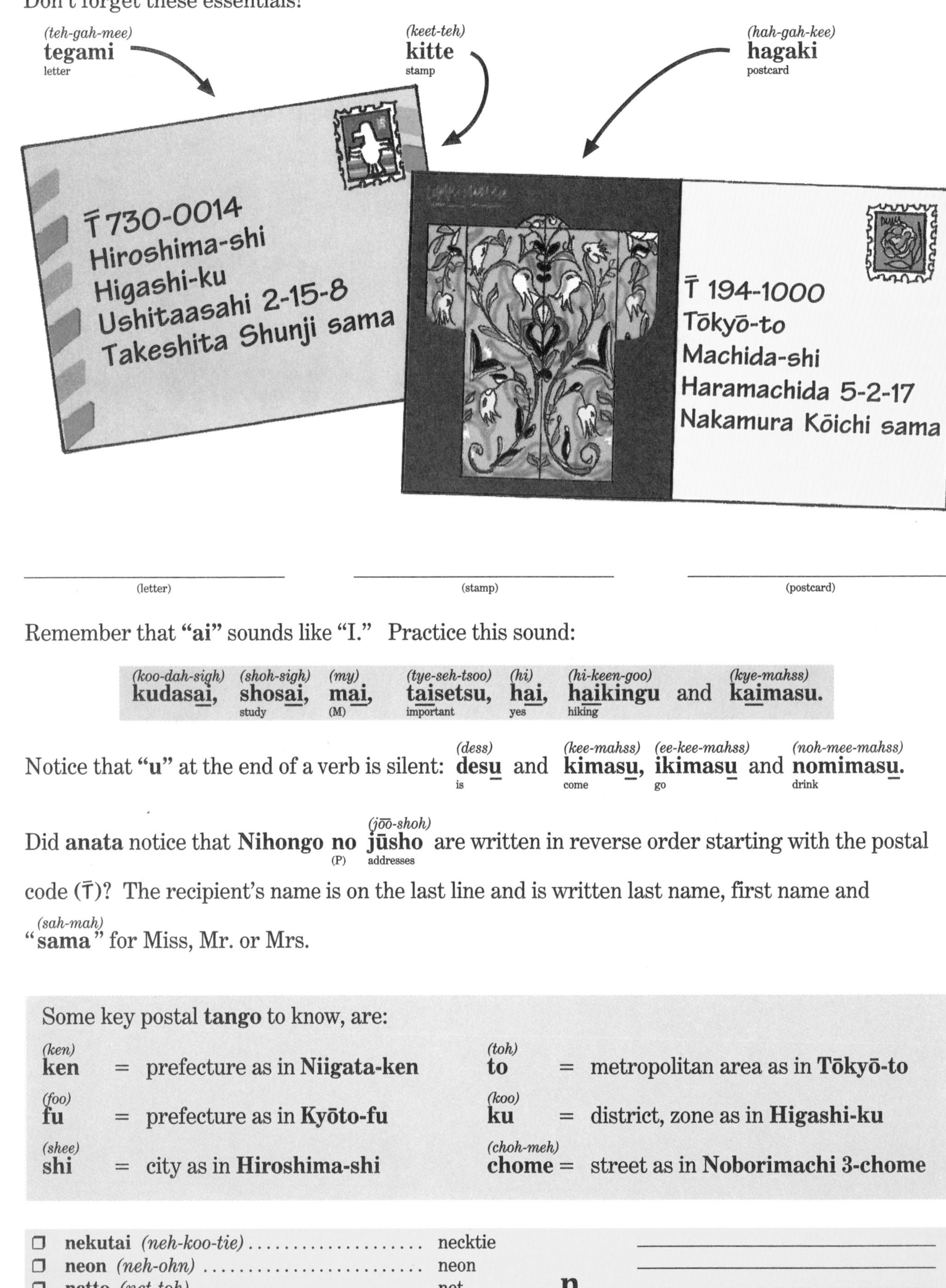

_______________ (letter) _______________ (stamp) _______________ (postcard)

Remember that **"ai"** sounds like "I." Practice this sound:

(koo-dah-sigh) **kudasai**, *(shoh-sigh)* **shosai** (study), *(my)* **mai** (M), *(tye-seh-tsoo)* **taisetsu** (important), *(hi)* **hai** (yes), *(hi-keen-goo)* **haikingu** (hiking) and *(kye-mahss)* **kaimasu.**

Notice that **"u"** at the end of a verb is silent: *(dess)* **desu** (is) and *(kee-mahss)* **kimasu** (come), *(ee-kee-mahss)* **ikimasu** (go) and *(noh-mee-mahss)* **nomimasu** (drink).

Did **anata** notice that **Nihongo no** (P) *(jōō-shoh)* **jūsho** (addresses) are written in reverse order starting with the postal code (〒)? The recipient's name is on the last line and is written last name, first name and *(sah-mah)* "**sama**" for Miss, Mr. or Mrs.

Some key postal **tango** to know, are:

(ken) **ken** = prefecture as in **Niigata-ken**

(foo) **fu** = prefecture as in **Kyōto-fu**

(shee) **shi** = city as in **Hiroshima-shi**

(toh) **to** = metropolitan area as in **Tōkyō-to**

(koo) **ku** = district, zone as in **Higashi-ku**

(choh-meh) **chome** = street as in **Noborimachi 3-chome**

n

- ❒ **nekutai** *(neh-koo-tie)* .... necktie ____________
- ❒ **neon** *(neh-ohn)* .... neon ____________
- ❒ **netto** *(net-toh)* .... net ____________
- ❒ **nōto** *(nōh-toh)* .... note ____________
- ❒ **nyūsu** *(nyōō-zoo)* .... news ____________

Simple, isn't it? **Ima**, *(ee-mah)* after you fill in the blanks below, go back a second time and negate all these sentences by changing the final "**-su**" to "**-sen.**" Don't get discouraged! Just look at how much **anata wa** have already learned and think ahead to new and wonderful food and adventures.

(mee-mahss) **mimasu** see _______________

(neh-mahss) **nemasu** sleep _______________

(oh-koo-ree-mahss) **okurimasu** send _______________

(mah-chee-mahss) **machimasu** wait for _______________

(mee-mahss)
mimasu
see

Watashi wa beddo *(bed-doh)* (bed) **o** *(oh)* (P) _______________.

Kare / Kanojo wa hoteru *(hoh-teh-roo)* **o** _______________.

Anata wa resutoran *(ress-toh-rahn)* **o** _______________.

Watashitachi wa Fujisan *(foo-jee-sahn)* (Mt. Fuji) **o** _______________.

Karera wa ie *(ee-eh)* (house) **o** _______________.

(oh-koo-ree-mahss)
okurimasu
send

Watashi wa tegami *(teh-gah-mee)* (letter) **o** *(oh)* (P) _______________.

Kare / Kanojo wa hagaki *(hah-gah-kee)* (postcard) **o** _______________.

Anata wa hon *(hohn)* **o** _______________.

Watashitachi wa shinbun *(sheen-boon)* (newspaper) **o** _______________.

Karera wa zasshi *(zahsh-shee)* (magazine) **o** _______________.

(neh-mahss)
nemasu
sleep

Watashi wa shinshitsu *(sheen-shee-tsoo)* (bedroom) **de** *(deh)* (in) _______________.

Kare / Kanojo wa ie *(ee-eh)* (house) **de** (in) _______________.

Anata wa hoteru de _______________.

Watashitachi wa ryokan *(ryoh-kahn)* (inn) **de** _______________.

Karera wa beddo *(bed-doh)* **de** _______________.

(mah-chee-mahss)
machimasu
wait for

Watashi wa shinkansen *(sheen-kahn-sen)* (bullet train) **o** *(oh)* (P) _______________.

Kare / Kanojo wa basu *(bah-soo)* **o** _______________.

Anata wa takushī *(tah-koo-shēē)* (taxi) **o** _______________.

Watashitachi wa hoteru *(hoh-teh-roo)* **no** (P) **naka** *(nah-kah)* (inside) **de** _______________.

Karera wa resutoran *(ress-toh-rahn)* **no** (P) **naka** *(nah-kah)* (inside) **de** _______________.

O

- ❒ **ōbā** *(ōh-bāh)* .... overcoat _______________
- ❒ **ōbāshūzu** *(ōh-bāh-shōō-zoo)* .... overshoes _______________
- ❒ **ōdā** *(ōh-dāh)* .... order _______________
- ❒ **ofisu** *(oh-fee-soo)* .... office _______________
- ❒ **ōkē** *(ōh-kēh)* .... okay, all right _______________

Before **anata wa** proceed with the next step, identify all the **mono** below.

- ❒ **ōpun** *(ōh-poon)* .... open
- ❒ **orenji** *(oh-ren-jee)*...................... orange
- ❒ **orugan** *(oh-roo-gahn)*................... organ
- ❒ **ōtobai** *(ōh-toh-by)* .... motorbike
- ❒ **ōtomīru** *(ōh-toh-mēē-roo)* .... oatmeal

O

____

____

____

____

____

16 Yūbin (yōō-bean) mail

Anata wa know how to count, how to ask **shitsumon,** *(shee-tsoo-mohn)* questions, how to use **dōshi** *(dōh-shee)* with the "plug-in" formula and how to describe something, be it the location of a **hoteru** *(hoh-teh-roo)* **mata** *(mah-tah)* or **wa** *(wah)* **ie** *(ee-eh)* house **no** (P) **iro.** *(ee-roh)* color Let's take the basics that **anata** have learned and expand them in special areas that will be most helpful in your travels. What does everyone do on a holiday? Send **hagaki** *(hah-gah-kee)* of course. Let's learn exactly how the **Nihon no** (P) **yūbinkyoku** *(yōō-bean-kyoh-koo)* post office works.

Yūbinkyoku *(yōō-bean-kyoh-koo)* post office is where **anata** buy a **kitte,** *(keet-teh)* stamp send a **kozutsumi** *(koh-zoo-tsoo-mee)* package **mata** *(mah-tah)* or **wa** mail a **tegami.** *(teh-gah-mee)* letter
Yūbinkyoku *(yōō-bean-kyoh-koo)* is closed on **kyūjitsu** *(kyōō-jee-tsoo)* holidays and **Nichiyōbi.** *(nee-chee-yōh-bee)* Sundays In **Nihon, anata wa** can also obtain postal supplies at your **hoteru no** (P) **furonto.** *(foo-rohn-toh)* front desk

❒ **ōkesutora** *(ōh-keh-soo-toh-rah)*	orchestra		______
❒ **omuretsu** *(oh-moo-reh-tsoo)*	omelette		______
❒ **ōnā** *(ōh-nāh)*	owner	**O**	______
❒ **onsu** *(ohn-soo)*	ounce		______
❒ **opera** *(oh-peh-rah)*	opera		______

Koko ni are the necessary **tango** for the **yūbinkyoku** *(yōō-bean-kyoh-koo)* post office or your **hoteru no furonto.** *(foo-rohn-toh)* front desk Practice them aloud and write them in the blanks.

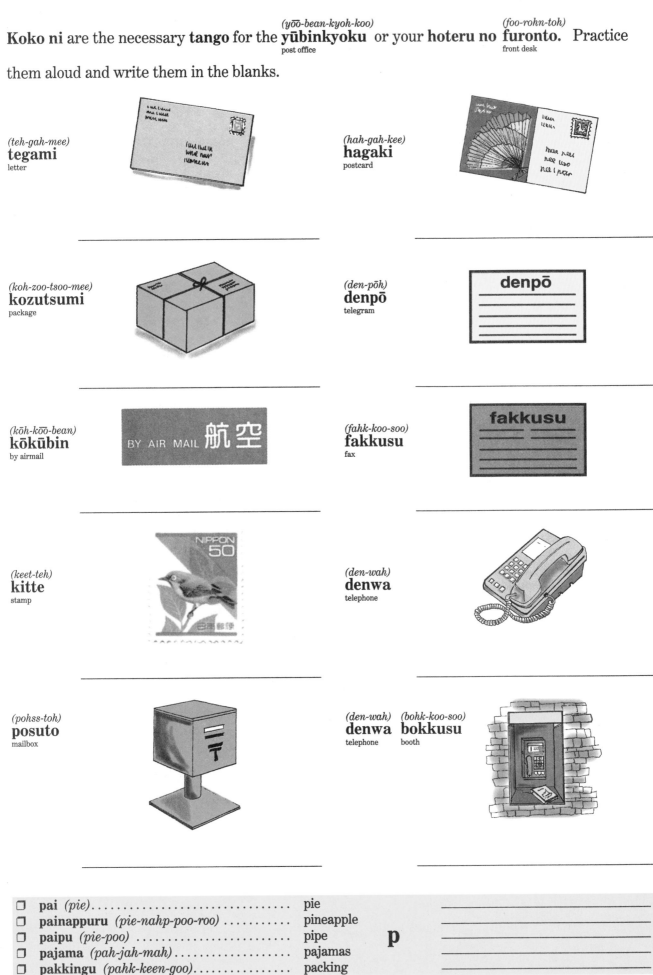

(teh-gah-mee)
tegami
letter

____

(hah-gah-kee)
hagaki
postcard

____

(koh-zoo-tsoo-mee)
kozutsumi
package

____

(den-pōh)
denpō
telegram

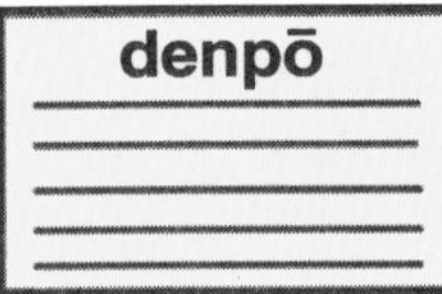

____

(kōh-kōō-bean)
kōkūbin
by airmail

____

(fahk-koo-soo)
fakkusu
fax

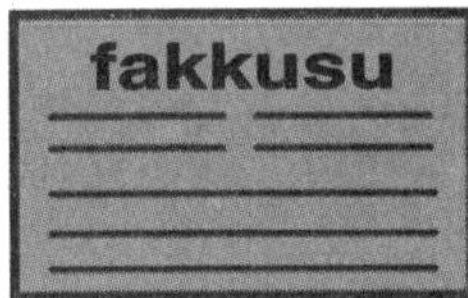

____

(keet-teh)
kitte
stamp

____

(den-wah)
denwa
telephone

____

(pohss-toh)
posuto
mailbox

____

(den-wah) *(bohk-koo-soo)*
denwa bokkusu
telephone booth

____

p

- ❐ **pai** *(pie)*. . . . . pie ______________________
- ❐ **painappuru** *(pie-nahp-poo-roo)* . . . . . . pineapple ______________________
- ❐ **paipu** *(pie-poo)* . . . . pipe ______________________
- ❐ **pajama** *(pah-jah-mah)*. . . . . pajamas ______________________
- ❐ **pakkingu** *(pahk-keen-goo)*. . . . . packing ______________________

Next step — **anata wa** ask **shitsumon** *(shee-tsoo-mohn)* like those **shita,** *(shtah)* below, depending on what **anata wa irimasu.** *(ee-ree-mahss)* need

Repeat these sentences aloud many times.

(keet-teh) **Kitte** (stamp) **wa doko** *(deh)* **de** (at) *(kye-mahss)* **kaimasu ka?** (do I buy one) ____________

(hah-gah-kee) **Hagaki** (postcard) **wa doko de** *(kye-mahss)* **kaimasu ka?** (do I buy one) ____________

(teh-gah-mee) **Tegami** (letter) **wa doko** *(deh)* **de** *(kye-mahss)* **kaimasu ka?** ____________

(pohss-toh) **Posuto** (mailbox) **wa doko desu ka?** ____________

(den-wah) **Denwa** (telephone) *(bohk-koo-soo)* **bokkusu** (booth) **wa doko desu ka?** ____________

(fahk-koo-soo) **Fakkusu** (fax) **wa doko** *(kah-rah)* **kara** (from) *(oh-koo-ree-mahss)* **okurimasu** (do I send one) **ka?** ____________

(koh-zoo-tsoo-mee) **Kozutsumi** (package) **wa doko kara** *(oh-koo-ree-mahss)* **okurimasu ka?** ____________

(hah-gah-kee) **Hagaki wa** *(ee-koo-rah)* **ikura** (how much) **desu ka?** ____________

Ima, quiz yourself. See if **anata wa** can translate the following thoughts into **Nihongo.**

1. Where is the telephone booth? ____________
2. How much does a stamp cost? ____________
3. Where is the front desk? ____________
4. Where is the post office? ____________
5. (At) where do I buy a stamp? ____________
6. How much is it? ____________
7. (From) where do I send a package? ____________
8. (From) where do I send a fax? ____________

KOTAE

1. **Denwa bokkusu wa doko desu ka?**
2. **Kitte wa ikura desu ka?**
3. **Furonto wa doko desu ka?**
4. **Yūbinkyoku wa doko desu ka?**
5. **Kitte wa doko de kaimasu ka?**
6. **Ikura desu ka?**
7. **Kozutsumi wa doko kara okurimasu ka?**
8. **Fakkusu wa doko kara okurimasu ka?**

Koko ni *(moht-toh)* **motto** *(ah-tah-rah-shēē)* **atarashii** *(dōh-shee)* **dōshi ga arimasu.**
here / more / verbs / are

(shee-mahss) **shimasu** (do) ______________________

(mee-seh-mahss) **misemasu** (show) ______________________

(kah-kee-mahss) **kakimasu** (write) ______________________

(hah-rye-mahss) **haraimasu** (pay) ______________________

Practice these verbs by not only filling in the blanks, but by saying them aloud many, many times until you are comfortable with the sounds and the words.

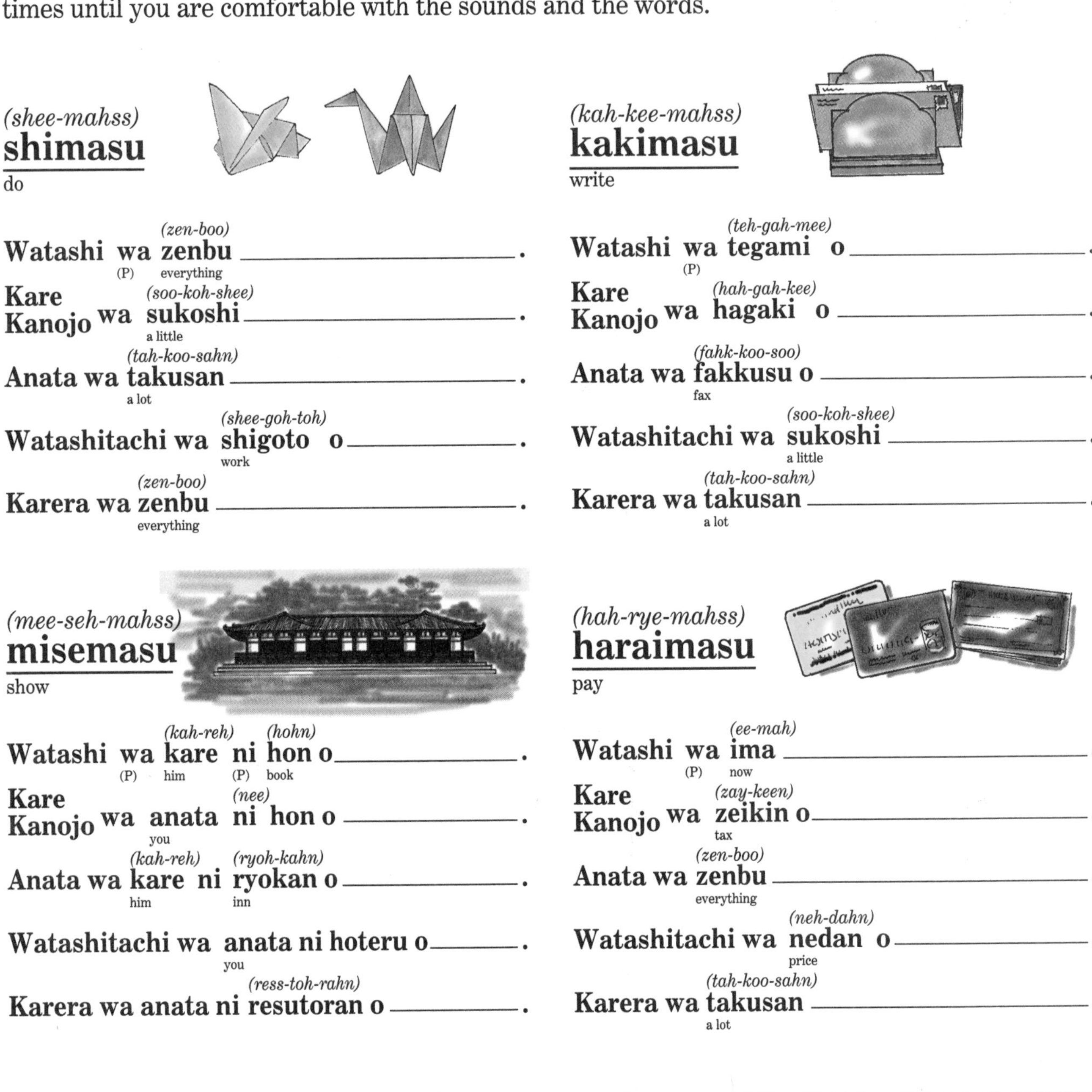

(shee-mahss)
shimasu
do

Watashi wa *(zen-boo)* **zenbu** ______________________.
(P) everything

Kare / Kanojo wa *(soo-koh-shee)* **sukoshi** ______________________.
a little

Anata wa *(tah-koo-sahn)* **takusan** ______________________.
a lot

Watashitachi wa *(shee-goh-toh)* **shigoto o** ______________________.
work

Karera wa *(zen-boo)* **zenbu** ______________________.
everything

(kah-kee-mahss)
kakimasu
write

Watashi wa *(teh-gah-mee)* **tegami o** ______________________.
(P)

Kare / Kanojo wa *(hah-gah-kee)* **hagaki o** ______________________.

Anata wa *(fahk-koo-soo)* **fakkusu o** ______________________.
fax

Watashitachi wa *(soo-koh-shee)* **sukoshi** ______________________.
a little

Karera wa *(tah-koo-sahn)* **takusan** ______________________.
a lot

(mee-seh-mahss)
misemasu
show

Watashi wa *(kah-reh)* **kare ni** *(hohn)* **hon o** ______________________.
(P) him (P) book

Kare / Kanojo wa anata ni *(nee)* **hon o** ______________________.
you

Anata wa *(kah-reh)* **kare ni** *(ryoh-kahn)* **ryokan o** ______________________.
him inn

Watashitachi wa anata ni hoteru o ______________________.
you

Karera wa anata ni *(ress-toh-rahn)* **resutoran o** ______________________.

(hah-rye-mahss)
haraimasu
pay

Watashi wa *(ee-mah)* **ima** ______________________.
(P) now

Kare / Kanojo wa *(zay-keen)* **zeikin o** ______________________.
tax

Anata wa *(zen-boo)* **zenbu** ______________________.
everything

Watashitachi wa *(neh-dahn)* **nedan o** ______________________.
price

Karera wa *(tah-koo-sahn)* **takusan** ______________________.
a lot

- ❐ **pankēki** *(pahn-kēh-kee)* .... pancake ______________________
- ❐ **panku** *(pahn-koo)* .... puncture ______________________
- ❐ **panorama** *(pah-noh-rah-mah)* .... panorama **p** ______________________
- ❐ **pantsu** *(pahn-tsoo)* .... pants ______________________
- ❐ **papaia** *(pah-pie-ah)* .... papaya ______________________

17 Basic Traffic Signs and Conversions

Some of these signs you probably recognize, but take a couple of minutes to review them anyway.

tsuukō kinshi
road closed to vehicles

zeikan
customs

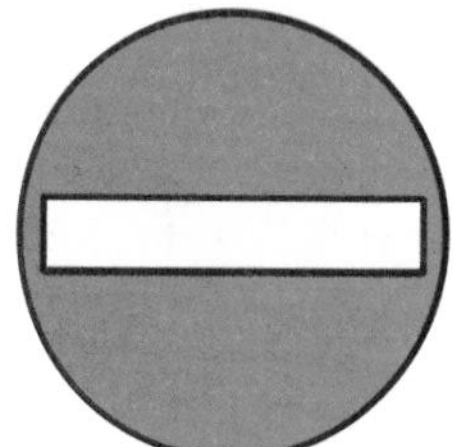

shinnyū kinshi
no entrance

chūsha ka
parking permitted

jokō
yield

seigen sokudo
speed limit

chūsha kinshi
no parking

oikoshi kinshi
no passing

ichiji teishi
stop

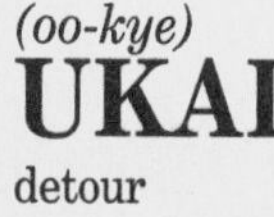

(oo-kye)
UKAI
detour

What follows are approximate conversions, so when you order something by liters, kilograms or grams you will have an idea of what to expect and not find yourself being handed one piece of candy when you thought you ordered an entire bag.

To Convert		Do the Math		
liters (l) to gallons, gallons to liters,	multiply by 0.26 multiply by 3.79	4 liters x 0.26 10 gal. x 3.79	= =	1.04 gallons 37.9 liters
kilograms (kg) to pounds, pounds to kilos,	multiply by 2.2 multiply by 0.46	2 kilograms x 2.2 10 pounds x 0.46	= =	4.4 pounds 4.6 kg
grams (g) to ounces, ounces to grams,	multiply by 0.035 multiply by 28.35	100 grams x 0.035 10 oz. x 28.35	= =	3.5 oz. 283.5 g.
meters (m) to feet, feet to meters,	multiply by 3.28 multiply by 0.3	2 meters x 3.28 6 feet x 0.3	= =	6.56 feet 1.8 meters

For fun, take your weight in pounds and convert it into kilograms. It sounds better that way, doesn't it? How many kilometers is it from your home to school, to work, to the post office?

The Simple Versions		
one liter	=	approximately one US quart
four liters	=	approximately one US gallon
one kilo	=	approximately 2.2 pounds
100 grams	=	approximately 3.5 ounces
500 grams	=	slightly more than one pound
one meter	=	slightly more than three feet

The distance between **New York** and **Tōkyō** is approximately 6,726 miles. How many kilometers would that be? It is 5,109 miles between **San Francisco** and **Tōkyō**. How many kilometers is that?

kilometers (km.) to miles, miles to kilometers,	multiply by 0.62 multiply by 1.6	1000 km. x 0.62 1000 miles x 1.6	= =	620 miles 1,600 km.

Inches 1	2	3	4	5	6	7

To convert centimeters into inches, multiply by 0.39 Example: 9 cm. x 0.39 = 3.51 in.

To convert inches into centimeters, multiply by 2.54 Example: 4 in. x 2.54 = 10.16 cm.

cm 1	2	3	4	5	6	7	8	9	10	11	12	13	14	15	16	17	18

18 Denpyō *(den-pyōh)* bills to *(toh)* and Ryōshūsho *(ryōh-shōō-shoh)* receipts

Hai, *(hi)* there are also **denpyō** *(den-pyōh)* bills to pay in **Nihon. Anata wa** have just finished your evening meal and **anata wa** would like the **denpyō** bill. **Dō** *(dōh)* how do **anata wa** go about this? **Anata wa** call for your **uētā** *(oo-ēh-tāh)* waiter **mata** *(mah-tah)* or **wa** *(wah)* **uētoresu** *(oo-ēh-toh-reh-soo)* waitress. The **uētā** *(oo-ēh-tāh)* will normally reel off what **anata** have eaten while writing rapidly. **Kare** will then give you **ichi** *(ee-chee)* one **mai** *(my)* sheet **no** (P) **kami** *(kah-mee)* paper. **Anata wa** take your **denpyō** *(den-pyōh)* bill to the **reji** *(reh-jee)* counter to pay the cashier. The cashier will say, "**Gōkei** *(gōh-kay)* total **de** of **gosen ni** 5,000 + 200 = 5,200 **hyaku** *(hyah-koo)* **en desu.**"

Remember that in **Nihon** it is not customary to leave a **chippu** *(cheep-poo)* tip because a service charge is already included in the **gōkei** *(gōh-kay)* total on the **denpyō. Anata wa** will notice that refills of **ocha** *(oh-chah)* are not included on the **denpyō.** In **Nihon** your **koppu** *(kohp-poo)* cup will be gladly refilled time and time again at no extra charge. After **anata** have paid the **denpyō,** your **uētā** *(oo-ēh-tāh)* or cashier will very likely say "**Mata** *(mah-tah)* **dōzo** *(dōh-zoh)*." please come again When **anata** dine out on your trip, it is always a good idea to make a reservation. It can be difficult to get into a popular **resutoran.** And remember, **anata wa** know enough **Nihongo** to make a reservation. Just speak slowly and clearly.

❑ **pārā** *(pāh-rāh)*	parlor	**p**	______
❑ **parashūto** *(pah-rah-shōō-toh)*	parachute		______
❑ **parasoru** *(pah-rah-soh-roo)*	parasol		______
❑ **pāsento** *(pāh-sen-toh)*	percent		______
❑ **paseri** *(pah-seh-ree)*	parsley		______

Remember these key **tango** when dining out in **Nihon.**

(oo-ēh-tāh)
uētā ______________________
waiter

(oo-ēh-toh-reh-soo)
uētoresu ______________________
waitress

(den-pyōh)
denpyō ______________________
bill (restaurant)

(shoo-koo-hah-koo-dye)
shukuhakudai ______________________
bill (hotel)

(meh-nyōō)
menyū ______________________
menu

(mah-tah) (dōh-zoh)
mata dōzo ______________________
please come again

(soo-mee-mah-sen)
sumimasen ______________________
excuse me, sorry to bother you

(dōh-moh)
dōmo ______________________
thank you

(koo-dah-sigh)
kudasai ______________________
please/please give me

(dōh) (ee-tah-shee-mahsh-teh)
dō itashimashite ______________________
you're welcome

Koko ni is a sample *(kye-wah)* **kaiwa** (conversation) involving paying the *(shoo-koo-hah-koo-dye)* **shukuhakudai** (bill) when leaving a **hoteru.**

Tanaka san: *(soo-mee-mah-sen)* **Sumimasen.** *(chek-koo)* **Chekku** (check out) *(ah-oo-toh)* **auto** *(shee-tye)* **shitai** (I would like) **no desu ga.**

____

(mah-nēh-jāh) Manējā (manager): *(heh-yah)* **Heya** (room) **wa nan** (what) **ban** (number) **desu ka?**

____

Tanaka san: **Yonhyakujū ban desu.**

____

Manējā: **Hai.** *(choht-toh)* **Chotto** (just a minute) *(maht-teh)* **matte** (wait) **kudasai.**

____

Tanaka san: *(ryōh-shōō-shoh)* **Ryōshūsho** (receipt) **o kudasai.**

____

If **anata** have any *(mohn-dye)* **mondai** (problem) with **bangō,** just ask someone to write them out so that **anata wa** *(wah-kah-ree-mahss)* **wakarimasu** (understand) everything correctly,

Bangō o *(kye-teh)* **kaite** (write) **kudasai. Arigatō gozaimasu.**

Practice: ______________________
(Please write the numbers. Thank you.)

- ❒ **pasu** *(pah-soo)* . . . . pass, free ticket ______________
- ❒ **pasupōto** *(pah-soo-pōh-toh)* . . . . passport ______________
- ❒ **pasuteru** *(pah-soo-teh-roo)* . . . . pastel ______________
- ❒ **pātī** *(pāh-tēē)* . . . . party ______________
- ❒ **pējento** *(pēh-jen-toh)* . . . . pageant ______________

p

Ima let's take a break from **denpyō** (bills) **to okane** *(oh-kah-neh)* (money) and learn some **atarashii** *(ah-tah-rah-shēē)* **tango. Anata** can always practice these **tango** by using your flash cards at the back of this **hon.** *(hohn)* Carry these flash cards in your purse, pocket, briefcase or knapsack and *use them!*

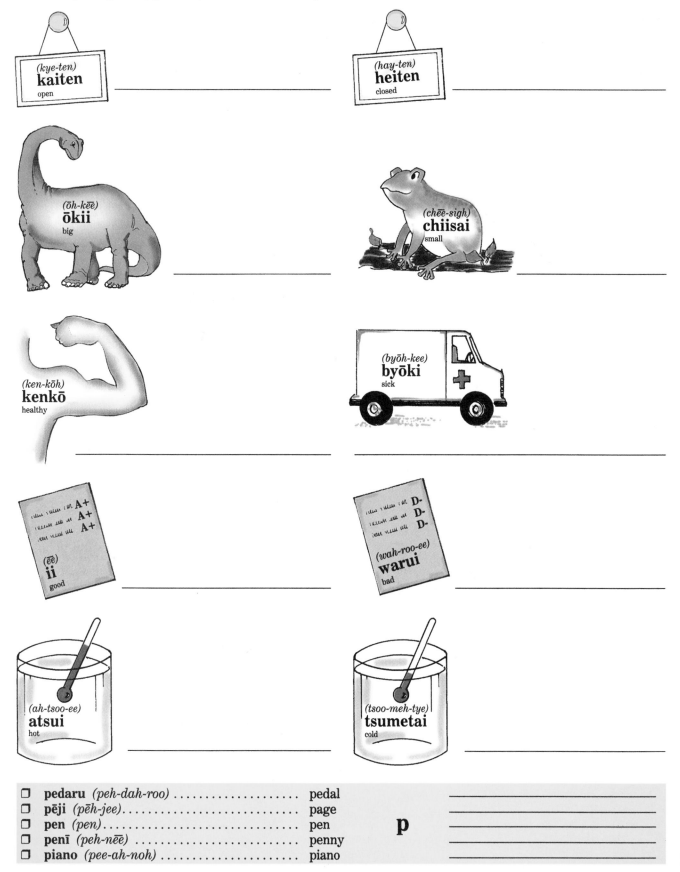

❒ **pedaru** *(peh-dah-roo)* .... pedal
❒ **pēji** *(pēh-jee)*.......................... page
❒ **pen** *(pen)*............................... pen
❒ **penī** *(peh-nēē)* .... penny
❒ **piano** *(pee-ah-noh)* .... piano

p

(mee-jee-kye)
mijikai ______________________
short

(nah-guy)
nagai ______________________
long

(oh-soy)
osoi ______________________
slow

(hah-yai)
hayai ______________________
fast

(tah-kye)
takai ______________________
tall, high

(hee-koo-ee)
hikui ______________________
short

(toh-shee-yoh-ree)
toshiyori ______________________
old

(wah-kye)
wakai ______________________
young

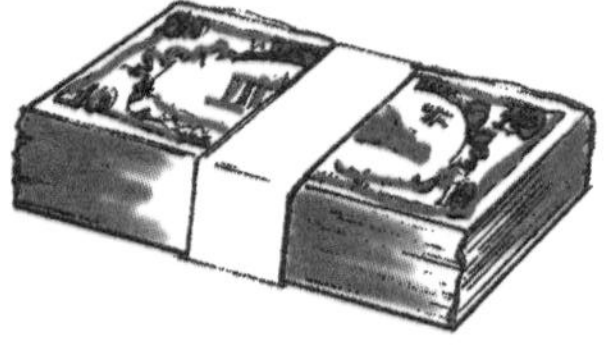

(tah-kye)
takai ______________________
expensive

(yah-soo-ee)
yasui ______________________
inexpensive

(kah-neh-moh-chee)
kanemochi ______________________
rich

(been-bōh)
binbō ______________________
poor

(tah-koo-sahn)
takusan ______________________
a lot

(soo-koh-shee)
sukoshi ______________________
a little

❒ **pikunikku** *(pee-koo-neek-koo)* .... picnic ______________________
❒ **pin** *(peen)* .... pin ______________________
❒ **poketto** *(poh-ket-toh)* .... pocket **p** ______________________
❒ **pondo** *(pohn-doh)* .... pound ______________________
❒ **ponpu** *(pohn-poo)* .... pump ______________________

(ah-tah-rah-shēē) (ah-ree-mahss)
Koko ni atarashii dōshi ga arimasu.
here are

(sheet-teh) (ee-mahss) **shitte imasu** know	______	(noh-ree-mahss) **norimasu** ride	______
(yoh-mee-mahss) **yomimasu** read	______	(ryoh-kōh) (shee-mahss) **ryokō shimasu** travel	______

Study the patterns below closely, as **anata** will use these verbs a lot.

Nishi Asahigaoka 4-8

(sheet-teh) (ee-mahss)
shitte imasu
know

Watashi wa Eigo o ______.
(P) (P)

Kare / Kanojo wa Nihongo o ______.

(soo-beh-teh)
Anata wa subete ______.
everything

(jōō-shoh)
Watashitachi wa jūsho o ______.
address

(foo-rahn-soo-goh)
Karera wa Furansugo o ______.
French

(noh-ree-mahss)
norimasu
ride

(jee-ten-shah)
Watashi wa jitensha ni ______.
(P) bicycle on

(jee-dōh-shah)
Kare / Kanojo wa jidōsha ni ______.
car in

(bah-soo)
Anata wa basu ni ______.
bus

(tah-koo-shēē)
Watashitachi wa takushī ni ______.
taxi

(chee-kah-teh-tsoo)
Karera wa chikatetsu ni ______.
subway

(yoh-mee-mahss)
yomimasu
read

(hohn)
Watashi wa hon o ______.
(P) (P)

(meh-nyōō)
Kare / Kanojo wa menyū o ______.

(tah-koo-sahn)
Anata wa takusan ______.
a lot

(zahsh-shee)
Watashitachi wa zasshi o ______.
magazine

(sheen-boon)
Karera wa shinbun o ______.
newspaper

(ryoh-kōh) (shee-mahss)
ryokō shimasu
travel

Watashi wa jitensha de ______.
(P) by

Kare / Kanojo wa jidōsha de ______.

Anata wa basu de ______.

(ōh-toh-by)
Watashitachi wa ōtobai de ______.
motorcycle

(foo-neh)
Karera wa fune de ______.
boat

p

- ❒ **posutā** *(poh-soo-tāh)* .... poster ______
- ❒ **pōtā** *(pōh-tāh)* .... porter ______
- ❒ **pudingu** *(poo-deen-goo)* .... pudding ______
- ❒ **purasu** *(poo-rah-soo)* .... plus ______
- ❒ **pūru** *(pōō-roo)* .... pool, swimming pool ______

Anata have been using three **hijō ni taisetsu** verbs which translate very similarly in **Eigo**, but are used quite differently in **Nihongo**.

(ah-ree-mahss) **arimasu** is, are (with things)	*(shtah)* **Kotae wa shita ni arimasu.** below / are	*(kah-doh) (bee-joo-tsoo-kahn)* **Kado ni Bijutsukan ga arimasu.** corner / art museum / is
(ee-mahss) **imasu** is, are (with people and animals)	*(ee-shah)* **Isha san wa hoteru ni imasu.** doctor / is	*(ee-shah)* **Isha san wa hoteru ni imasen.** is not
(dess) **desu** am, is, are	*(nee-hohn-jeen)* **Watashi wa Nihonjin desu.**	*(hohn) (hyah-koo)* **Hon wa hyaku en desu.** book / 100 / is

Don't worry about these nuances now, but be aware that they exist.

Can you translate the sentences *(shtah)* **shita** into **Nihongo?** *(koh-tah-eh)* **Kotae** (answers) **wa shita** (below) **ni arimasu.**

1. I know Japanese. ______________________________
2. They ride in a taxi. ______________________________
3. He reads the newspaper. ______________________________
4. We know everything. Watashitachi wa subete shitte imasu.
5. She knows a lot. ______________________________
6. We know French. ______________________________
7. I read the book. ______________________________
8. We travel by train. ______________________________
9. I know English. ______________________________
10. She reads the letter. ______________________________

KOTAE

1. **Watashi wa Nihongo o shitte imasu.**
2. **Karera wa takushī ni norimasu.**
3. **Kare wa shinbun o yomimasu.**
4. **Watashitachi wa subete shitte imasu.**
5. **Kanojo wa takusan shitte imasu.**
6. **Watashitachi wa Furansugo o shitte imasu.**
7. **Watashi wa hon o yomimasu.**
8. **Watashitachi wa densha de ryokō shimasu.**
9. **Watashi wa Eigo o shitte imasu.**
10. **Kanojo wa tegami o yomimasu.**

Ima, draw **sen** (lines) between the opposites (*shtah*) **shita.** (below) Do not forget to say them out loud. Say these **tango** every day to describe the **mono** in **anata** (your) **no** (P) (*ee-eh*) **ie,** (home) **anata** (your) **no** (*gahk-kōh*) **gakkō** (school) and **anata no** (*shoh-sigh*) **shosai.** (office)

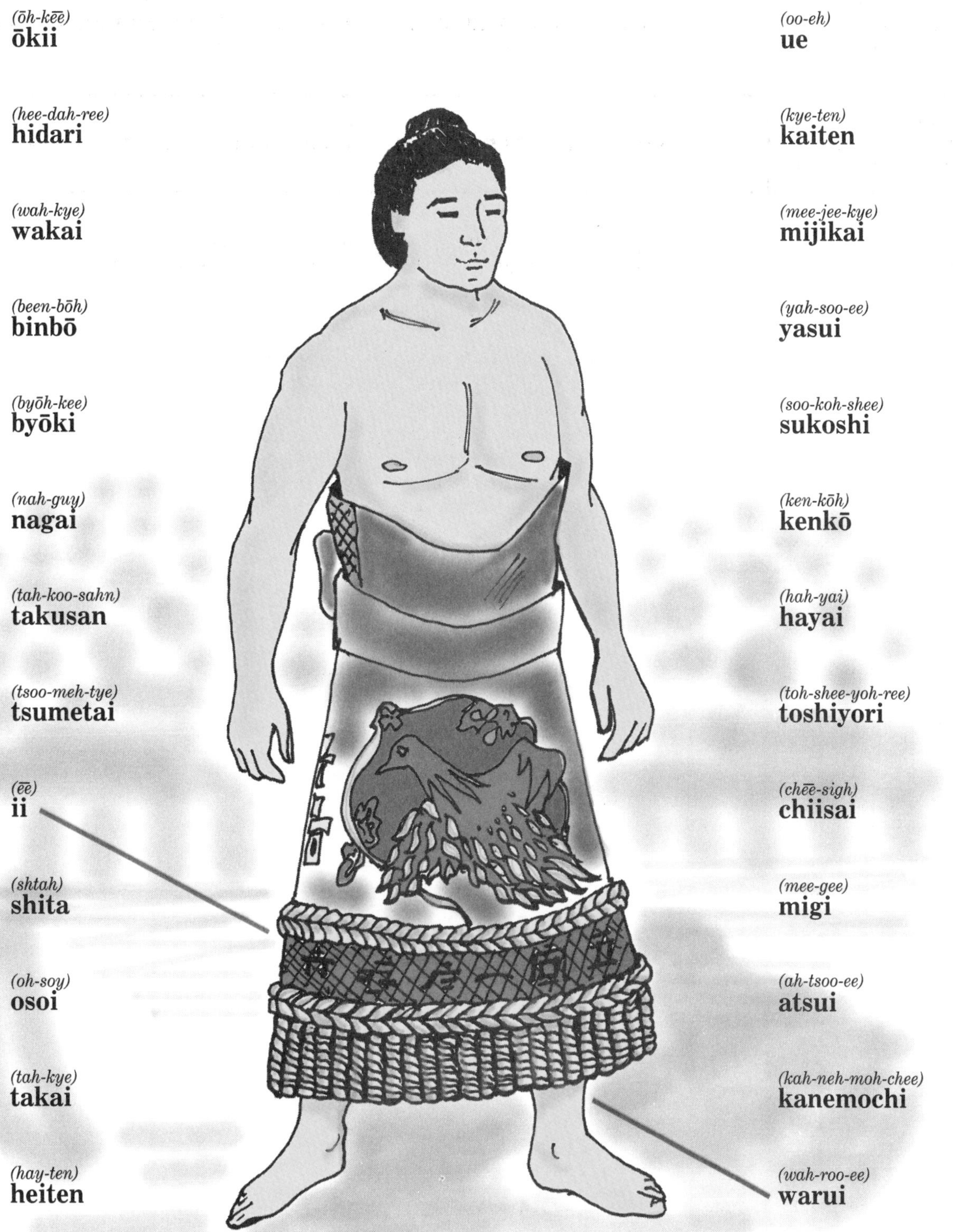

(*ōh-kēē*) **ōkii**

(*hee-dah-ree*) **hidari**

(*wah-kye*) **wakai**

(*been-bōh*) **binbō**

(*byōh-kee*) **byōki**

(*nah-guy*) **nagai**

(*tah-koo-sahn*) **takusan**

(*tsoo-meh-tye*) **tsumetai**

(*ēē*) **ii**

(*shtah*) **shita**

(*oh-soy*) **osoi**

(*tah-kye*) **takai**

(*hay-ten*) **heiten**

(*oo-eh*) **ue**

(*kye-ten*) **kaiten**

(*mee-jee-kye*) **mijikai**

(*yah-soo-ee*) **yasui**

(*soo-koh-shee*) **sukoshi**

(*ken-kōh*) **kenkō**

(*hah-yai*) **hayai**

(*toh-shee-yoh-ree*) **toshiyori**

(*chēē-sigh*) **chiisai**

(*mee-gee*) **migi**

(*ah-tsoo-ee*) **atsui**

(*kah-neh-moh-chee*) **kanemochi**

(*wah-roo-ee*) **warui**

- ❒ **rajio** (*rah-jee-oh*) . . . . radio
- ❒ **raketto** (*rah-ket-toh*) . . . . racket
- ❒ **rasshuawā** (*rahs-shoo-ah-wāh*) . . . . rush hour
- ❒ **raudosupīkā** (*rah-oo-doh-soo-pēē-kāh*) . . . . . loudspeaker
- ❒ **referī** (*reh-feh-rēē*) . . . . referee

r ____________________

19 Ryokō Shimasu

(ryoh-kōh) (shee-mahss)
travel

(kee-nōh) **Kinō wa Tōkyō!** (yesterday)

(kyōh) **Kyō wa Kyōto!** (today)

(ahsh-tah) (ōh-sah-kah) **Ashita wa Ōsaka!** (tomorrow)

If you know a few key **tango,** traveling can be easy, clean and **hijō** *(hee-jōh)* [very] **ni omoshiroi** *(oh-moh-shee-roy)* [interesting]**. Nihon** is **shimaguni** *(shee-mah-goo-nee)* [island country] and is roughly the size of **Kariforunia** *(kah-ree-foh-roo-nee-ah)* [California]. There are many **ryokō** [travel] **no** [(P)] **hōhō** *(hōh-hōh)* [ways] in **Nihon. Anata wa nani** *(nah-nee)* [what] **de** *(deh)* [by] **ryokō** *(ryoh-kōh)* [travel] **shimasu ka?** *(shee-mahss)*

Tanaka san wa jidōsha *(jee-dōh-shah)* [car] **de** [by] **ryokō** *(ryoh-kōh)* [travels] **shimasu.** *(shee-mahss)*

Kazuko wa shinkansen *(sheen-kahn-sen)* [bullet train] **de** [by] **ryokō shimasu.**

Yōko wa fune *(foo-neh)* [boat] **de ryokō shimasu.**

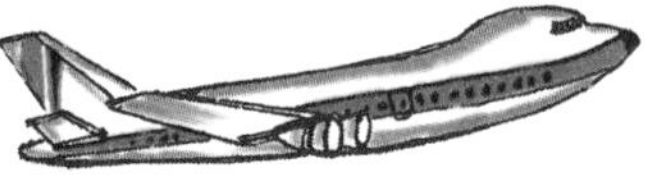

Itō san wa hikōki *(hee-kōh-kee)* [airplane] **de ryokō shimasu.**

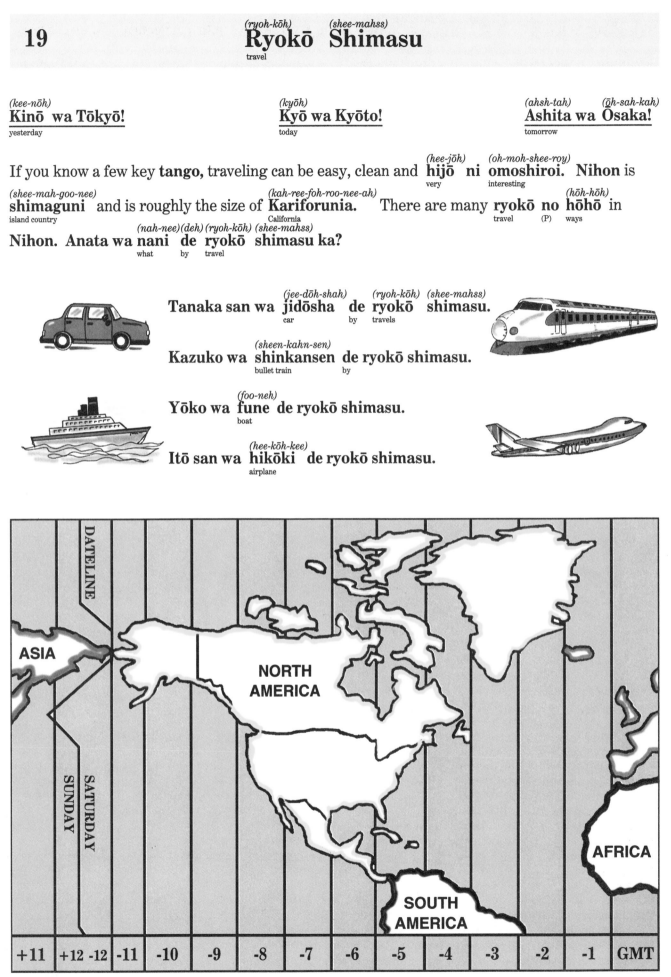

DATELINE
ASIA
NORTH AMERICA
SATURDAY
SUNDAY
AFRICA
SOUTH AMERICA

+11	+12 -12	-11	-10	-9	-8	-7	-6	-5	-4	-3	-2	-1	GMT

While **anata wa** are traveling, **anata wa** will want to tell others your nationality and **anata wa** will meet people from all corners of the world. Can you guess where someone is from if they say one of the following? **Kotae** are in your glossary beginning on page 108.

Watashi wa Igirisu kara kimashita. _(ee-gee-ree-soo) (kah-rah) (kee-mahsh-tah)_ (kara = from, kimashita = come) ____________________

Watashitachi wa Doitsu kara kimashita. _(doy-tsoo) (kee-mahsh-tah)_ (Watashitachi = we) ____________________

Watashi wa Furansu kara kimashita. _(foo-rahn-soo)_ ____________________

Watashi wa Supein kara kimashita. _(soo-pain)_ ____________________

Kanojo wa Itaria kara kimashita. _(kah-noh-joh) (ee-tah-ree-ah)_ (Kanojo = she) ____________________

Kanojo wa Chūgoku kara kimashita. _(chōō-goh-koo) (kee-mahsh-tah)_ ____________________

Kare wa Kankoku kara kimashita. _(kah-reh) (kahn-koh-koo)_ (Kare = he) ____________________

Watashi wa Ōsutoraria kara kimashita. _(ōh-soo-toh-rah-ree-ah)_ ____________________

Watashi wa Shingapōru kara kimashita. _(sheen-gah-pōh-roo)_ ____________________

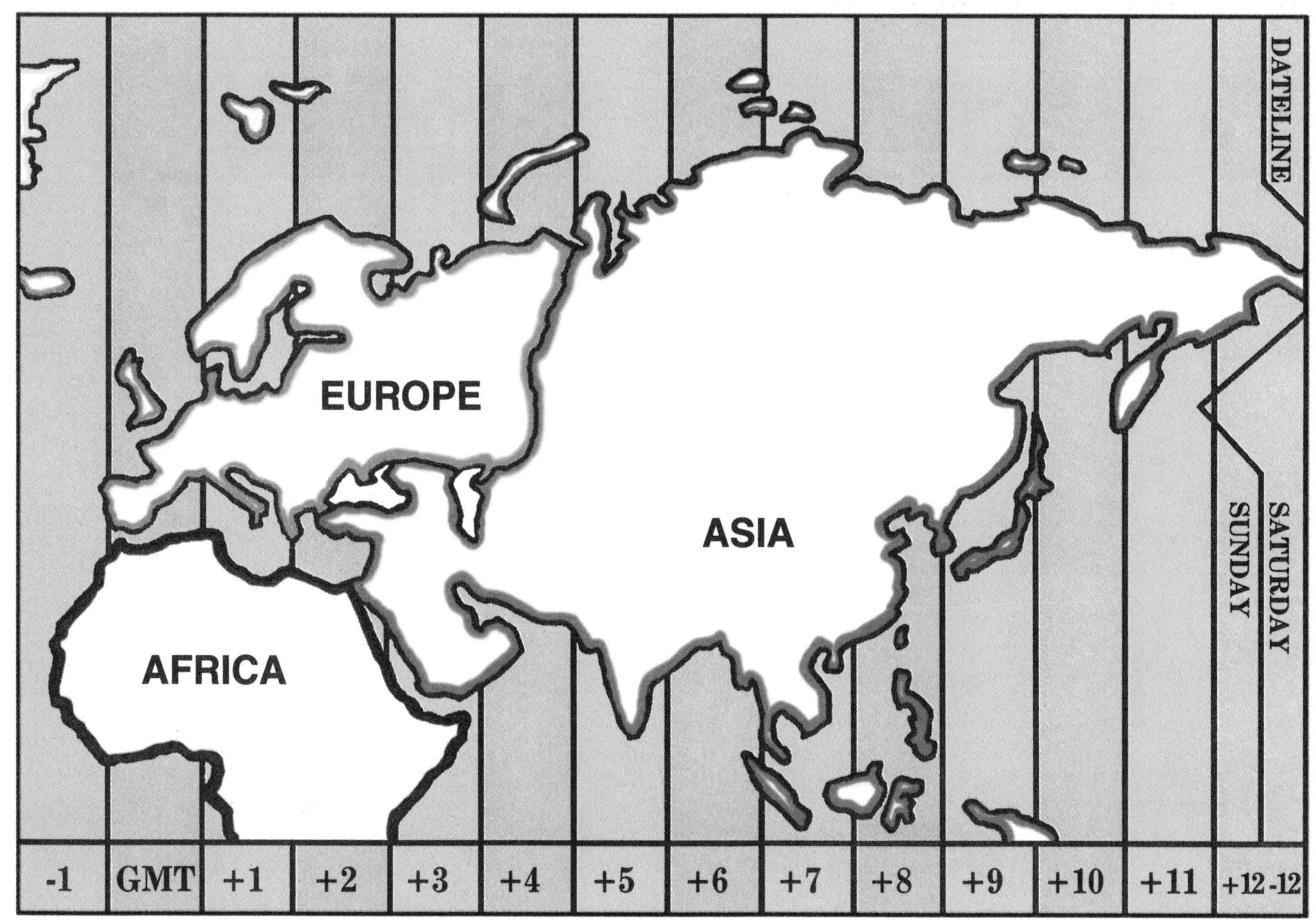

The **tango "ryokō"** means "journey" or "trip." Many **tango** revolve around the concept of travel which is exactly what **anata** wish to do. Practice the following **tango** many times. **Anata wa** will use them often.

(ryoh-kōh) (shee-mahss)
ryokō shimasu ______________________
travel

(ryoh-kōh-guy-shah)
ryokōgaisha ______________________
travel agency

(ryoh-kōh-shah)
ryokōsha ______________________
traveler

(dōh-zoh) (yoy) (ryoh-kōh) (oh)
Dōzo yoi ryokō o ! ______________________
have a good trip

If **anata** choose *(jee-dōh-shah)* **jidōsha** (car) *(deh)* **de** *(ee-koo)* **iku,** (go) **koko ni** a few key **tango ga** *(ah-ree-mahss)* **arimasu.** (are)

(kōh-soh-koo) (dōh-rōh)
kōsoku dōrō ______________________
freeway

(ren-tah) (kāh)
renta kā ______________________
rental car

(mee-chee)
michi ______________________
road

(shohp-poo)
renta kā shoppu ______________________
car-rental agency

(tōh-ree)
tōri ______________________
street

(gah-soh-reen) (soo-tahn-doh)
gasorin sutando ______________________
service station / stand

(shtah)
Shita ni (below) are some basic signs which **anata** sould learn to recognize quickly. Many of **kono tango** are based on the root " *(koo-chee)* **kuchi.**" (mouth) *(ee-ree-goo-chee)* **Iriguchi** (entrance) means "into the mouth" and *(deh-goo-chee)* **deguchi** (exit) means "out of the mouth."

IRIGUCHI 入口

DEGUCHI 出口

(ee-ree-goo-chee)
iriguchi ______________________
entrance

(deh-goo-chee)
deguchi ______________________
exit

(sheen-nyōō) (keen-shee)
shinnyū kinshi ______________________
do not enter

(hee-jōh-goo-chee)
hijōguchi ______________________
emergency exit

OSU 押す

HIKU 引く

(oh-soo)
osu ______________________
push (doors)

(hee-koo)
hiku ______________________
pull (doors)

r

- ❒ **rekōdo** *(reh-kōh-doh)* .... record ______________________
- ❒ **remon** *(reh-mohn)* .... lemon ______________________
- ❒ **ribon** *(ree-bohn)* .... ribbon ______________________
- ❒ **robī** *(roh-bēē)* .... lobby ______________________
- ❒ **rubī** *(roo-bēē)* .... ruby ______________________

Let's learn the basic travel verbs. Take out a piece of paper and make up your own sentences with these **atarashii** *(ah-tah-rah-shēē)* **dōshi.** Follow the same pattern **anata** have in previous Steps.

tobimasu *(toh-bee-mahss)* fly ____________

tsukimasu *(tsoo-kee-mahss)* arrive ____________

demasu *(deh-mahss)* leave, depart ____________

arimasu/ imasu/ desu *(ah-ree-mahss) (ee-mahss) (dess)* is, are, am ____________

yoyaku shimasu *(yoh-yah-koo) (shee-mahss)* make a reservation, book ____________

unten shimasu *(oon-ten) (shee-mahss)* drive ____________

nizukuri shimasu *(nee-zoo-koo-ree) (shee-mahss)* pack ____________

norikaemasu *(noh-ree-kah-eh-mahss)* transfer (vehicles) ____________

Koko ni some **atarashii tango** for your **ryokō** *(ryoh-kōh)* (trip) **ga arimasu** *(ah-ree-mahss)* (are).

kūkō *(kōō-kōh)* airport

____

hōmu *(hōh-moo)* platform

____

jikokuhyō *(jee-koh-koo-hyōh)* timetable

Tōkyō kara Ōsaka made (from ... to)		
Shuppatsu	**Ressha**	**Tōchaku**
07:40	14	10:55
10:00	322	13:15
12:15	784	15:30
14:30	1214	17:45

____

eki *(eh-kee)* station

____

S

- ❒ **sābisu** *(sāh-bee-soo)* .... service ____________
- ❒ **saidā** *(sigh-dāh)* .... cider ____________
- ❒ **sain** *(sign)* .... sign ____________
- ❒ **sairen** *(sigh-ren)* .... siren ____________
- ❒ **sakkarin** *(sahk-kah-reen)* .... saccharin ____________

With **kono tango, anata wa** are ready for any **ryokō,** anywhere. **Anata wa** should have no **mondai** *(mohn-dye)* problems with **kono dōshi,** just remember the basic "plug-in" formula **anata** already learned. Use that knowledge to translate the following thoughts into **Nihongo. Kotae wa shita** *(shtah)* below **ni arimasu.**

1. This airplane flies to Japan. ______________________________
2. I transfer trains in Tokyo. ______________________________
3. I book (reserve) an inn. ______________________________
4. We arrive tomorrow. ______________________________
5. We buy three tickets to Kobe. ______________________________
6. They drive to Nagasaki. ______________________________
7. Where is the train to Kyoto? ______________________________
8. I leave tomorrow. ______________________________

Koko ni some **hijō ni taisetsu** *(tye-seh-tsoo)* **na** (P) **tango** for the **ryokōsha** *(ryoh-kōh-shah)* traveler **ga arimasu** *(ah-ree-mahss)* are.

Tōkyō kara (from) Hiroshima made (to)		
Shuppatsu	**Ressha**	**Tōchaku**
08:00	17	13:00
10:30	325	15:30
14:00	787	19:00
18:30	1217	23:00
Dōzo yoi ryokō o!		

tsukatte imasu *(tsoo-kaht-teh) (ee-mahss)* occupied, being used ______________________________

aite imasu *(eye-teh) (ee-mahss)* free, open ______________________________

yukisaki *(yoo-kee-sah-kee)* destination ______________________________

seki *(seh-kee)* seat ______________________________

shuppatsu *(shoop-pah-tsoo)* departure ______________________________

tōchaku *(tōh-chah-koo)* arrival ______________________________

gaikoku no *(guy-koh-koo)* foreign (P) ______________________________

kokunai no *(koh-koo-nye)* domestic (P) ______________________________

KOTAE

1. Kono hikōki wa Nihon e tobimasu.
2. Watashi wa Tōkyō de densha o norikaemasu.
3. Watashi wa ryokan o yoyaku shimasu.
4. Watashitachi wa ashita tsukimasu.
5. Watashitachi wa Kōbe yuki no kippu o san mai kaimasu.
6. Karera wa Nagasaki made unten shimasu.
7. Kyōto yuki no densha wa doko desu ka?
8. Watashi wa ashita demasu.

Increase your *(ryoh-kōh)* **ryokō** (travel) **no tango** (P) by writing out the **tango** below and practicing the sample sentences out loud. Practice asking *(shee-tsoo-mohn)* **shitsumon** with **"doko."** It will help you later.

(yoo-kee)
yuki ______________________________
to
Tōkyō yuki no ressha wa doko desu ka?

(gēh-toh)
gēto ______________________________
gate
Nana ban gēto wa doko desu ka?

(sen)
sen ______________________________
track
Nana ban sen wa doko desu ka?

(pōh-tāh)
pōtā ______________________________
porter
Pōtā wa doko desu ka?

(hee-kōh-kee)
hikōki ______________________________
flight
Kono hikōki wa doko made desu ka?

(ahn-nye-joh)
annaijo ______________________________
information office
Annaijo wa doko desu ka?

(ryōh-gah-eh-joh)
ryōgaejo ______________________________
foreign-currency exchange
Ryōgaejo wa doko desu ka?

(kah-oon-tāh)
kauntā ______________________________
counter
Hachi ban no kauntā wa doko desu ka?

(mah-chee-eye-shee-tsoo)
machiaishitsu ______________________________
waiting room
Machiaishitsu wa doko desu ka?

(shoh-koo-dōh-shah)
shokudōsha ______________________________
dining car
Shokudōsha wa doko desu ka?

(sheen-dye-shah)
shindaisha ______________________________
sleeping car
Shindaisha wa doko desu ka?

(kee-tsoo-en-shah)
kitsuensha ______________________________
smoking car
Kitsuensha wa doko desu ka?

______ (when)

Ressha wa ______ (when) *(deh-mahss)* **demasu ka?** (leaves)

______ (what)

______________ (what) **desu ka?** (is it)

❒ **sandoitchi** *(sahn-doh-eet-chee)*	sandwich		______________
❒ **sarada** *(sah-rah-dah)*	salad		______________
❒ **semento** *(seh-men-toh)*	cement	**S**	______________
❒ **shanpen** *(shahn-pen)*	champagne		______________
❒ **shinhonī** *(sheen-hoh-nēē)*	symphony		______________

(tsoo-gee)
Can **anata wa** read **tsugi** **no** paragraph?
following (P)

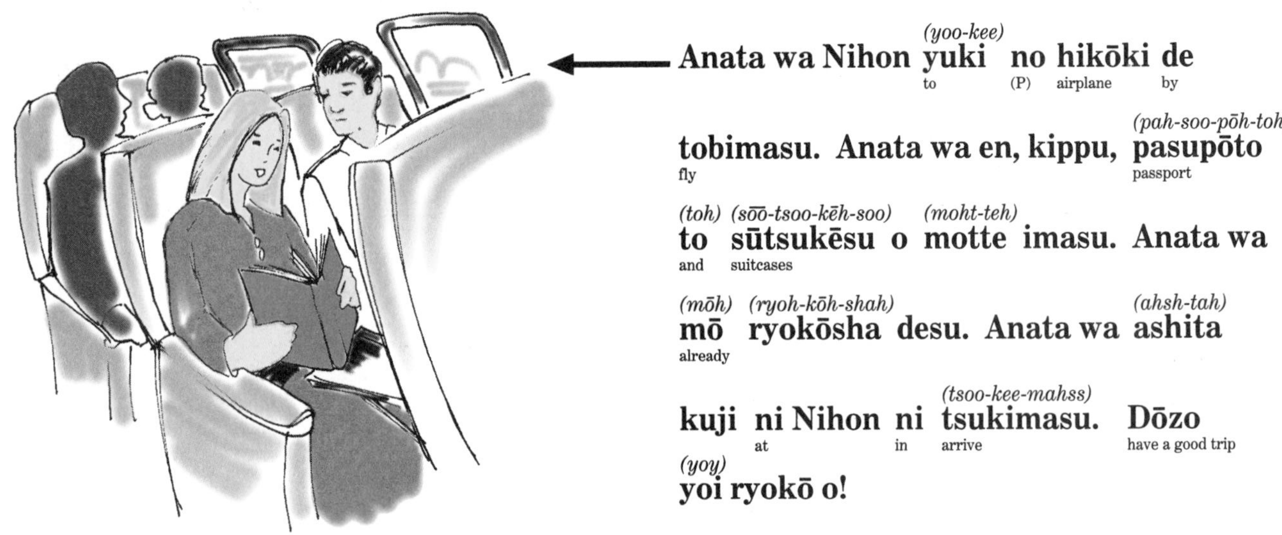

(yoo-kee)
Anata wa Nihon yuki no hikōki de
to (P) airplane by

(pah-soo-pōh-toh)
tobimasu. Anata wa en, kippu, pasupōto
fly passport

(toh) (sōō-tsoo-kēh-soo) (moht-teh)
to sūtsukēsu o motte imasu. Anata wa
and suitcases

(mōh) (ryoh-kōh-shah) (ahsh-tah)
mō ryokōsha desu. Anata wa ashita
already

(tsoo-kee-mahss)
kuji ni Nihon ni tsukimasu. Dōzo
at in arrive have a good trip

(yoy)
yoi ryokō o!

(toh)
Ressha wa come in many different shapes, sizes **to** speeds in **Nihon. Ressha** that go the fastest

(sheen-kahn-sen) (sheen-kahn-sen) (noh-zoh-mee) (hee-kah-ree) (koh-dah-mah)
are called **shinkansen.** There are three kinds of **shinkansen: nozomi, hikari** and **kodama.**
bullet trains bullet trains super express express ordinary

If **anata wa** plan to travel a long distance, **anata wa** may wish to catch one of the **shinkansen.**

❐ **sētā** *(sēh-tāh)*	sweater		______________________
❐ **sōda** *(sōh-dah)*	soda		______________________
❐ **sōsu** *(sōh-soo)*	sauce	**S**	______________________
❐ **suchuwādesu** *(soo-choo-wāh-deh-soo)*	stewardess		______________________
❐ **sukejūru** *(soo-keh-jōō-roo)*	schedule		______________________

Knowing these travel **tango** will make your holiday twice as enjoyable and at least three times as easy. Review these **tango** by doing the crossword puzzle below. Drill yourself on this Step by selecting other destinations and ask your own **shitsumon** about **ressha, basu** or **hikōki** *(hee-kōh-kee)* that go there. Select more **atarashii tango** from your **jisho** *(jee-shoh)* dictionary and ask your own questions beginning with **doko, itsu** and **ikura.** **Kotae** to the crossword puzzle are at the bottom of the next page.

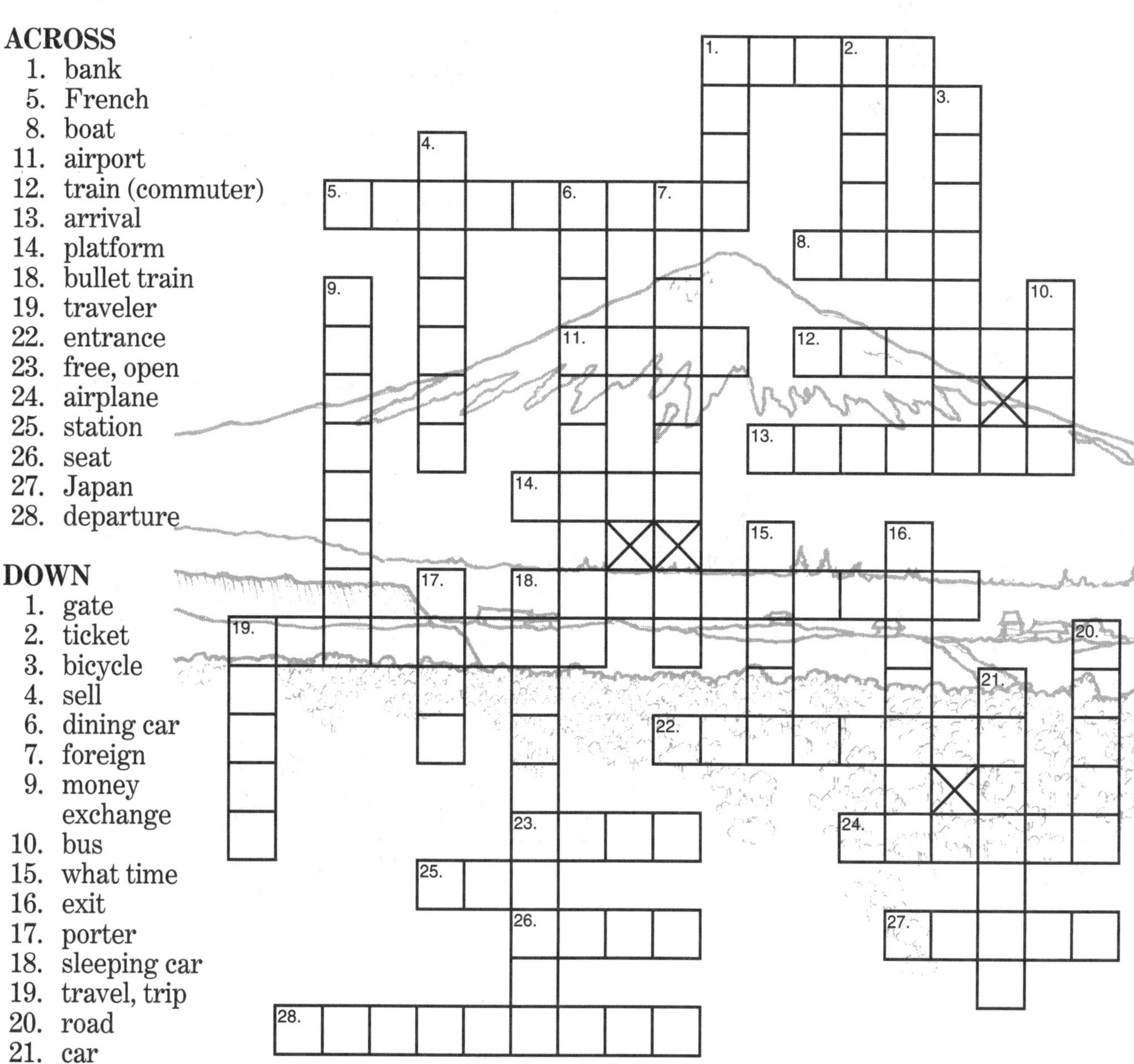

ACROSS
1. bank
5. French
8. boat
11. airport
12. train (commuter)
13. arrival
14. platform
18. bullet train
19. traveler
22. entrance
23. free, open
24. airplane
25. station
26. seat
27. Japan
28. departure

DOWN
1. gate
2. ticket
3. bicycle
4. sell
6. dining car
7. foreign
9. money exchange
10. bus
15. what time
16. exit
17. porter
18. sleeping car
19. travel, trip
20. road
21. car

Fujisan (Mt. Fuji) is Japan's highest mountain, rising to a height of 12,388 feet. **Fujisan,** located in the **Fuji Hakone Izu** National Park, is only an hour's train trip from **Tōkyō** and well worth the journey.

S

- ❒ **sukī** *(soo-kēē)* .... ski ______________
- ❒ **sukurīn** *(soo-koo-rēēn)* .... screen ______________
- ❒ **supōtsu** *(soo-pōh-tsoo)* .... sports ______________
- ❒ **sūpu** *(sōō-poo)* .... soup (Western-style) ______________
- ❒ **sutēki** *(soo-tēh-kee)* .... steak ______________

(keep-poo) (neh-dahn) (shee-tsoo-mohn)
What about inquiring about **kippu no nedan? Anata wa** can ask **kono shitsumon,** too!
ticket (P) price

(yoo-kee) (keep-poo) (ee-koo-rah)
Ōsaka yuki no kippu wa ikura desu ka? ______
to (P) ticket how much

(yoo-kee) (keep-poo)
Tōkyō yuki no kippu wa ikura desu ka? ______
(P)

(ee-koo-rah)
Nagoya yuki no kippu wa ikura desu ka? ______
(P)

(kah-tah-mee-chee)
katamichi ______
one-way

(ōh-foo-koo)
ōfuku ______
round-trip

(shoop-pah-tsoo) (tōh-chah-koo)
What about times of **shuppatsu** and **tōchaku? Anata wa** can ask **kono shitsumon.**
departures arrivals

(ee-tsoo) (deh-mahss)
Kōbe yuki no ressha wa itsu demasu ka? ______
to (P) when leaves

(hee-kōh-kee) (deh-mahss)
Kōbe yuki no hikōki wa itsu demasu ka? ______
(P) airplane

(kah-rah) (ee-tsoo) (tsoo-kee-mahss)
Sapporo kara no ressha wa itsu tsukimasu ka? ______
from (P) when arrives

(hee-kōh-kee) (tsoo-kee-mahss)
Sapporo kara no hikōki wa itsu tsukimasu ka? ______
(P)

Nagasaki yuki no ressha wa itsu demasu ka? ______
(P)

(eh-kee) (ee-mahss)
Anata wa have just arrived in **Nihon. Anata wa eki ni imasu.** Where would you like to go?
station at are

(ee-kee-tye) (dess)
In **Nihongo,** "would like to go" is "**ikitai desu.**" Tell the person selling tickets where you wish to go! **Kyōto? Nagoya? Tōkyō?**

(nee) (ee-kee-tye)
Watashi wa Kyōto ni ikitai desu. ______
to would like to go

(nee) (ee-kee-tye)
Watashi wa Nagoya ni ikitai desu. ______

Watashi wa Tōkyō ni ikitai desu. ______

KOTAE

ACROSS
1. ginkō
5. Furansugo
8. fune
11. kūkō
12. densha
13. tōchaku
14. hōmu
18. shinkansen
19. ryokōsha
22. iriguchi
23. aite
24. hikōki
25. eki
26. seki
27. Nihon
28. shuppatsu

DOWN
1. gēto
2. kippu
3. jitensha
4. urimasu
6. shokudōsha
7. gaikoku no
9. ryōgaejo
10. basu
15. nanji
16. deguchi
17. pōtā
18. shindaisha
19. ryokō
20. michi
21. jidōsha

Ima that **anata wa** know the words essential for traveling in **Nihon,** what are some specialty items **anata** might go in search of?

(den-kee) (say-heen)
denki seihin
electronic goods

(oh-mee-yah-geh)
omiyage
souvenirs

(nee-hohn) (neen-gyōh)
Nihon ningyō
Japanese dolls

(oh-ree-gah-mee)
origami
origami paper

(tohk-koo-ree)(toh) (sah-kah-zoo-kee)
tokkuri to sakazuki
sake bottles / sake cups

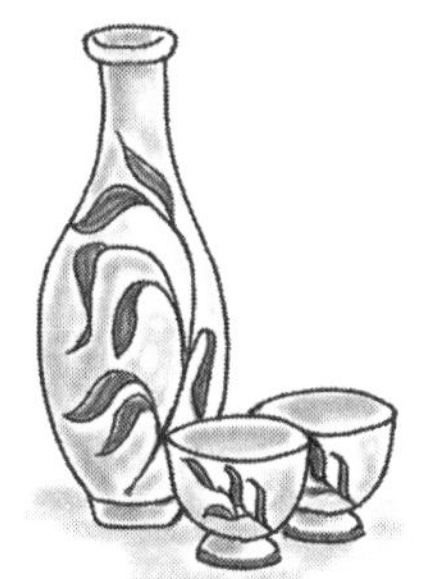

(yoo-noh-mee) (jah-wahn) (toh) (kyōō-soo)
yunomi jawan to kyūsu
tea cups / tea pots

Consider using JAPANESE *a language map*™ as well. JAPANESE *a language map*™ is the perfect companion for your travels when **anata** may not wish to take along this **hon.** Each section focuses on essentials for your **ryoko.** Your *Language Map*™ is not meant to replace learning **Nihongo**, but will help you in the event **anata** forget something and need a little bit of help. For more information about the *Language Map*™ Series, please turn to page 132.

t

- ❒ **tabako** *(tah-bah-koh)* .... tobacco
- ❒ **taipu** *(tie-poo)* .... type
- ❒ **tairu** *(tie-roo)* .... tile
- ❒ **taiya** *(tie-yah)* .... tire
- ❒ **takushī** *(tah-koo-shēē)* .... taxi

20 Menyū (meh-nyōō)
menu

Ima anata wa Nihon **ni** (nee) in **imasu.** (ee-mahss) are Anata wa **hoteru** (hoh-teh-roo) **ni imasu.** You are hungry, but **ii** (ēē) good **resutoran wa doko desu ka?** First of all, there are different types of places to eat. Let's learn them.

resutoran (ress-toh-rahn) ____________________
serves a variety of meals, usually specializing in Western dishes

udonya / sobaya (oo-dohn-yah) (soh-bah-yah) ____________________
a noodle shop that offers a variety of noodle dishes

sushiya (soo-shee-yah) ____________________
resutoran serving only **sashimi** (raw fish) and **sushi** (vinegared rice and fish)

ryōriya / ryōtei (ryōh-ree-yah) (ryōh-tay) ____________________
resutoran specializing exclusively in **Nihon no** dishes

kissaten (kees-sah-ten) ____________________
coffee shop / teahouse serving light meals **to** snacks throughout the day and into the evening

If **anata** look around you in a **Nihon no** (P) **resutoran, anata wa** will see that some **shūkan** (shōō-kahn) customs might be different from yours. **Ohashi** (oh-hah-shee) chopsticks are generally used as eating utensils and **anata wa** may be seated on **tatami.** (tah-tah-mee) straw mats Remember, shoes are not allowed on **tatami.** (tah-tah-mee) **Anata wa** will be greeted with **"Irasshaimase."** (ee-rahs-shy-mah-seh) welcome Oftentimes customers will say **"Itadakimasu"** (ee-tah-dah-kee-mahss) Thank you for the food. I will start to eat. when they are served.

Your turn to practice now.

____
(Thank you for the food. I will start to eat.)

And at least one more time for practice!

____
(Thank you for the food. I will start to eat.)

- ❒ **tanku** *(tahn-koo)*........................ tank
- ❒ **taoru** *(tah-oh-roo)*........................ towel
- ❒ **tāru** *(tāh-roo)*........................ tar
- ❒ **tēburu** *(tēh-boo-roo)*........................ table
- ❒ **tenisu** *(teh-nee-soo)*........................ tennis

t

Start imagining now all the new taste treats you will experience abroad. Try all of the different

types of eating establishments mentioned on the previous page. Experiment. Sharing **tēburu** with others is a common and pleasant **shūkan** *(shōō-kahn)* (custom)**.** When **anata** see a vacant **seki,** *(seh-kee)* (seat) just ask "**Sumimasen** *(soo-mee-mah-sen)* (but) **ga kono seki wa aite** *(eye-teh)* (free) **imasu ka?**" When you sit down, **anata** can politely say, "**Sumimasen.**" If **anata** need a **menyū,** *(meh-nyōō)* catch the attention of the **uētā** *(oo-ēh-tāh)* (waiter) or **uētoresu,** *(oo-ēh-toh-reh-soo)* (waitress) saying,

Chotto, *(choht-toh)* (just a moment) **menyū o misete** *(mee-seh-teh)* (show) **kudasai.** *(koo-dah-sigh)*

____
(Just a moment, show me the menu please.)

In most **resutoran,** plastic replicas of the food served as well as the **nedan** *(neh-dahn)* (prices) are on display in a **shouuindō.** *(shoh-oo-een-dōh)* (show window) **Anata wa** can simply point out to the **uētā** *(oo-ēh-tāh)* what **anata** would like to order.

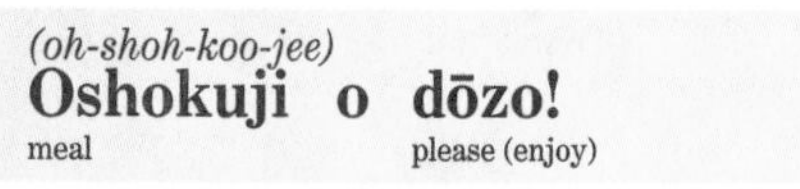

Oshokuji *(oh-shoh-koo-jee)* (meal) **o dōzo!** (please (enjoy))

Most **resutoran** offer **tokubetsu** *(toh-koo-beh-tsoo)* (special) **na** *(nah)* **ryōri** *(ryōh-ree)* (dishes) prepared by the chef or **shokuji** *(shoh-koo-jee)* (meals) prepared with regional ingredients.

❒ **tento** *(ten-toh)*	tent		______
❒ **tēpu** *(tēh-poo)*	tape		______
❒ **terebi** *(teh-reh-bee)*	television	**t**	______
❒ **tomato** *(toh-mah-toh)*	tomato		______
❒ **ton** *(tohn)*	ton		______

(nee-hohn-jeen) *(shoh-koo-jee)* *(goh-goh)*
Nihonjin have three **shokuji** to enjoy every day, plus perhaps snacks in **gogo.**
Japanese (people) meals afternoon

(chōh-shoh-koo) *(ah-sah-goh-hahn)*
chōshoku / asagohan ______________________________
breakfast

In **hoteru no resutoran, kono shokuji** usually consists of **kōhī** or **kōcha,** toast **to batā.**
(P) black tea

In **ryokan,** a traditional **Nihon no chōshoku,** consisting of **gohan,** seaweed, **shirumono,**
(P) rice soup

raw **tamago to yakizakana** is served.
egg grilled fish

(chōō-shoh-koo) *(hee-roo-goh-hahn)*
chūshoku / hirugohan ______________________________
lunch

generally served from 11:30 to 14:00;

(yōō-shoh-koo) *(bahn-goh-hahn)*
yūshoku / bangohan ______________________________
dinner

generally served from 17:00 to 21:00 and sometimes later;
after 21:00 snacks are usually served.

Ima for a preview of delights to come . . . At the back of **kono hon, anata wa** will find a sample **Nihon no menyū.** Read the **menyū** and learn the **atarashii** *(ah-tah-rah-shēē)* **tango.** When **anata** are ready to leave for **Nihon,** cut out the **menyū,** fold it, and carry it in your pocket, wallet or purse. Before you go, how do **anata wa** say these **san** *(sahn)* phrases which are so very important for the hungry traveler?

(P) after **no**

Thank you for the food. I will start to eat. ______________________________

Just a moment, show me the menu please. ______________________________

Please enjoy your meal! ______________________________

__________ **ga yasai** *(yah-sigh)* **o tabemasu ka?**
(who) vegetables (P) eats

__________ **ga sake o nomimasu ka?**
(who) rice wine drinks

__________ (who)

__________ **ga Nihon o ryokō shimasu ka?** *(shee-mahss)*
(who) to travels

❐	**tonneru** *(tohn-neh-roo)*	tunnel		______________
❐	**torakku** *(toh-rahk-koo)*	truck		______________
❐	**toranku** *(toh-rahn-koo)*	trunk	**t**	______________
❐	**torofī** *(toh-roh-fēē)*	trophy		______________
❐	**tōsutā** *(tōh-soo-tāh)*	toaster		______________

The menu below has the main categories **anata** will find in most restaurants. Learn them **kyō** *(kyōh)* today so that **anata** will easily recognize them when you dine **Tōkyō de** *(deh)* in or **Kōbe de.** Be sure to write the words in the blanks below.

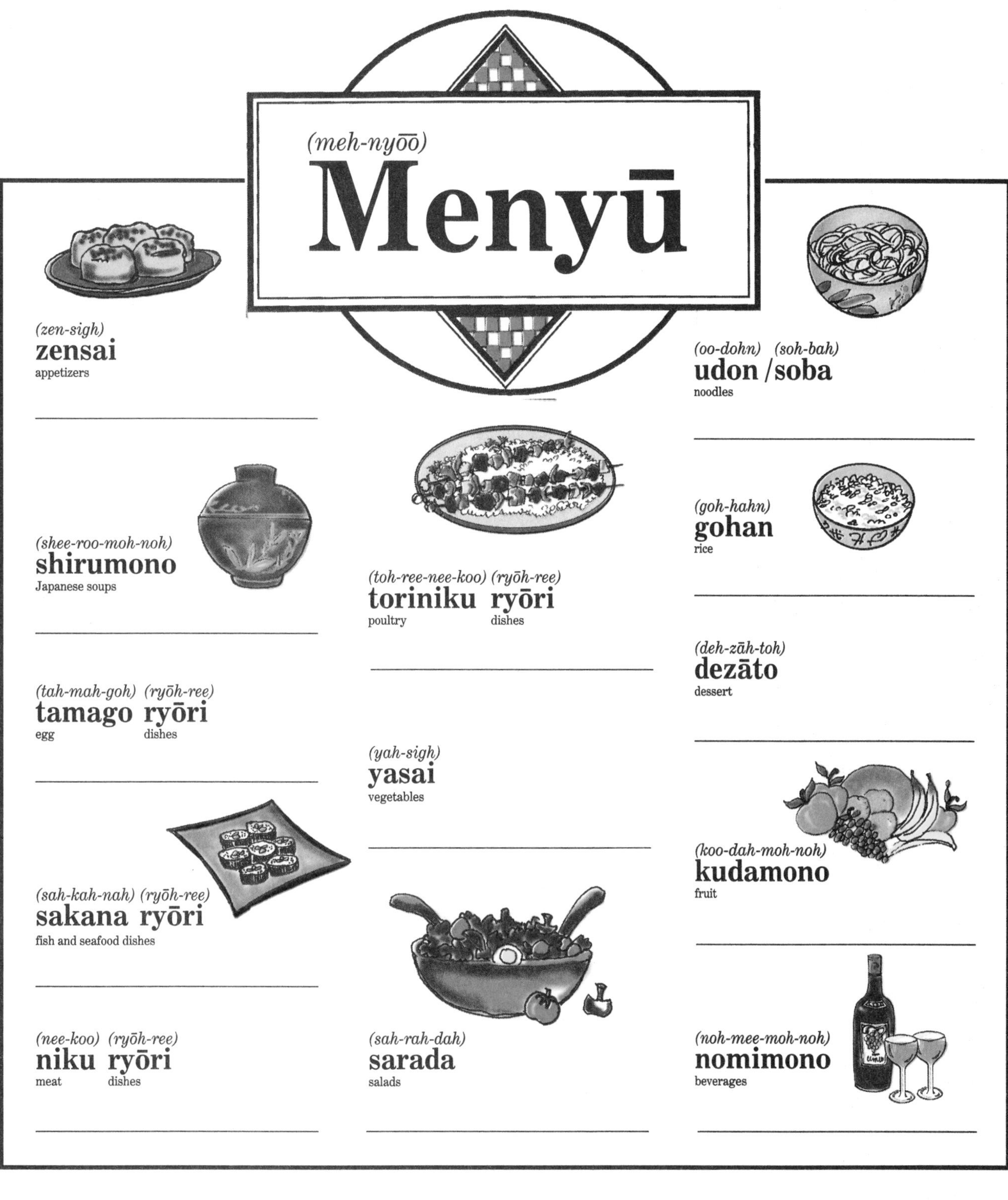

(meh-nyōō)
Menyū
(zen-sigh)
zensai
appetizers
(shee-roo-moh-noh)
shirumono
Japanese soups
(tah-mah-goh) (ryōh-ree)
tamago ryōri
egg dishes
(sah-kah-nah) (ryōh-ree)
sakana ryōri
fish and seafood dishes
(nee-koo) (ryōh-ree)
niku ryōri
meat dishes
(toh-ree-nee-koo) (ryōh-ree)
toriniku ryōri
poultry dishes
(yah-sigh)
yasai
vegetables
(sah-rah-dah)
sarada
salads
(oo-dohn) (soh-bah)
udon / soba
noodles
(goh-hahn)
gohan
rice
(deh-zāh-toh)
dezāto
dessert
(koo-dah-moh-noh)
kudamono
fruit
(noh-mee-moh-noh)
nomimono
beverages

Learning the following should help you identify what kind of meat you have ordered and how it will be prepared.

- ❒ **gyūniku** *(gyōō-nee-koo)* . . . . beef ______________________
- ❒ **koushiniku** *(koh-oo-shee-nee-koo)* . . . . veal ______________________
- ❒ **butaniku** *(boo-tah-nee-koo)* . . . . pork ______________________
- ❒ **toriniku** *(toh-ree-nee-koo)* . . . . poultry ______________________

Anata wa may also get **shirumono** (shee-roo-moh-noh) *soup*, **gohan** (goh-hahn) *rice* **to** (toh) **tsukemono** (tsoo-keh-moh-noh) *pickled vegetables* with **anata** *your* **no** *(P)* **shokuji** (shoh-koo-jee) *meal*. One day at an **ichiba** (ee-chee-bah) *market* will teach you **namae** for all the different kinds of **yasai** (yah-sigh) **to kudamono** (koo-dah-moh-noh) *fruit*, plus it will be a delightful experience for **anata. Anata wa** can always consult your menu guide at the back of **kono hon** if **anata** forget **tadashii** (tah-dah-shēē) *correct* **namae. Ima anata wa** are seated and **uētā** (oo-ēh-tāh) **ga kimasu** (kee-mahss) *comes*.

Menyū o misete kudasai.
Nomimono wa nani ni shimasu ka?
Shirowain o kudasai.

Chōshoku *breakfast* is a **hijō** *very* **ni** *(P)* simple **shokuji** (shoh-koo-jee). A Western-style **chōshoku** is usually available for **ryokōsha** (ryoh-kōh-shah) *tourists* in their **hoteru.** A traditional **Nihon no** *(P)* **chōshoku** is served in **ryokan.** Here is what you can expect to greet you in the **asa** (ah-sah) *morning*.

Nomimono	Chōshoku
kōhī	**pan**
kōcha *black tea*	**rōru pan** (rōh-roo) *rolls*
hotto (hoht-toh) *hot* **chokorēto** (choh-koh-rēh-toh) *chocolate*	**batā**
kokoa *cocoa*	**tōsuto** (tōh-soo-toh) *toast*
orenji *orange* **jūsu** *juice*	**hamu** (hah-moo) **eggu** (eg-goo) *ham and eggs*
tomato jūsu	**medamayaki** *sunny-side up (eggs)*
miruku	**iri** (ee-ree) *scrambled* **tamago**
mizu	**gohan** (goh-hahn) *rice*

- ❒ **sakana** *(sah-kah-nah)* .... fish ____________________
- ❒ **kani** *(kah-nee)* .... crab ____________________
- ❒ **namamomo** *(nah-mah-moh-noh)* .... raw ____________________
- ❒ **yudeta** *(yoo-deh-tah)* .... boiled in water ____________________
- ❒ **nita** *(nee-tah)* .... boiled in sauce ____________________

(shtah)
Shita ni wa is an example of what **anata** might select for your evening meal. Using your menu guide on pages 117 and 118, as well as what **anata** have learned in this Step, fill in the blanks *in English* with what **anata** believe your **uētā** will bring you. **Kotae wa** *(shtah)* **shita ni arimasu** (are).

Zensai
Kaisō moriawase
Shirumono
Akadashi
Sakana ryōri
Yakizakana, gohan, yasai
Dezāto
Anmitsu
(when)
(how)
(why)

KOTAE

Appetizer:	Selected seaweed
Soup:	Red bean-paste soup
Fish Dish:	Broiled fish, rice and vegetables
Dessert:	Boiled black-eyed peas with honey and agar-agar

Ima is a good time for a quick review. Draw lines between the matching *(ay-goh)* **Eigo** *(toh)* **to** **Nihongo** **no** (P) **tango** below.

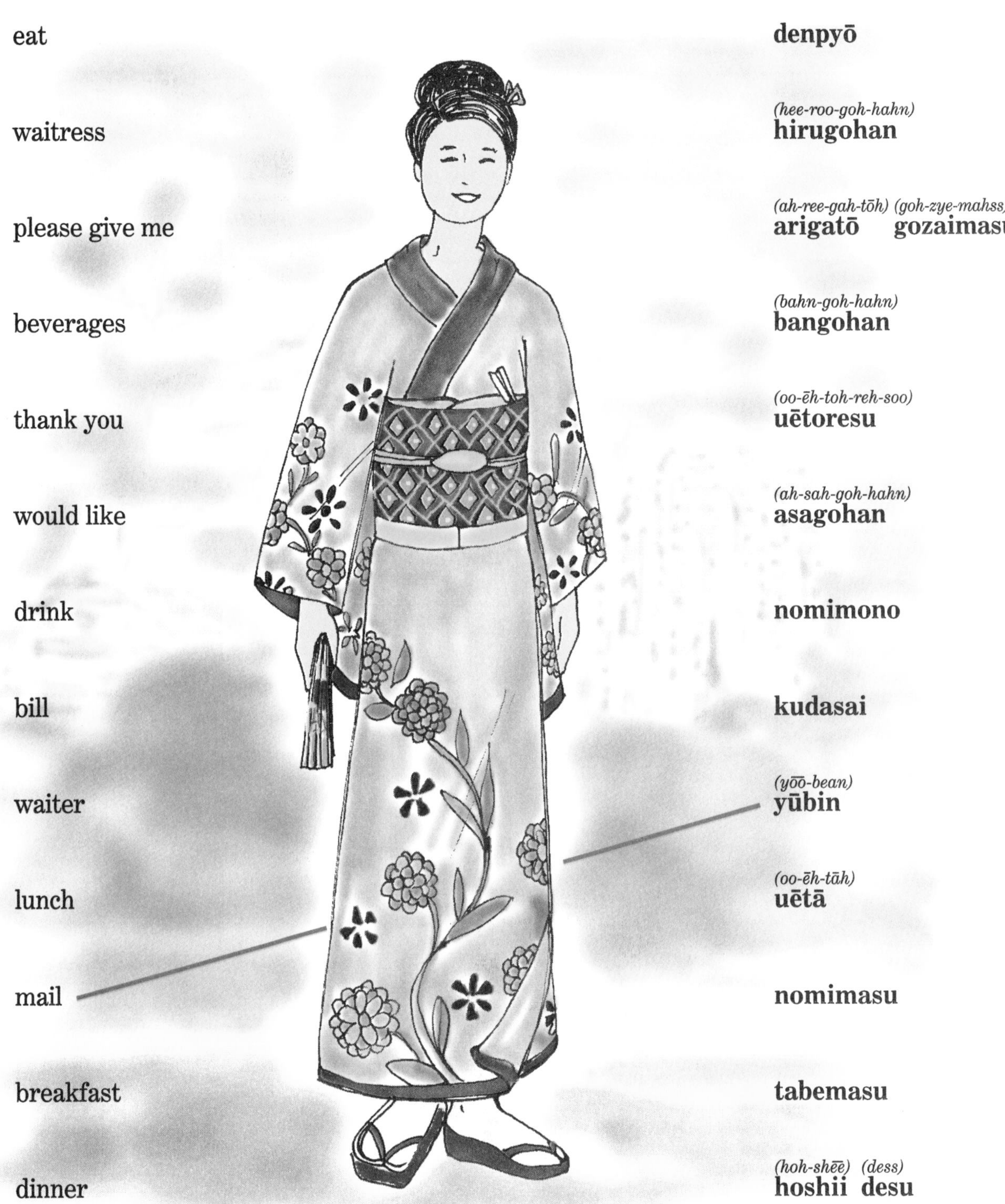

eat	**denpyō**
waitress	*(hee-roo-goh-hahn)* **hirugohan**
please give me	*(ah-ree-gah-tōh) (goh-zye-mahss)* **arigatō gozaimasu**
beverages	*(bahn-goh-hahn)* **bangohan**
thank you	*(oo-ēh-toh-reh-soo)* **uētoresu**
would like	*(ah-sah-goh-hahn)* **asagohan**
drink	**nomimono**
bill	**kudasai**
waiter	*(yōō-bean)* **yūbin**
lunch	*(oo-ēh-tāh)* **uētā**
mail	**nomimasu**
breakfast	**tabemasu**
dinner	*(hoh-shēē) (dess)* **hoshii desu**

- ❒ **tsukemono ni shita** *(tsoo-keh-moh-noh)(nee)(shtah)*. pickled __________
- ❒ **mushita** *(moo-shtah)* .... steamed __________
- ❒ **yaita** *(yai-tah)* .... baked / grilled __________
- ❒ **itameta** *(ee-tah-meh-tah)*.......................... stir-fried __________
- ❒ **ageta** *(ah-geh-tah)*.......................... deep-fried __________

21 *(den-wah)* Denwa
telephone

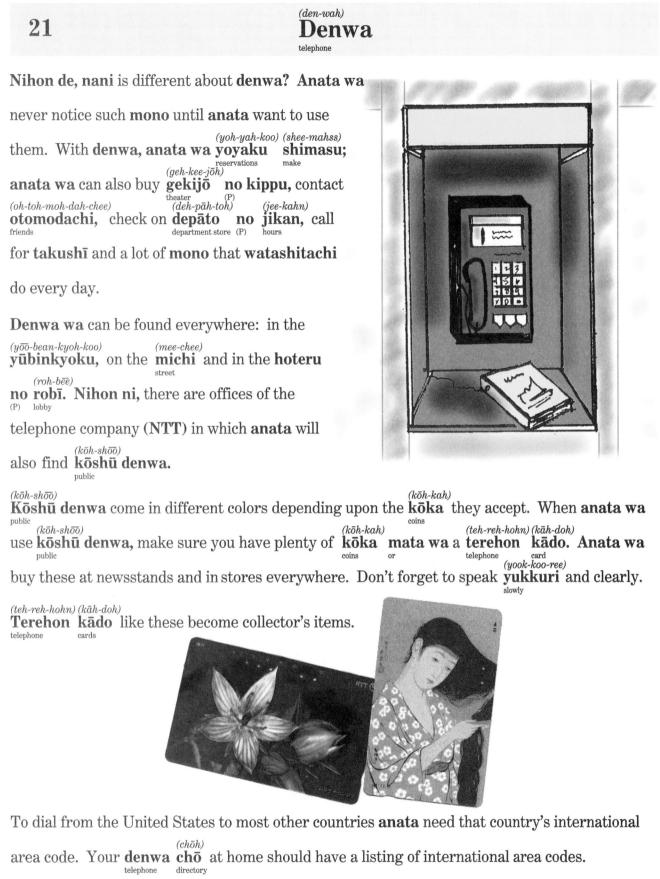

Nihon de, nani is different about **denwa? Anata wa** never notice such **mono** until **anata** want to use

(yoh-yah-koo) (shee-mahss)
them. With **denwa, anata wa yoyaku shimasu;**
reservations make

(geh-kee-jōh)
anata wa can also buy **gekijō no kippu,** contact
theater (P)

(oh-toh-moh-dah-chee) (deh-pāh-toh) (jee-kahn)
otomodachi, check on **depāto no jikan,** call
friends department store (P) hours

for **takushī** and a lot of **mono** that **watashitachi** do every day.

Denwa wa can be found everywhere: in the

(yōō-bean-kyoh-koo) (mee-chee)
yūbinkyoku, on the **michi** and in the **hoteru**
street

(roh-bēē)
no robī. Nihon ni, there are offices of the
(P) lobby

telephone company **(NTT)** in which **anata** will

(kōh-shōō)
also find **kōshū denwa.**
public

(kōh-shōō) (kōh-kah)
Kōshū denwa come in different colors depending upon the **kōka** they accept. When **anata wa**
public coins

(kōh-shōō) (kōh-kah) (teh-reh-hohn) (kāh-doh)
use **kōshū denwa,** make sure you have plenty of **kōka mata wa** a **terehon kādo. Anata wa**
public coins or telephone card

(yook-koo-ree)
buy these at newsstands and in stores everywhere. Don't forget to speak **yukkuri** and clearly.
slowly

(teh-reh-hohn) (kāh-doh)
Terehon kādo like these become collector's items.
telephone cards

To dial from the United States to most other countries **anata** need that country's international

(chōh)
area code. Your **denwa chō** at home should have a listing of international area codes.
telephone directory

Koko ni some very useful words built around the word **"denwa" ga arimasu.**

- ❒ **denwa bokkusu** *(den-wah)(bohk-koo-soo)* .... telephone booth
- ❒ **kōshū denwa** *(kōh-shōō)(den-wah)* .... public telephone
- ❒ **kokusai denwa** *(koh-koo-sigh)(den-wah)* .... international telephone call
- ❒ **shinai denwa** *(shee-nye)(den-wah)* .... local telephone call

When **anata** leave your contact numbers with friends, family and business colleagues, **anata** should include your destination country's area code and city code whenever possible . For example,

City Codes		City Codes	
Tōkyō	3	Kōbe	78
Ōsaka	6	Hiroshima	82
Yokohama	45	Kawasaki	44

The country code for Japan is — 81 —

To call from one city to another **anata wa** may need to call **kōkanshu** *(kōh-kahn-shoo)* (operator). Tell the **kōkanshu,**

"**Tōkyō ni** *(nee)* (to) **denwa o** ((telephone) call) **kaketai desu.**" *(kah-keh-tye)* (I would like to make) or "**Shikago** *(shee-kah-goh)* (Chicago) **ni** (to) **denwa o kaketai desu.**" *(kah-keh-tye)* (I would like to make)

Now you try it: ______________________________
(I would like to make a call to . . . .)

When answering the **denwa, anata** pick up the receiver and say,

Moshi-moshi. *(moh-shee-moh-shee)* (hello) ______________ (your name) **to** *(toh)* (P) **mōshimasu.** *(mōh-shee-mahss)* (speaking)

When saying goodbye, **anata wa iimasu** (say) "**Sayōnara,**" *(sah-yōh-nah-rah)* (good-bye) or "**Dewa** *(deh-wah)* (until) **mata.**" *(mah-tah)* (again) Your turn —

____
(Hello. . . . speaking.)

______________________________ (good-bye)

______________________________ (until again)

Don't forget that **anata wa** can always ask . . .

Amerika e *(eh)* (to) **no** (P) **kokusai** *(koh-koo-sigh)* (international telephone call) **denwa wa ikura** *(ee-koo-rah)* (how much) **desu ka?** ______________________________

Kanada e no (to (P)) **kokusai denwa wa ikura desu ka?** ______________________________

Koko ni some countries **anata** may wish to call.

- ❐ **Ōsutoraria** *(ōh-soo-toh-rah-ree-ah)* . . . . Australia ______________
- ❐ **Kanada** *(kah-nah-dah)* . . . . Canada ______________
- ❐ **Chūgoku** *(chōō-goh-koo)* . . . . China ______________
- ❐ **Igirisu** *(ee-gee-ree-soo)* . . . . England ______________

Koko ni some sample sentences for the **denwa ga arimasu.** Write them in the blanks *(shtah)* **shita** (below).

Boston *(nee)* **ni** (to) **denwa o** *(kah-keh-tye)* **kaketai** (I would like to make) **desu.** ______________________

(nah-ree-tah) **Narita** *(kōō-kōh)* **Kūkō** (airport) **ni denwa o kaketai desu.** ______________________

San Francisco ni (to) **denwa o kaketai desu.** ______________________

(sigh-tōh) **Saitō san** (Mr. Saito) **ni denwa o kaketai desu.** ______________________

Denwa *(bahn-gōh)* **bangō** (number) **wa** *(nahn)* **nan** *(bahn)* **ban desu ka?** ______________________

Denwa bangō wa 473 - 6440 desu. ______________________

Christine: *(moh-shee-moh-shee)* **Moshi-moshi. Christine** *(toh)* **to** *(mōh-shee-mahss)* **mōshimasu** (speaking). **Sumimasen ga Yamamoto san** (Mr. Yamamoto) **wa** *(ee-rahs-shy-mahss)* **irasshaimasu** (is in) **ka?**

____

(hee-shoh) Hisho (secretary): *(choht-toh)* **Chotto** (just) *(maht-teh)* **matte** (wait) **kudasai. Sumimasen. Ima** *(hah-nah-shee-chōō)* **hanashichū** (line busy) **desu.**

____

Christine: *(mōh)* **Mō** *(ee-chee-doh)* **ichido** (more once) *(hah-nahsh-teh)* **hanashite** (speak) **kudasai.** *(moht-toh)* **Motto** (more) *(yook-koo-ree)* **yukkuri** (slowly) **hanashite kudasai.**

____

Hisho: **Sumimasen. Ima** *(hah-nah-shee-chōō)* **hanashichū desu.**

____

Christine: **Dōmo.** *(sah-yōh-nah-rah)* **Sayōnara.**

____

Anata wa are ready to use any **Nihon no denwa.** Just take it *(yook-koo-ree)* **yukkuri** (slowly) and speak clearly.

- ❒ **Airurando** *(ah-ee-roo-rahn-doh)* .... Ireland
- ❒ **Isuraeru** *(ee-soo-rah-eh-roo)* .... Israel ________
- ❒ **Kankoku** *(kahn-koh-koo)* .... Korea ________
- ❒ **Marēshia** *(mah-rēh-shee-ah)* .... Malaysia ________
- ❒ **Nyūjīrando** *(nyōō-jēē-rahn-doh)* .... New Zealand ________

22 *(chee-kah-teh-tsoo)* Chikatetsu
subway

(chee-kah-teh-tsoo) (shoo-yōh) (toh-shee)
An excellent means of transportation is the **chikatetsu.** **Shuyō** **toshi** in **Nihon** have
subway major cities

(chee-kah-teh-tsoo) (toh-shee) (toh) (tah-koo-shēē) (ben-ree)
chikatetsu. In smaller **toshi, basu, densha to takushī** are **hijō ni benri** forms of
subways taxi very convenient

(mee-chee) (shoo-yōh)
transportation. **Takushī** can be hailed from the **michi** or found at most **shuyō** hotels.
street major

(noh-ree-bah) (deh-pāh-toh) (eh-kee)
There are also **takushī noriba** in front of many **Nihon no depāto** and **eki.**
stands (P) department stores stations

(chee-kah-teh-tsoo)
chikatetsu
subway

(bah-soo)
basu
bus

(den-shah)
densha
train (commuter)

(chee-kah-teh-tsoo) (eh-kee)
chikatetsu no eki
(P) station

(bah-soo-tay)
basutei
bus stop

(tah-koo-shēē) (noh-ree-bah)
takushī noriba
taxi stand

(chee-zoo) (sen) (toh) (eh-kee) (shoo-yōh) (nah) (eh-kee)
Chizu displaying the various **sen to eki** are available at most **shuyō na eki** and even
maps lines stations major stations

some **hoteru.** **Sen** are color-coded to facilitate reading, just like your example on the next page.
lines

(keep-poo) (kye-mahss)
Anata wa kippu o kaimasu from a vending machine at the **eki no iriguchi.** Be sure to keep
ticket buy entrance

(deh-goo-chee)
your **kippu,** as it will be collected at the **eki no deguchi.**
exit

- ❒ **Doitsu** *(doy-tsoo)* .... Germany ______
- ❒ **Shingapōru** *(sheen-gah-pōh-roo)* .... Singapore ______
- ❒ **Minami Afurika** *(mee-nah-mee)(ah-foo-ree-kah)* .... South Africa ______
- ❒ **Suisu** *(soo-ee-soo)* .... Switzerland ______
- ❒ **Amerika** *(ah-meh-ree-kah)* .... United States ______

Other than having foreign words, the **chikatetsu** *(chee-kah-teh-tsoo)* functions just like **New York de** *(deh)* in or **London de.**

Locate your destination, select the correct line on your practice **chikatetsu** and hop on board.

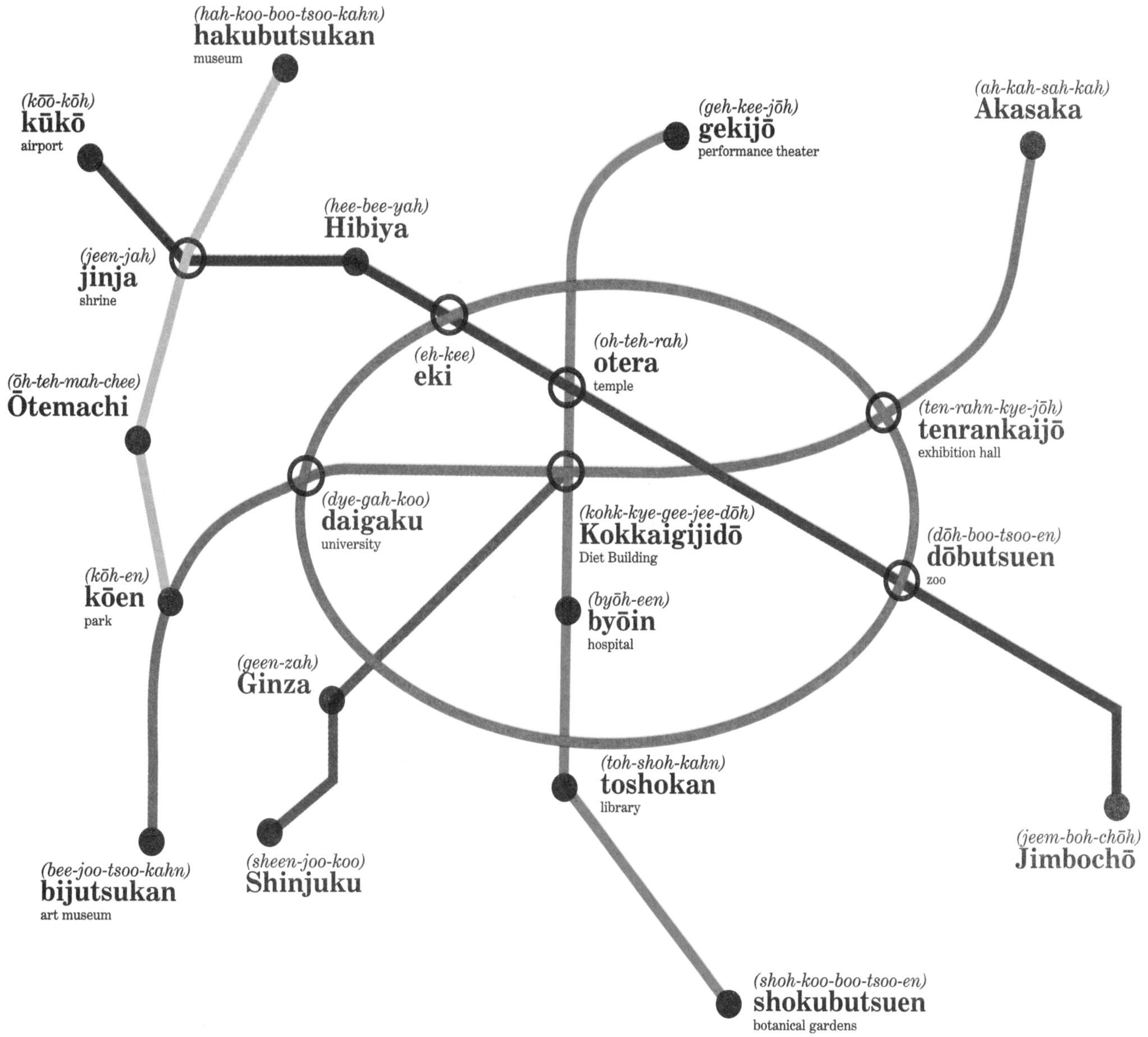

(hah-koo-boo-tsoo-kahn)
hakubutsukan
museum

(kōō-kōh)
kūkō
airport

(geh-kee-jōh)
gekijō
performance theater

(ah-kah-sah-kah)
Akasaka

(hee-bee-yah)
Hibiya

(jeen-jah)
jinja
shrine

(eh-kee)
eki

(oh-teh-rah)
otera
temple

(ōh-teh-mah-chee)
Ōtemachi

(ten-rahn-kye-jōh)
tenrankaijō
exhibition hall

(dye-gah-koo)
daigaku
university

(kohk-kye-gee-jee-dōh)
Kokkaigijidō
Diet Building

(dōh-boo-tsoo-en)
dōbutsuen
zoo

(kōh-en)
kōen
park

(byōh-een)
byōin
hospital

(geen-zah)
Ginza

(toh-shoh-kahn)
toshokan
library

(jeem-boh-chōh)
Jimbochō

(bee-joo-tsoo-kahn)
bijutsukan
art museum

(sheen-joo-koo)
Shinjuku

(shoh-koo-boo-tsoo-en)
shokubutsuen
botanical gardens

Say these questions aloud many times and don't forget you need **kippu** *(keep-poo)* ticket for the **chikatetsu!**

Chikatetsu no eki *(eh-kee)* station **wa doko desu ka?**

Basutei *(bah-soo-tay)* bus stop **wa doko desu ka?**

Takushī noriba *(noh-ree-bah)* stand **wa doko desu ka?**

Koko ni a few holidays you might experience during your visit **ga arimasu.**

- ❒ **Ōmisoka** *(ōh-mee-soh-kah)* . . . . New Year's Eve ____________
- ❒ **Oshōgatsu** *(oh-shōh-gah-tsoo)* . . . . New Year's Day ____________
- ❒ **Midori no Hi** *(mee-doh-ree)(noh)(hee)* . . . . Green Day (April 29) ____________
- ❒ **Kodomo no Hi** *(koh-doh-moh)(noh)(hee)* . . . . Children's Day (May 5) ____________

Practice the following basic questions out loud and then write them in the blanks below.

1. **Chikatetsu no** *(keep-poo)* **kippu** (ticket) **wa doko de** (at) *(kye-mahss)* **kaimasu** (does one buy) **ka?** ______________________

(no = (P))

Densha no kippu wa doko de (at) *(kye-mahss)* **kaimasu** (does one buy) **ka?** ______________________

2. **Chikatetsu wa** *(ee-tsoo)* **itsu** (when) *(deh-mahss)* **demasu** (leaves) **ka?** ______________________

Basu wa itsu demasu ka? ______________________

Densha wa itsu demasu ka? ______________________

3. *(ee-koo-rah)* **Ikura** (how much) **desu ka?** (is it) ______________________

(chee-kah-teh-tsoo) **Chikatetsu no** *(keep-poo)* **kippu wa ikura desu ka?** ______________________

Basu no kippu wa ikura desu ka? ______________________

(ryoh-keen) **Ryokin** (fare) **wa ikura** (how much) **desu ka?** ______________________

4. **Chikatetsu no** *(eh-kee)* **eki wa doko desu ka?** ______________________

(bah-soo-tay) **Basutei wa doko desu ka?** ______________________

Takushī *(noh-ree-bah)* **noriba wa doko desu ka?** ______________________

Let's change directions and learn three new verbs. **Anata wa** know the basic "plug-in" formula, so write out your own sentences using these new verbs.

(ah-rye-mahss) **araimasu** — wash ______________________

(nah-koo-shee-mahss) **nakushimasu** — lose ______________________

(kah-kah-ree-mahss) **kakarimasu** — take (time) ______________________

Koko ni a few special greetings which **anata** may wish to use **ga arimasu.**

- ❐ **Merī kurisumasu** *(meh-rēē)(koo-ree-soo-mahss)* . . . . Merry Christmas
- ❐ **Omedetō gozaimasu** *(oh-meh-deh-tōh)(goh-zye-mahss)* . . . . Congratulations
- ❐ **Otanjōbi omedetō gozaimasu** *(oh-tahn-jōh-bee)(oh-meh-deh-tōh)(goh-zye-mahss)* . . . Happy Birthday
- ❐ **Akemashite omedetō gozaimasu** *(ah-keh-mahsh-teh)(oh-meh-deh-tōh)(goh-zye-mahss)* . . . Happy New Year

23 Urimasu to Kaimasu

(oo-ree-mahss) **Urimasu** (sell) *(toh)* **to** (and) *(kye-mahss)* **Kaimasu** (buy)

Shopping abroad is exciting. The simple everyday task of buying a *(reet-toh-roo)* **rittoru** (liter) **no** **miruku** (milk) *(mah-tah)* **mata** (or) **wa** *(reen-goh)* **ringo** (apple) becomes a challenge that **anata** should **ima** be able to meet quickly and easily. Of course, **anata wa** will purchase *(oh-mee-yah-geh)* **omiyage** (souvenirs) **to** (and) *(keet-teh)* **kitte** **to** *(hah-gah-kee)* **hagaki** but do not forget those many other items ranging from shoelaces to *(ah-soo-pee-reen)* **asupirin** (aspirin) that **anata** might need unexpectedly. Locate your store, draw a line to it and, as always, write your new words in the blanks provided.

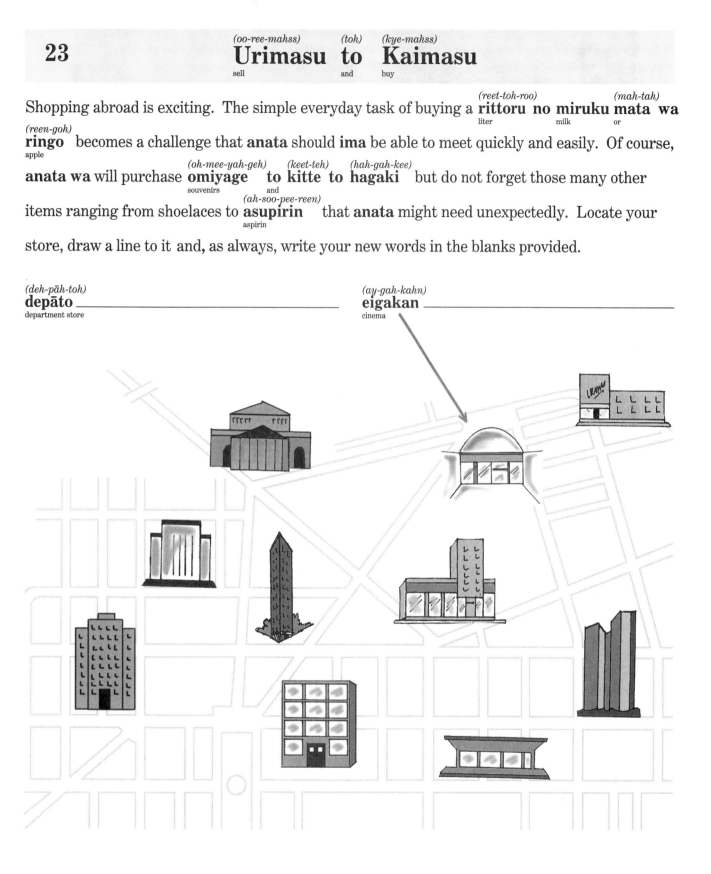

(deh-pāh-toh) **depāto** (department store) ______________________

(ay-gah-kahn) **eigakan** (cinema) ______________________

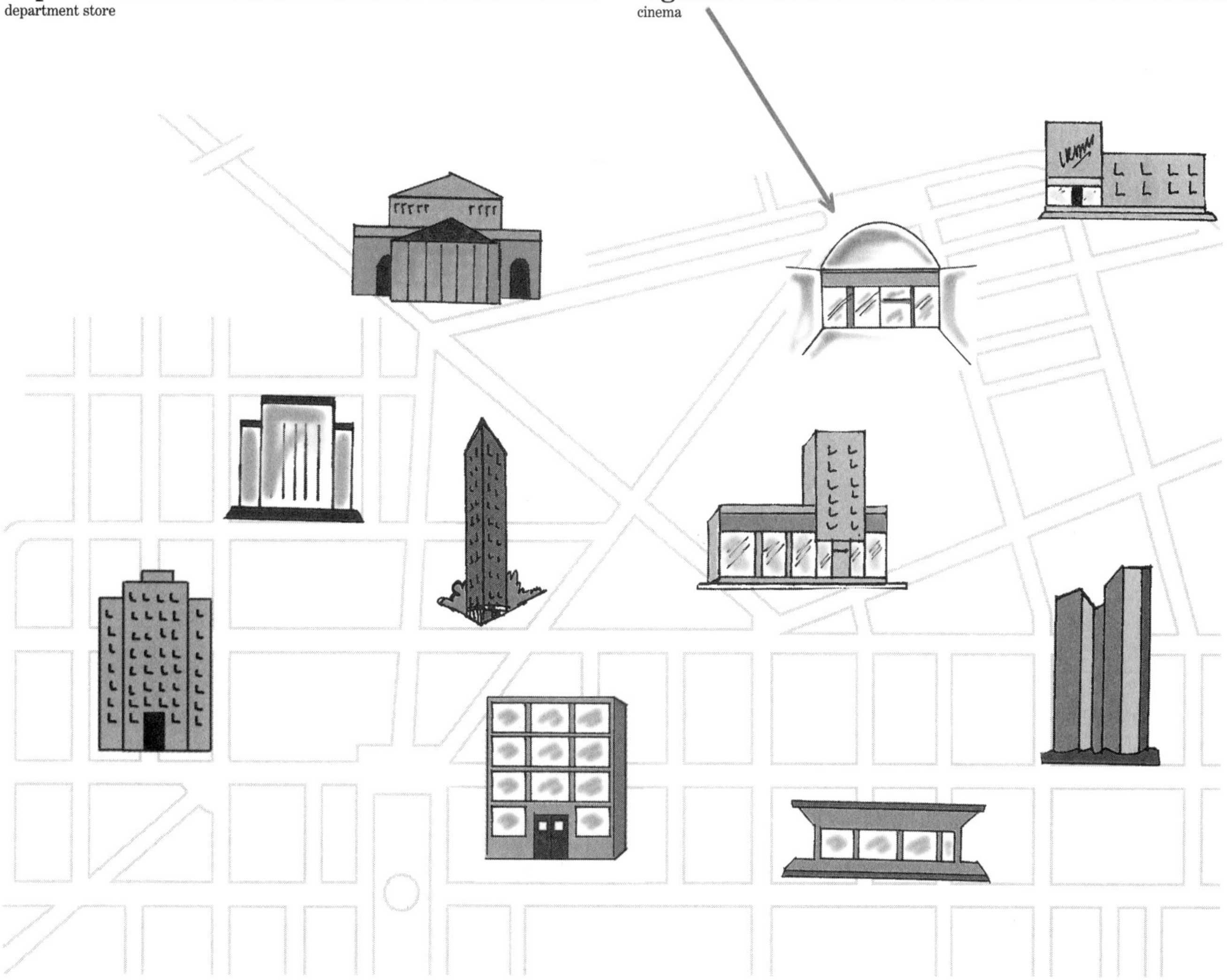

(yōō-bean-kyoh-koo) **yūbinkyoku** (post office) ______________________

(geen-kōh) **ginkō** (bank) ______________________

(hoh-teh-roo) **hoteru** (hotel) ______________________

(gah-soh-reen) **gasorin** (gasoline) *(soo-tahn-doh)* **sutando** (stand / station) ______________________

Most stores are open *(geh-tsoo-yōh-bee)* **Getsuyōbi** (Monday) through *(doh-yōh-bee)* **Doyōbi.** Some stores in the *(shōh-ten-guy)* **shōtengai** (shopping centers) are open on *(nee-chee-yōh-bee)* **Nichiyōbi.** (Sunday)

(nee-koo-yah) **nikuya** butcher shop ____________

(hohn-yah) **honya** bookstore ____________

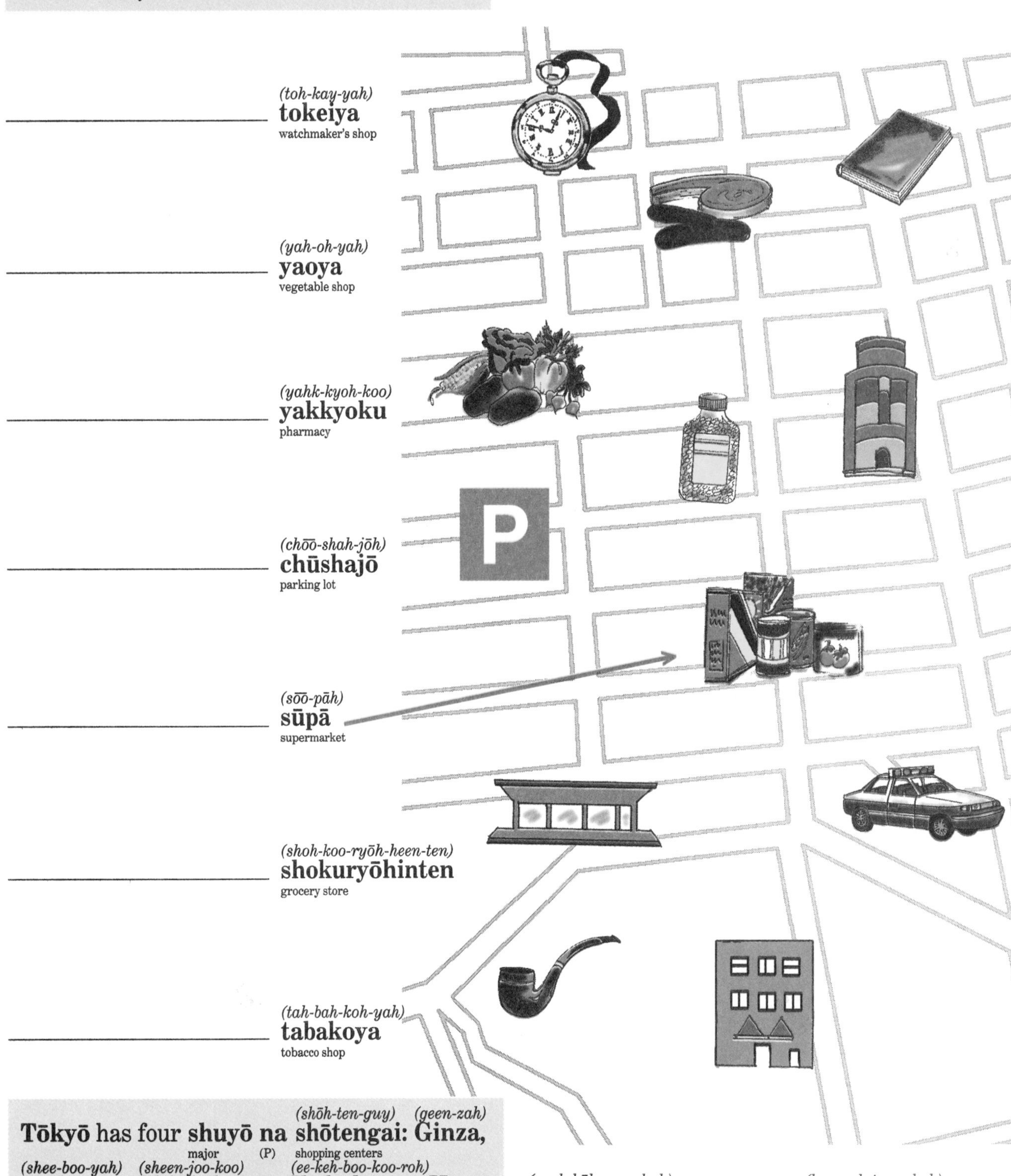

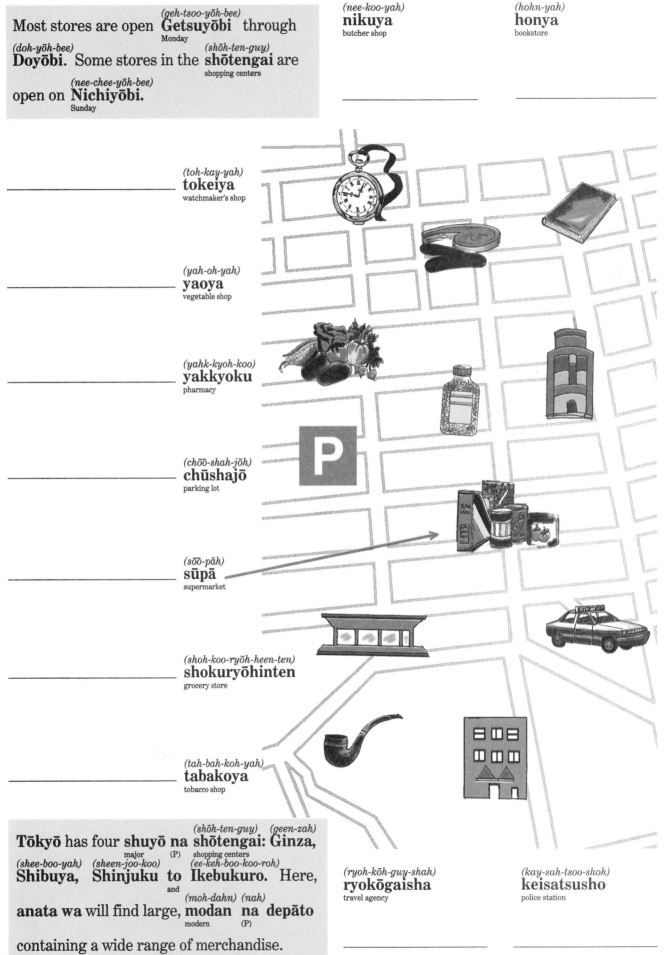

____________ *(toh-kay-yah)* **tokeiya** watchmaker's shop

____________ *(yah-oh-yah)* **yaoya** vegetable shop

____________ *(yahk-kyoh-koo)* **yakkyoku** pharmacy

____________ *(chōō-shah-jōh)* **chūshajō** parking lot

____________ *(sōō-pāh)* **sūpā** supermarket

____________ *(shoh-koo-ryōh-heen-ten)* **shokuryōhinten** grocery store

____________ *(tah-bah-koh-yah)* **tabakoya** tobacco shop

Tōkyō has four **shuyō na** (major (P)) *(shōh-ten-guy)* **shōtengai:** (shopping centers) *(geen-zah)* **Ginza,** *(shee-boo-yah)* **Shibuya,** *(sheen-joo-koo)* **Shinjuku to** (and) *(ee-keh-boo-koo-roh)* **Ikebukuro.** Here, **anata wa** will find large, *(moh-dahn)* **modan** (modern) *(nah)* **na** (P) **depāto** containing a wide range of merchandise.

(ryoh-kōh-guy-shah) **ryokōgaisha** travel agency ____________

(kay-sah-tsoo-shoh) **keisatsusho** police station ____________

(gyōō-nyōō-ten)
gyūnyūten
dairy

(hah-nah-yah)
hanaya
florist

(sah-kah-nah-yah)
sakanaya ____________________
fish market

(koo-dah-moh-noh-yah)
kudamonoya ____________________
fruit shop

(ee-chee-bah)
ichiba ____________________
market

(kohn-bee-nee-en-soo) (soo-toh-ah)
konbiniensu sutoa ____________________
convenience store

(doh-rye) (koo-rēē-neen-goo-yah)
dorai kurīninguya ____________________
dry cleaner's

(pahn-yah)
panya panya, panya, panya
bakery

(kees-sah-ten)
kissaten ____________________
coffe shop, teahouse

(koh-een-rahn-doh-rēē)
koinrandorī ____________________
laundry

(boon-bōh-goo-yah)
bunbōguya
stationery store

(bee-yōh-een)
biyōin
hairdresser (women's)

3.	*(sahn) (guy)* **san gai**	=	third floor
2.	*(nee) (kye)* **ni kai**	=	second floor
1.	*(eek-kye)* **ikkai**	=	first / ground floor
B.	*(chee-kah)* **chika**	=	basement

Depāto

(deh-pāh-toh) department store

At this point, **anata wa** should just about be ready for your **Nihon no** (P) **ryokō** (ryoh-kōh) trip. **Anata wa** have gone shopping for those last-minute odds 'n ends. Most likely, the store directory at your local **depāto** (deh-pāh-toh) department store did not look like the one **shita!** (shtah) **Anata wa** know that **"kodomo"** (koh-doh-moh) is **Nihongo** for "child" so if **anata** need something for a **kodomo, anata wa** would probably look on the **san** (sahn) third **gai,** (guy) floor wouldn't you? Time to buy a dictionary, isn't it?

4.	**hon** **chizu** **terebi**	**gakki** **kamera** **zasshi**	**shinbun** **bunbōgu** **resutoran**
3.	**kodomo yōhin** **fujin fuku** **fujin bōshi**	**shinshi fuku** **shinshi gutsu** **fujin gutsu**	**kottō** **nyūyōji yōhin** **omocha**
2.	**kagi** **tōki** **setomono**	**mizugi** **shitagi** **hankachi**	**supōtsu yōhin** **kyanpu yōhin** **kōgu**
1.	**kasa** **hōseki** **shinshi bōshi**	**tebukuro** **beruto** **kutsushita**	**tokei** **kōsui** **keshōhin**
B	**pan** **kissa** **osake**	**shokuhin** **yasai** **kudamono**	**wain** **niku** **yōshu**

Let's start a checklist for **anata** your **no** (P) **ryokō.** Besides **fuku,** (foo-koo) clothing **nani** what **ga irimasu** (ee-ree-mahss) need **ka?** As you learn these **tango,** assemble these items in a **kado** (kah-doh) corner of **anata no** your **ie.** (ee-eh) house Check and make sure that they are **kirei** (kee-ray) clean and ready for **anata no ryokō.** Be sure to do the same with the other **mono** (moh-noh) things that **anata** pack. On the next pages, match each item to its picture and write out the word many times. As **anata** organize these things, check them off on this list. Do not forget to take the next group of sticky labels and label these **mono** today!

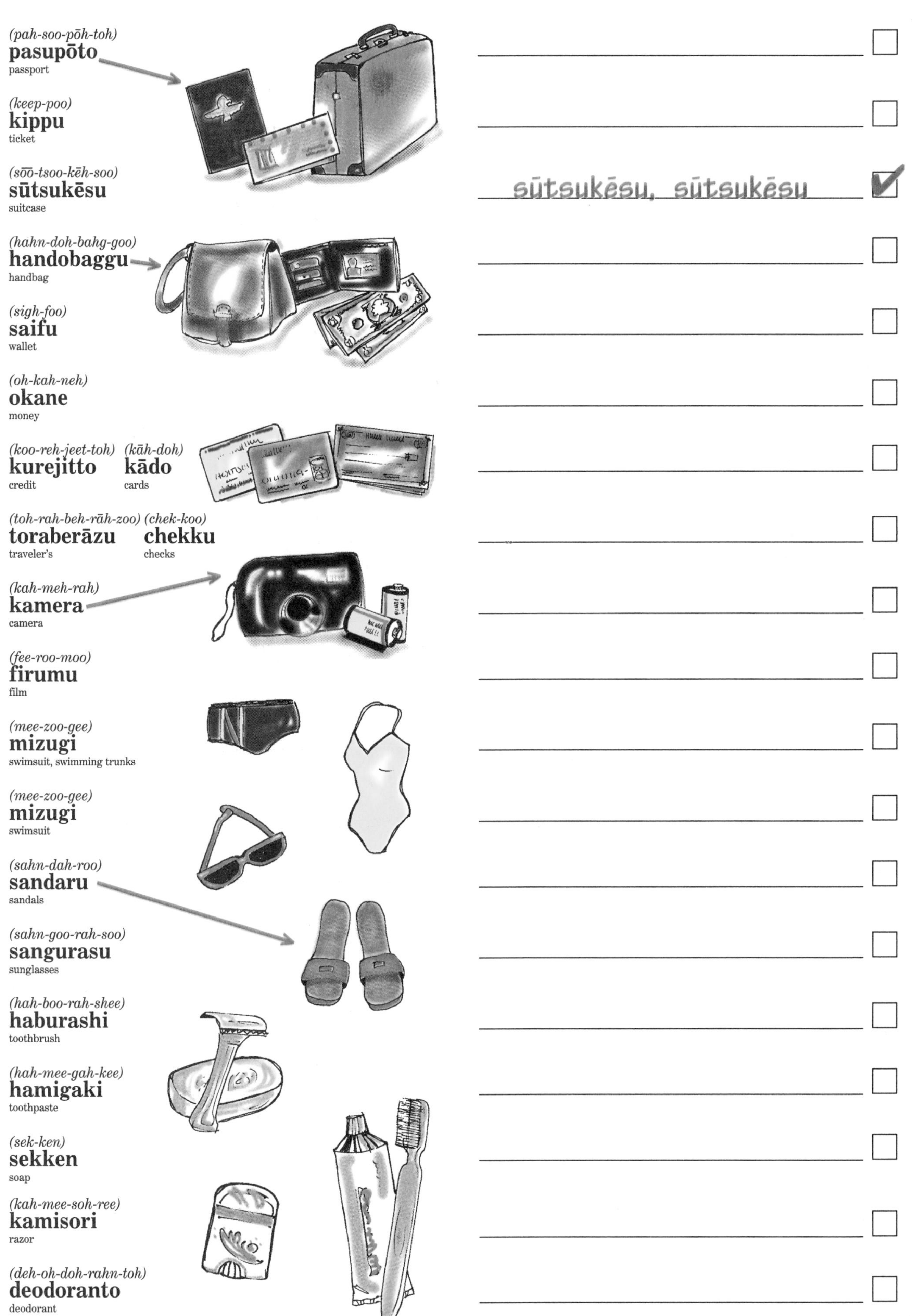

(pah-soo-pōh-toh)
pasupōto
passport

(keep-poo)
kippu
ticket

(sōō-tsoo-kēh-soo)
sūtsukēsu
suitcase

sūtsukēsu, sūtsukēsu ✔

(hahn-doh-bahg-goo)
handobaggu
handbag

(sigh-foo)
saifu
wallet

(oh-kah-neh)
okane
money

(koo-reh-jeet-toh) *(kāh-doh)*
kurejitto kādo
credit cards

(toh-rah-beh-rāh-zoo) *(chek-koo)*
toraberāzu chekku
traveler's checks

(kah-meh-rah)
kamera
camera

(fee-roo-moo)
firumu
film

(mee-zoo-gee)
mizugi
swimsuit, swimming trunks

(mee-zoo-gee)
mizugi
swimsuit

(sahn-dah-roo)
sandaru
sandals

(sahn-goo-rah-soo)
sangurasu
sunglasses

(hah-boo-rah-shee)
haburashi
toothbrush

(hah-mee-gah-kee)
hamigaki
toothpaste

(sek-ken)
sekken
soap

(kah-mee-soh-ree)
kamisori
razor

(deh-oh-doh-rahn-toh)
deodoranto
deodorant

(*koo-shee*)
kushi
comb

kushi, kushi, kushi ✔

(*rain-kōh-toh*)
reinkōto
raincoat

(*kah-sah*)
kasa
umbrella

(*ōh-bāh*)
ōbā
overcoat

(*teh-boo-koo-roh*)
tebukuro
gloves

(*bōh-shee*)
bōshi
hat

(*nah-gah-goo-tsoo*)
nagagutsu
boots

(*koo-tsoo*)
kutsu
shoes

(*teh-nee-soo*) (*shōō-zoo*)
tenisu shūzu
tennis shoes

(*sōō-tsoo*)
sūtsu
suit

(*neh-koo-tie*)
nekutai
tie

(*shah-tsoo*)
shatsu
shirt

(*hahn-kah-chee*)
hankachi
handkerchief

(*jah-ket-toh*)
jaketto
jacket, blazer

(*zoo-bohn*)
zubon
trousers

(*jēēn-zoo*)
jīnzu
jeans

(*shōh-toh*) (*pahn-tsoo*)
shōto pantsu
shorts

(*tēē*) (*shah-tsoo*)
tī shatsu
T-shirt

(*pahn-tsoo*)
pantsu
underpants

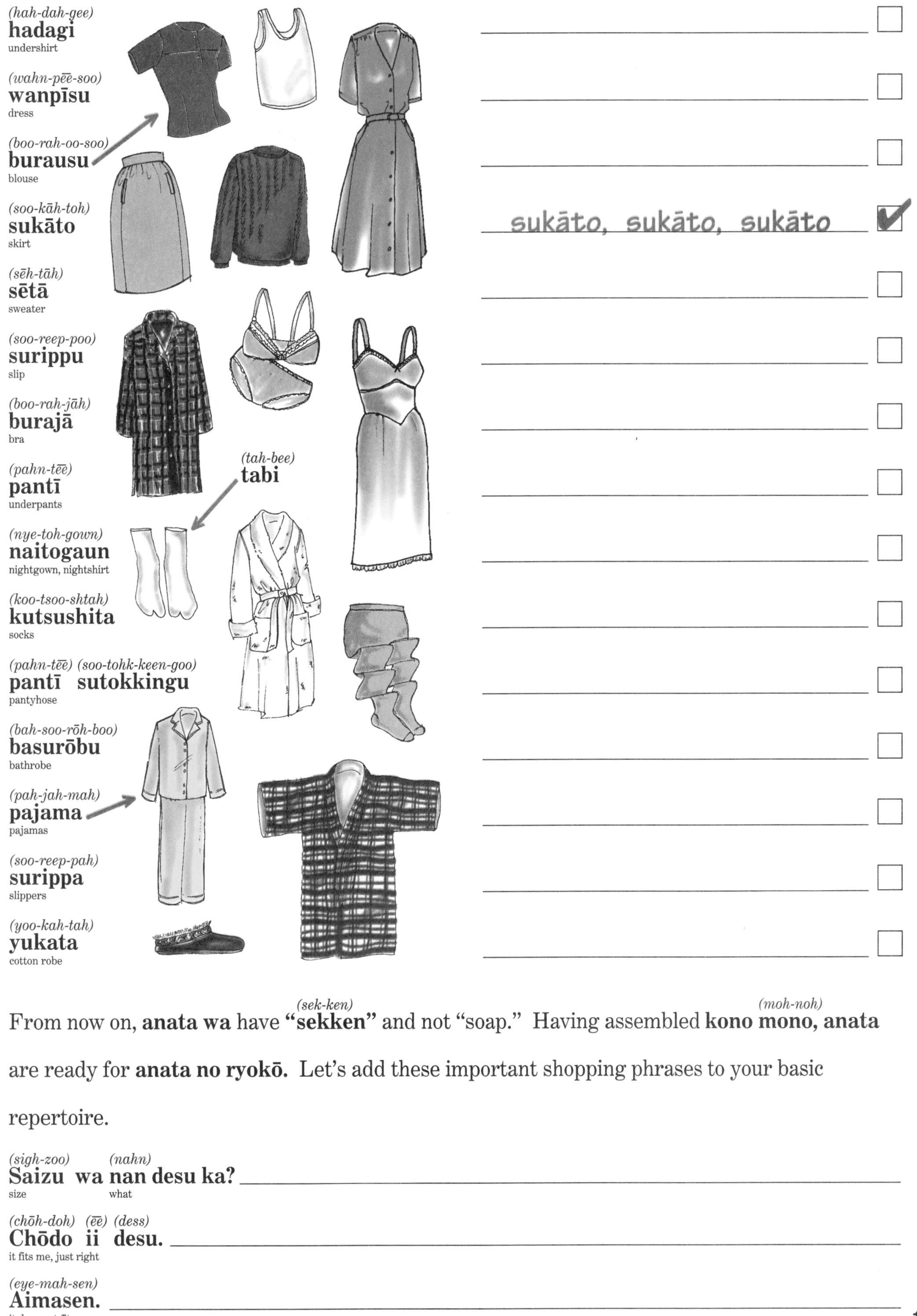

(hah-dah-gee)
hadagi
undershirt

(wahn-pē-soo)
wanpīsu
dress

(boo-rah-oo-soo)
burausu
blouse

(soo-kāh-toh)
sukāto
skirt

sukāto, sukāto, sukāto

(sēh-tāh)
sētā
sweater

(soo-reep-poo)
surippu
slip

(boo-rah-jāh)
burajā
bra

(pahn-tē)
pantī
underpants

(tah-bee)
tabi

(nye-toh-gown)
naitogaun
nightgown, nightshirt

(koo-tsoo-shtah)
kutsushita
socks

(pahn-tē) (soo-tohk-keen-goo)
pantī sutokkingu
pantyhose

(bah-soo-rōh-boo)
basurōbu
bathrobe

(pah-jah-mah)
pajama
pajamas

(soo-reep-pah)
surippa
slippers

(yoo-kah-tah)
yukata
cotton robe

From now on, **anata wa** have **"sekken"** *(sek-ken)* and not "soap." Having assembled **kono mono** *(moh-noh)*, **anata** are ready for **anata no ryokō.** Let's add these important shopping phrases to your basic repertoire.

(sigh-zoo) *(nahn)*
Saizu wa nan desu ka? ____________________
size — what

(chōh-doh) (ē) (dess)
Chōdo ii desu. ____________________
it fits me, just right

(eye-mah-sen)
Aimasen. ____________________
it does not fit me

Treat yourself to a final review. **Anata wa** (mee-seh) **mise** (stores) **no namae o** (P) (sheet-teh) **shitte** (know) **imasu,** so let's practice shopping. Just remember your key question **tango** that you learned in Step 2. Whether **anata** need to buy a (hohn) **hon** or a (bōh-shee) **bōshi** (hat) the necessary **tango** are the same.

1. First step — (doh-koh) **doko?**

(pahn-yah) **Panya** (bakery) **wa doko desu ka?** (geen-kōh) **Ginkō** (bank) **wa doko desu ka?** (hohn-yah) **Honya** (bookstore) **wa doko desu ka?**

____

(Where is the department store?)

____

(Where is the grocery store?)

____

(Where is the market?)

2. Second step — tell them what **anata wa** (ee-ree-mahss) **irimasu** (need) **mata wa** (or) (hoh-shēē) **hoshii** (would like) (dess) **desu.**

Watashi wa (I) ________ (?) **ga** (ee-ree-mahss) **irimasu.** (need)

________ (?) **ga** (ah-ree-mahss) **arimasu ka?** (are there / do you have)

Watashi wa (I) ________ (?) **ga** (hoh-shēē) **hoshii** (would like) (dess) **desu.**

____

(Do you have postcards?)

____

(I would like four stamps.)

____

(I need toothpaste.)

____

(Do you have film?)

____

(Do you have coffee?)

Go through the glossary at the end of **kono hon** and select **nijū** *(nee-jōō)* twenty **no tango.** Drill the above patterns with **kono nijū no tango.** Don't cheat. Drill them **kyō.** *(kyōh)* **Ima,** take **sara** *(sah-rah)* more **ni** *(nee)* (P) **nijū no tango** from the glossary and do the same.

3. Third step — find out **ikura** *(ee-koo-rah)* how much **desu ka.** *(dess)*

(koh-reh) *(ee-koo-rah)*
Kore wa ikura desu ka?
this how much

(hohn)
Hon wa ikura desu ka?

(keet-teh)
Kitte wa ikura desu ka?

____
(How much does the toothpaste cost?)

____
(How much does the soap cost?)

____
(How much does a cup of tea cost?)

4. Fourth step — success! I found it!

Once **anata** find what you would like, **anata** say,

Kore ga hoshii desu. _______________________________

or

Kore o kudasai. Kore o kudasai. Kore o kudasai.
please

(mah-tah)
Mata wa if **anata** would not like it, **anata** say,
or

(hoh-shee-koo) *(ah-ree-mah-sen)*
Kore wa hoshiku arimasen. _______________________________
would not like

or

(ēē-eh) *(kek-kōh)* *(dess)*
Iie, kekkō desu. _______________________________
no thank you

Congratulations! You have finished. By now you should have stuck your labels, flashed your cards, cut out your menu guide and packed your suitcases. You should be very pleased with your accomplishment. You have learned what it sometimes takes others years to achieve and you hopefully had fun doing it. **Dōzo yoi ryokō o!** *(yoy)* have a good trip **Tanoshinde kudasai!** *(tah-noh-sheen-deh)* have fun

Glossary

This glossary contains words used in this book only. It is not meant to be a dictionary. Consider purchasing a dictionary which best suits your needs - small for traveling, large for reference, or specialized for specific vocabulary needs.

A

ageta *(ah-geh-tah)* .... deep-fried
aida *(eye-dah)* .... between
aimasen *(eye-mah-sen)* .... it does not fit
airon *(eye-rohn)* .... iron
Airurando *(ah-ee-roo-rahn-doh)* .... Ireland
aisu hokkē *(eye-soo)(hohk-kēh)* .... ice hockey
aisu kurīmu *(eye-soo)(koo-rēē-moo)* .... ice cream
aisu sukēto *(eye-soo)(soo-kēh-toh)* .... ice skating
aite imasu *(eye-teh)(ee-mahss)* .... free, open
Ajia *(ah-jee-ah)* .... Asia
akai *(ah-kai)* .... red
aki *(ah-kee)* .... autumn
ame *(ah-meh)* .... rain
Amerika *(ah-meh-ree-kah)* .... America
Amerikajin *(ah-meh-ree-kah-jeen)* .... American
anata *(ah-nah-tah)* .... you
anata no *(ah-nah-tah)(noh)* .... your
anaunsā *(ah-noun-sāh)* .... announcer
annaijo *(ahn-nye-joh)* .... information desk
ano *(ah-noh)* .... that over there
aoi *(ah-oy)* .... blue
apāto *(ah-pāh-toh)* .... apartment
appuru pai *(ahp-poo-roo)(pie)* .... apple pie
araimasu *(ah-rye-mahss)* .... wash
arigatō gozaimasu *(ah-ree-gah-tōh)(goh-zye-mahss)* .... thank you
arimasu *(ah-ree-mahss)* .... is, are (with things)
arubamu *(ah-roo-bah-moo)* .... album
asa *(ah-sah)* .... morning
asagohan *(ah-sah-goh-hahn)* .... breakfast
ashita *(ahsh-tah)* .... tomorrow
asuparagasu *(ah-soo-pah-rah-gah-soo)* .... asparagus
asupirin *(ah-soo-pee-reen)* .... aspirin
atarashii *(ah-tah-rah-shēē)* .... new
ate *(ah-teh)* .... to
atsui *(ah-tsoo-ee)* .... hot

B

badominton *(bah-doh-meen-tohn)* .... badminton
bai *(by)* .... measure (M) word with glasses
ban *(bahn)* .... number
ban *(bahn)* .... evening
banana *(bah-nah-nah)* .... banana
bangō *(bahn-gōh)* .... number
bangohan *(bahn-goh-hahn)* .... dinner
basu *(bah-soo)* .... bus
basukettobōru *(bah-soo-ket-toh-bōh-roo)* .... basketball
basurōbu *(bah-soo-rōh-boo)* .... bathrobe
basutei *(bah-soo-tay)* .... bus stop
batā *(bah-tāh)* .... butter
batterī *(bah-teh-rēē)* .... battery
beddo *(bed-doh)* .... bed
bēkon *(bēh-kohn)* .... bacon
benri *(ben-ree)* .... convenient
bēsubōru *(bēh-soo-bōh-roo)* .... baseball
bīfusutēki *(bēē-foo-stēh-kee)* .... beefsteak
bīru *(bēē-roo)* .... beer
bijinesuman *(bee-jee-neh-soo-mahn)* .... businessman
bijutsukan *(bee-joo-tsoo-kahn)* .... art museum
bin *(been)* .... bottle
binbō *(been-bōh)* .... poor
bitamin *(bee-tah-meen)* .... vitamin
biyōin *(bee-yōh-een)* .... hairdresser
bōshi *(bōh-shee)* .... hat
botan *(boh-tahn)* .... button
Bukkyō *(book-kyōh)* .... Buddhism
Bukkyōto *(book-kyōh-toh)* .... Buddhist
bunbōguya *(boon-bōh-goo-yah)* .... stationery store
burajā *(boo-rah-jāh)* .... bra
burausu *(boo-rah-oo-soo)* .... blouse
burēki *(boo-rēh-kee)* .... brake
butaniku *(boo-tah-nee-koo)* .... pork
byō *(byōh)* .... second (time)
byōin *(byōh-een)* .... hospital
byōki *(byōh-kee)* .... sick

C

chairoi *(chy-roy)* .... brown
channeru *(chahn-neh-roo)* .... channel
chekku *(chek-koo)* .... check
chekku auto *(chek-koo)(ah-oo-toh)* .... check out (hotel)
chesu *(cheh-soo)* .... chess
chichi *(chee-chee)* .... father
chikashitsu *(chee-kah-shee-tsoo)* .... basement
chikatetsu *(chee-kah-teh-tsoo)* .... subway
chikin *(chee-keen)* .... chicken
chippu *(cheep-poo)* .... tip, gratuity
chīsai *(chēē-sigh)* .... small
chizu *(chee-zoo)* .... map
chīzu *(chēē-zoo)* .... cheese
chōdo ii desu *(chōh-doh)(ēē)(dess)* .... it fits me, just right
chome *(choh-meh)* .... street (address)
chōshoku *(chōh-shoh-koo)* .... breakfast
chotto *(choht-toh)* .... just a minute, just wait, say!
chotto matte *(choht-toh)(maht-teh)* .... just wait
Chūgoku *(chōō-goh-koo)* .... China
Chūgokugo *(chēē-goh-koo-goh)* .... Chinese language
chūmon shimasu *(chōō-mohn)(shee-mahss)* .... order
chūshajō *(chōō-shah-jōh)* .... parking lot
chūshoku *(chōō-shoh-koo)* .... lunch

D

daidokoro *(dye-doh-koh-roh)* .... kitchen
daigaku *(dye-gah-koo)* .... university
dainingu *(die-neen-goo)* .... dining room
daiyamondo *(die-yah-mohn-doh)* .... diamond
dama *(dah-mah)* .... coins
dare *(dah-reh)* .... who
deguchi *(deh-goo-chee)* .... exit
dekorēshon *(deh-koh-rēh-shohn)* .... decoration
demasu *(deh-mahss)* .... leave, depart
demo *(deh-moh)* .... demonstration
denpō *(den-pōh)* .... telegram
denpyō *(den-pyōh)* .... bill
densha *(den-shah)* .... train (commuter)
denwa *(den-wah)* .... telephone
denwa bokkusu *(den-wah)(bohk-koo-soo)* .... telephone booth

denwa chō *(den-wah)(chōh)* ...... telephone directory
deodoranto *(deh-oh-doh-rahn-toh)*........ deodorant
depāto *(deh-pāh-toh)*.............. department store
deshita *(desh-tah)* .... was
desu *(dess)* .... are, is, have
dewa arimasen *(deh-wah)(ah-ree-mah-sen)*.......... .... am not, is not, are not
dewa mata *(deh-wah)(mah-tah)* .... until again
dezain *(deh-zine)*...................... design
dezāto *(deh-zāh-toh)* .... dessert
direkutā *(dee-reh-koo-tāh)*................ director
do *(doh)* .... degree
dō *(dōh)* .... how
dō itashimashite *(dōh)(ee-tah-shee-mahsh-teh)* .... you're welcome
doa *(doh-ah)* .... door
dōbutsuen *(dōh-boo-tsoo-en)* .... zoo
Doitsu *(doy-tsoo)*..................... Germany
doko *(doh-koh)*........................... where
dōmo *(dōh-moh)* ..... very much, thank you, I'm sorry
dorai kurīningu *(doh-rye)(koo-rēē-neen-goo)* .... dry cleaning
dorama *(doh-rah-mah)*.................... drama
doru *(doh-roo)* .... dollar
dōshi *(dōh-shee)*.......................... verb
dōshite *(dōh-shtay)*........................ why
Doyōbi *(doh-yōh-bee)* .... Saturday
dōzo *(dōh-zoh)* .... please
Dōzo yoi ryokō o! *(dōh-zoh)(yoy)(ryoh-kōh)(oh)*...... .... Have a good trip!

E

e *(eh)* .... picture
echiketto *(eh-chee-ket-toh)* .... etiquette
eiga *(ay-gah)* .... movie
eigakan *(ay-gah-kahn)*......... movie theater, cinema
Eigo *(ay-goh)* .... English language
eki *(eh-kee)* .... station (train, subway)
ekisu *(eh-kee-soo)* .... extract
ekurea *(eh-koo-reh-ah)*..................... éclair
en *(en)* .... yen
enameru *(eh-nah-meh-roo)* .... enamel
enerugī *(eh-neh-roo-gēē)* .... energy
enjin *(ehn-jeen)* .... engine
enpitsu *(en-pee-tsoo)*...................... pencil
epuron *(eh-poo-rohn)* .... apron
erebētā *(eh-reh-bēh-tāh)*.................. elevator
esukarētā *(ess-kah-rēh-tāh)* .... escalator
etchingu *(et-cheen-goo)* .... etching

F

fairu *(fy-roo)* .... file
fakkusu *(fahk-koo-soo)*...................... fax
fantajī *(fahn-tah-jēē)* .... fantasy
fasshon *(fahs-shohn)* .... fashion
feminisuto *(feh-mee-nee-soo-toh)*.......... feminist
fenshingu *(fen-sheen-goo)* .... fencing
firumu *(fee-roo-moo)* .... film
fōku *(fōh-koo)*............................. fork
fu *(foo)*............................... prefecture
Fujisan *(foo-jee-sahn)* .... Mt. Fuji
fukimasu *(foo-kee-mahss)* .... blow
fuku *(foo-koo)*.......................... clothing
fune *(foo-neh)*............................. boat
Furansu *(foo-rahn-soo)* .... France
Furansugo *(foo-rahn-soo-goh)* ...... French language
furimasu *(foo-ree-mahss)* .... fall (verb)
furoba *(foo-roh-bah)* .... bathroom
furonto *(foo-rohn-toh)* .... front desk (hotel)
furui *(foo-roo-ee)* .... old
furūtsu *(foo-rōō-tsoo)* .... fruit
futtobōru *(foot-toh-bōh-roo)* .... football
fuyu *(foo-yoo)*........................... winter

G

ga *(gah)* .... but
ga *(gah)* .... particle (P) word
gaido *(guy-doh)* .... guide
gaikoku *(guy-koh-koo)*............. foreign country
gaikoku no *(guy-koh-koo)(noh)* .... foreign
gakkō *(gahk-kōh)* .... school
ganbatte! *(gahn-baht-teh)* .... go fot it!
garēji *(gah-rēh-jee)* .... garage
gasorin *(gah-soh-reen)* .... gasoline
gasu renji *(gah-soo)(ren-jee)*............. gas range
gāze *(gāh-zeh)* .... gauze
gekijō *(geh-kee-jōh)*............ performance theater
gēmu *(gēh-moo)* .... game
gēto *(gēh-toh)* .... gate
Getsuyōbi *(geh-tsoo-yōh-bee)* .... Monday
ginkō *(geen-kōh)* .... bank
go *(goh)* .... five
gochisōsama *(goh-chee-sōh-sah-mah)*... it was delicious
Gogatsu *(goh-gah-tsoo)* .... May
gogo *(goh-goh)* .... afternoon
gohan *(goh-hahn)* .... rice
gohyaku *(goh-hyah-koo)* .... five hundred
goji *(goh-jee)*........................ five o'clock
gojū *(goh-jōō)* .... fifty
gōkei *(gōh-kay)* .... total
gomibako *(goh-mee-bah-koh)* ...... wastepaper basket
gomu *(goh-moo)*..................... rubber, gum
gorufu *(goh-roo-foo)* .... golf
guramu *(goo-rah-moo)* .... gram
gurasu *(goo-rah-soo)*....................... glass
gurē *(goo-rēh)*............................. grey
gurūpu *(goo-rōō-poo)* .... group
gyūniku *(gyōō-nee-koo)* .... beef
gyūnyūten *(gyōō-nyōō-ten)* .... dairy

H

haburashi *(hah-boo-rah-shee)*........... toothbrush
hachi *(hah-chee)* .... eight
Hachigatsu *(hah-chee-gah-tsoo)*............. August
hachijū *(hah-chee-jōō)* .... eighty
hadagi *(hah-dah-gee)* .... undershirt
hagaki *(hah-gah-kee)* .... postcard
haha *(hah-hah)* .... mother
hai *(hi)*................................... yes
haikingu *(hi-keen-goo)*..................... hiking
hajimarimasu *(hah-jee-mah-ree-mahss)* .... begin
hakubutsukan *(hah-koo-boo-tsoo-kahn)*..... museum
hamigaki *(hah-mee-gah-kee)* .... toothpaste
han *(hahn)* .... half
hana *(hah-nah)* .... flower
hanashichū *(hah-nah-shee-chōō)* ..... the line is busy
hanashimasu *(hah-nah-shee-mahss)*........... speak
hanashite *(han-nahsh-teh)* .... speak!
hanaya *(hah-nah-yah)* .... florist
hanbāgā *(hahn-bāh-gāh)* .... hamburger
handobaggu *(hahn-doh-bahg-goo)* .... handbag
hankachi *(hahn-kah-chee)*............. handkerchief
hanmā *(hahn-māh)*....................... hammer
haraimasu *(hah-rye-mahss)* .... pay
haru *(hah-roo)* .... spring
hayai *(hah-yai)* .... fast

heiten *(hay-ten)* .... closed
herikoputā *(heh-ree-koh-poo-tāh)* .... helicopter
heya *(heh-yah)* .... room
hi *(hee)* .... day
hidari *(hee-dah-ree)* .... left
higashi *(hee-gah-shee)* .... east
hijō ni *(hee-jōh)(nee)* .... very
hijōguchi *(hee-jōh-goo-chee)* .... emergency exit
hikari *(hee-kah-ree)* .... express bullet train
hikōki *(hee-kōh-kee)* .... airplane
hiku *(hee-koo)* .... pull
hikui *(hee-koo-ee)* .... low
hirugohan *(hee-roo-goh-hahn)* .... lunch
hītā *(hēē-tāh)* .... heater
hito *(hee-toh)* .... person
hitto *(heet-toh)* .... hit
hōhō *(hōh-hōh)* .... way
hokkē *(hohk-kēh)* .... hockey
hōkō *(hōh-kōh)* .... direction
hōmu *(hōh-moo)* .... platform
hon *(hohn)* .... measure (M) word for long, cylindrical
hon *(hohn)* .... book
honya *(hohn-yah)* .... bookstore
hoshii desu *(hoh-shēē)(dess)* .... would like
hoshiku arimasen *(hoh-shee-koo)(ah-ree-mah-sen)* ... . would not like
hosuteru *(hoh-soo-teh-roo)* .... hostel
hoteru *(hoh-teh-roo)* .... hotel
hotto chokorēto *(hoht-toh)(choh-koh-rēh-toh)* .... hot chocolate
hotto doggu *(hoht-toh)(dohg-goo)* .... hot dog
hotto kēki *(hoht-toh)(kēh-kee)* ..... hot cake (pancake)
howaito sōsu *(hoh-why-toh)(sōh-soo)* ..... white sauce
hyaku *(hyah-koo)* .... one hundred

I

ichi *(ee-chee)* .... one
ichi mai *(ee-chee)(my)* .... one sheet
ichiba *(ee-chee-bah)* .... market
Ichigatsu *(ee-chee-gah-tsoo)* .... January
ichijikan *(ee-chee-jee-kahn)* .... one hour
ichiman *(ee-chee-mahn)* .... ten thousand
ichinen *(ee-chee-nen)* .... one year
ie *(ee-eh)* .... house
Igirisu *(ee-gee-ree-soo)* .... England
ii *(ēē)* .... good
iie *(ēē-eh)* .... no
iie, kekkō desu *(ēē-eh)(kek-kōh)(dess)* .... no thank you
iimasu *(ēē-mahss)* .... say, one says
ikaga *(ee-kah-gah)* .... how
ikimasu *(ee-kee-mahss)* .... go
ikitai desu *(ee-kee-tye)(dess)* .... would like to go
ikkai *(eek-kye)* .... first/ground floor
ikura *(ee-koo-rah)* .... how much
ikutsu *(ee-koo-tsoo)* .... how many
ima *(ee-mah)* .... living room
ima *(ee-mah)* .... now
imasu *(ee-mahss)* ... is, are, am (with people and animals)
imēji *(ee-mēh-jee)* .... image
imitēshon *(ee-mee-tēh-shohn)* .... imitation
inchi *(een-chee)* .... inch
inku *(een-koo)* .... ink
intabyū *(een-tah-byōō)* .... interview
inu *(ee-noo)* .... dog
ippai *(eep-pie)* .... one cup
ippan *(eep-pahn)* .... general
ippun *(eep-poon)* .... one minute
irasshaimase *(ee-rahs-shy-mah-seh)* .... welcome

iriguchi *(ee-ree-goo-chee)* .... entrance
irimasu *(ee-ree-mahss)* .... need
iro *(ee-roh)* .... color
isha san *(ee-shah)(sahn)* .... doctor
isshūkan *(eesh-shōō-kahn)* .... (one) week
isu *(ee-soo)* .... chair
Isuraeru *(ee-soo-rah-eh-roo)* .... Israel
itameta *(ee-tah-meh-tah)* .... stir-fried
Itaria *(ee-tah-ree-ah)* .... Italy
Itariago *(ee-tah-ree-ah-goh)* .... Italian language
itsu *(ee-tsoo)* .... when

J

jaketto *(jah-ket-toh)* .... jacket
jamu *(jah-moo)* .... jam
jānarisuto *(jāh-nah-ree-soo-toh)* .... journalist
janguru *(jahn-goo-roo)* .... jungle
jazu *(jah-zoo)* .... jazz (music)
jerī *(jeh-rēē)* .... jelly
jettoki *(jet-toh-kee)* .... jet airplane
jidōsha *(jee-dōh-shah)* .... car
jīnzu *(jēēn-zoo)* .... jeans
jikan *(jee-kahn)* .... time, hour
jikokuhyō *(jee-koh-koo-hyōh)* ..... schedule, timetable
jinja *(jeen-jah)* .... shrine
jinjaeru *(jeen-jāh-ēh-roo)* .... ginger ale
jīppu *(jēē-poo)* .... jeep
jisho *(jee-shoh)* .... dictionary
jitensha *(jee-ten-shah)* .... bicycle
jōku *(jōh-koo)* .... joke
jū *(jōō)* .... ten
Jūgatsu *(jōō-gah-tsoo)* .... October
jūgo *(jōō-goh)* .... fifteen
jūgofun *(jōō-goh-foon)* .... quarter, 15 minutes
jūhachi *(jōō-hah-chee)* .... eighteen
jūichi *(jōō-ee-chee)* .... eleven
Jūichigatsu *(jōō-ee-chee-gah-tsoo)* .... November
jūku *(jōō-koo)* .... nineteen
jūkyū *(jōō-kyōō)* .... nineteen
jūnana *(jōō-nah-nah)* .... seventeen
jūni *(jōō-nee)* .... twelve
Jūnigatsu *(jōō-nee-gah-tsoo)* .... December
juppun *(joop-poon)* .... ten minutes
jūroku *(jōō-roh-koo)* .... sixteen
jūsan *(jōō-sahn)* .... thirteen
jūshi *(jōō-shee)* .... fourteen
jūshichi *(jōō-shee-chee)* .... seventeen
jūsho *(jōō-shoh)* .... address, residence
jūsu *(jōō-soo)* .... juice
jūyon *(jōō-yohn)* .... fourteen

K

ka *(kah)* .... indicates a question
kābu *(kāh-boo)* .... curve
kādigan *(kāh-dee-gahn)* .... cardigan
kado *(kah-doh)* .... corner
kādo *(kāh-doh)* .... card
kafe *(kah-feh)* .... café, coffeehouse
kagami *(kah-gah-mee)* .... mirror
kagetsu *(kah-geh-tsoo)* .... month
kai *(kye)* .... floor
kaimasu *(kye-mahss)* .... buy
kaite *(kye-teh)* .... write!
kaiten *(kye-ten)* .... open
kaiwa *(kye-wah)* .... conversation
kakarimasu *(kah-kah-ree-mahss)* .... hang
kakarimasu *(kah-kah-ree-mahss)* .... take (time)
kakebuton *(kah-keh-boo-tohn)* .... quilt

kaketai desu *(kah-keh-tye)(dess)* ... would like to make
kākī *(kāh-kēē)* ... khaki
kakimasu *(kah-kee-mahss)* ... write
kamera *(kah-meh-rah)* ... camera
kami *(kah-mee)* ... paper
kamisori *(kah-mee-soh-ree)* ... razor
Kanada *(kah-nah-dah)* ... Canada
Kanadajin *(kah-nah-dah-jeen)* ... Canadian
kanbasu *(kahn-bah-soo)* ... canvas
kanemochi *(kah-neh-moh-chee)* ... rich
kānēshon *(kāh-nēh-shohn)* ... carnation
kangarū *(kahn-gah-rōō)* ... kangaroo
kani *(kah-nee)* ... crab
kānibaru *(kāh-nee-bah-roo)* ... carnival
Kankoku *(kahn-koh-koo)* ... Korea (South)
kanojo *(kah-noh-joh)* ... she, her
kanū *(kah-nōō)* ... canoe
kāpetto *(kāh-pet-toh)* ... carpet
kappu *(kahp-poo)* ... cup
kara *(kah-rah)* ... from
karā *(kah-rāh)* ... collar
karatto *(kah-raht-toh)* ... carat
kare *(kah-reh)* ... he, him
karē *(kah-rēh)* ... curry
karendā *(kah-ren-dāh)* ... calendar
karera *(kah-reh-rah)* ... they
karifurawā *(kah-ree-foo-rah-wāh)* ... cauliflower
karorī *(kah-roh-rēē)* ... calorie
kasa *(kah-sah)* ... umbrella
kashi *(kah-shee)* ... Fahrenheit
kashimia *(kah-shee-mee-ah)* ... cashmere
katamichi *(kah-tah-mee-chee)* ... one-way
katarogu *(kah-tah-roh-goo)* ... catalogue
kategorī *(kah-teh-goh-rēē)* ... category
kāten *(kāh-ten)* ... curtain
Katorikkukyōto *(kah-toh-reek-koo-kyōh-toh)* .. Catholic
katto *(kaht-toh)* ... cut
kauntā *(kah-oon-tāh)* ... counter
Kayōbi *(kah-yōh-bee)* ... Tuesday
kaze *(kah-zeh)* ... wind
kazoku *(kah-zoh-koo)* ... family
kazu *(kah-zoo)* ... number
kēburu *(kēh-boo-roo)* ... cable
kēburukā *(kēh-boo-roo-kāh)* ... cable car
kechappu *(keh-chahp-poo)* ... ketchup
keisatsusho *(kay-sah-tsoo-shoh)* ... police station
kēki *(kēh-kee)* ... cake
ken *(ken)* ... prefecture
kenkō *(ken-kōh)* ... healthy
kī *(kēē)* ... key
kiiroi *(kēē-roy)* ... yellow
kimashita *(kee-mahsh-tah)* ... came
kimasu *(kee-mahss)* ... come
kinō *(kee-nōh)* ... yesterday
Kinyōbi *(keen-yōh-bee)* ... Friday
kion *(kee-ohn)* ... temperature
kippu *(keep-poo)* ... ticket
kirei *(kee-ray)* ... clean
kiri *(kee-ree)* ... fog
kiro *(kee-roh)* ... kilometer
kissaten *(kees-sah-ten)* ... coffe shop, teahouse
kita *(kee-tah)* ... north
kitsuensha *(kee-tsoo-en-shah)* ... smoking compartment
kitte *(keet-teh)* ... stamp
ko *(koh)* ... measure (M) word
kōcha *(kōh-chah)* ... black tea
kodama *(koh-dah-mah)* ... ordinary bullet train
kodomo *(koh-doh-moh)* ... child

kōen *(kōh-en)* ... park
kōhī *(kōh-hēē)* ... coffee
koinrandorī *(koh-een-rahn-doh-rēē)* ... laundry
kōka *(kōh-kah)* ... coin
kōkanshu *(kōh-kahn-shoo)* ... operator
kokku *(kohk-koo)* ... cook
koko *(koh-koh)* ... here
kokoa *(koh-koh-ah)* ... cocoa
kōkūbin *(kōh-kōō-bean)* ... by airmail
kokunai no *(koh-koo-nye)(noh)* ... domestic
kokusai denwa *(koh-koo-sigh)(den-wah)* ... international telephone call
komedian *(koh-meh-dee-ahn)* ... comedian
konbanwa *(kohn-bahn-wah)* ... good evening
konbīfu *(kohn-bēē-foo)* ... corned beef
konbinēshon *(kohn-bee-nēh-shohn)* ... combination
konbiniensu sutoa *(kohn-bee-nee-en-soo)(soo-toh-ah)* ... convenience store
kondakutā *(kohn-dah-koo-tāh)* ... conductor
kone *(koh-neh)* ... connection
konkurīto *(kohn-koo-rēē-toh)* ... concrete
konma *(kohn-mah)* ... comma
konnichiwa *(kohn-nee-chee-wah)* ... good day, hello
kono *(koh-noh)* ... this
konpakuto kā *(kohn-pah-koo-toh)(kāh)* ... compact car
konpasu *(kohn-pah-soo)* ... compass
konpyūtā *(kohn-pyōō-tāh)* ... computer
konsāto *(kohn-sāh-toh)* ... concert
konsome *(kohn-soh-meh)* ... consommé
kōnsutāchi *(kōhn-soo-tāh-chee)* ... cornstarch
kontena *(kohn-teh-nah)* ... container
kontorasuto *(kohn-toh-rah-soo-toh)* ... contrast
kontorōru *(kohn-toh-rōh-roo)* ... control
kopī *(koh-pēē)* ... copy
koppu *(kohp-poo)* ... glass, cup
kōrasu *(kōh-rah-soo)* ... chorus
kore *(koh-reh)* ... this
korekushon *(koh-reh-koo-shohn)* ... collection
koruku *(koh-roo-koo)* ... cork
koshō *(koh-shōh)* ... pepper
kōshū denwa *(kōh-shōō)(den-wah)* ... public telephone
kōsoku dōro *(kōh-soh-koo)(dōh-roh)* ... freeway
kōsu *(kōh-soo)* ... course (class)
kosuto *(koh-soo-toh)* ... cost
kotae *(koh-tah-eh)* ... answer
kōto *(kōh-toh)* ... coat
koushiniku *(koh-oo-shee-nee-koo)* ... veal
kozutsumi *(koh-zoo-tsoo-mee)* ... package
ku *(koo)* ... nine
ku *(koo)* ... district, zone (address)
kuchi *(koo-chee)* ... mouth
kudamono *(koo-dah-moh-noh)* ... fruit
kudamonoya *(koo-dah-moh-noh-yah)* ... fruit shop
kudasai *(koo-dah-sigh)* ... please, please give me
Kugatsu *(koo-gah-tsoo)* ... September
kukkī *(kook-kēē)* ... cookie
kūkō *(kōō-kōh)* ... airport
kurejitto kādo *(koo-reh-jeet-toh)(kāh-doh)* ... credit card
kurīmu *(koo-rēē-moo)* ... cream
kurikaeshimasu *(koo-ree-kah-eh-shee-mahss)* ... repeat
kuroi *(koo-roy)* ... black
kurosuwādo *(koo-roh-soo-wāh-doh)* ... crossword puzzle
kuruma *(koo-roo-mah)* ... car, automobile
kushi *(koo-shee)* ... comb
kutsu *(koo-tsoo)* ... shoe
kutsushita *(koo-tsoo-shtah)* ... sock
kyō *(kyōh)* ... today

kyōkai *(kyōh-kai)* .... church
kyū *(kyōō)* .... nine
kyūjitsu *(kyōō-jee-tsoo)* .... holiday
kyūjū *(kyōō-jōō)* .... ninety
kyūsu *(kyōō-soo)* .... tea pots

M

māchi *(māh-chee)* .... march
machiaishitsu *(mah-chee-eye-shee-tsoo)* . waiting room
machimasu *(mah-chee-mahss)* .... wait for
machinē *(mah-chee-nēh)* .... matinée
madamu *(mah-dah-moo)* .... madam
mado *(mah-doh)* .... window
mae *(mah-eh)* .... in front of, before
magajin *(mah-gah-jeen)* .... magazine
magarimasu *(mah-gah-ree-mahss)* .... turn
māgarin *(māh-gah-reen)* .... margarine
mai *(my)* ...... measure (M) word for thin, flat sheets
maikurohon *(my-koo-roh-hohn)* .... microphone
mainasu *(my-nah-soo)* .... minus
mairu *(my-roo)* .... mile
majikku *(mah-jeek-koo)* .... magic
makaroni *(mah-kah-roh-nee)* .... macaroni
māketto *(māh-ket-toh)* .... market
māku *(māh-koo)* .... mark, label
makura *(mah-koo-rah)* .... pillow
māmarēdo *(māh-mah-rēh-doh)* .... marmalade
mandorin *(mahn-doh-reen)* .... mandolin
manējā *(mah-nēh-jāh)* .... manager
manekin *(mah-neh-keen)* .... mannequin
marason *(mah-rah-sohn)* .... marathon
Marēshia *(mah-rēh-shee-ah)* .... Malaysia
maruku *(mah-roo-koo)* .... mark
massāji *(mahs-sāh-jee)* .... massage
massugu *(mahs-soo-goo)* .... straight ahead
masukotto *(mah-soo-koht-toh)* .... mascot
masuku *(mah-soo-koo)* .... mask, respirator
masuto *(mah-soo-toh)* .... mast
mata dōzo *(mah-tah)(dōh-zoh)* ..... please come again
mata wa *(mah-tah)(wah)* .... or
matchi *(maht-chee)* .... match, box of matches
matte *(maht-teh)* .... wait
mattoresu *(maht-toh-reh-soo)* .... mattress
mayonēzu *(mah-yoh-nēh-zoo)* .... mayonnaise
medaru *(meh-dah-roo)* .... medal
mēdo *(mēh-doh)* .... maid
megahon *(meh-gah-hohn)* .... megaphone
megane *(meh-gah-neh)* .... eyeglasses
memo *(meh-moh)* .... memo
menyū *(meh-nyōō)* .... menu
meron *(meh-rohn)* .... melon
messēji *(mess-sēh-jee)* .... message
mētoru *(mēh-toh-roo)* .... meter
mezamashi dokei *(meh-zah-mah-shee)(doh-kay)* .... alarm clock
michi *(mee-chee)* .... road, street
midori *(mee-doh-ree)* .... green
migi *(mee-gee)* .... right
migi ni *(mee-gee)(nee)* .... to the right
mijikai *(mee-jee-kye)* .... short
mimasu *(mee-mahss)* .... see
minami *(mee-nah-mee)* .... south
Minami Afurika *(mee-nah-mee)(ah-foo-ree-kah)* .... South Africa
miruku *(mee-roo-koo)* .... milk
mise *(mee-seh)* .... shop, store
misemasu *(mee-seh-mahss)* .... show
misete *(mee-seh-teh)* .... show!
mishin *(mee-sheen)* .... sewing machine
mizu *(mee-zoo)* .... water
mizugi *(mee-zoo-gee)* .... swimsuit
mo *(moh)* .... also
mō *(mōh)* .... already
mō ichido *(mōh)(ee-chee-doh)* .... once more
modan *(moh-dahn)* .... modern
moderu *(moh-deh-roo)* .... model
Mokuyōbi *(moh-koo-yōh-bee)* .... Thursday
mondai *(mohn-dye)* .... problem
mono *(moh-noh)* .... thing
monorēru *(moh-noh-rēh-roo)* .... monorail
moshi-moshi *(moh-shee-moh-shee)* .... hello
mōshimasu *(mōh-shee-mahss)* .... speaking
mōtā *(mōh-tāh)* .... motor
motte imasu *(moht-teh)(ee-mahss)* .... have
motto *(moht-toh)* .... more
mottō *(moht-tōh)* .... motto
mushita *(moo-shtah)* .... steamed
musuko *(moo-soo-koh)* .... son
musume *(moo-soo-meh)* .... daughter

N

nagagutsu *(nah-gah-goo-tsoo)* .... boots
nagai *(nah-guy)* .... long
naifu *(nye-foo)* .... knife
naitogaun *(nye-toh-gown)* .... nightgown
naka *(nah-kah)* .... inside
nakushimasu *(nah-koo-shee-mahss)* .... lose
namae *(nah-mah-eh)* .... name
namamono *(nah-mah-moh-noh)* .... raw
nan *(nahn)* .... what
nana *(nah-nah)* .... seven
nanajū *(nah-nah-jōō)* .... seventy
nani *(nah-nee)* .... what
nanji *(nahn-jee)* .... what time
Nanji desu ka? *(nahn-jee)(dess)(kah)* ... What time is it?
Nanji ni? *(nahn-jee)(nee)* .... At what time?
napukin *(nah-poo-keen)* .... napkin
naraimasu *(nah-rye-mahss)* .... learn
natsu *(nah-tsoo)* .... summer
nattsu *(naht-tsoo)* .... nut
naze *(nah-zeh)* .... why
nedan *(neh-dahn)* .... price
nekkachīfu *(nek-kah-chēē-foo)* .... neckerchief
nekkuresu *(nek-koo-reh-soo)* .... necklace
neko *(neh-koh)* .... cat
nekutai *(neh-koo-tie)* .... necktie
nemasu *(neh-mahss)* .... sleep
neon *(neh-ohn)* .... neon
netto *(net-toh)* .... net
ni *(nee)* .... two
ni *(nee)* .... in, into, at, on
ni *(nee)* .... particle (P) word
ni kai *(nee)(kye)* .... second floor
nibanme *(nee-bahn-meh)* .... second (rank)
nichi *(nee-chee)* .... day
Nichiyōbi *(nee-chee-yōh-bee)* .... Sunday
Nigatsu *(nee-gah-tsoo)* .... February
Nihon *(nee-hohn)* .... Japan
Nihon ningyō *(nee-hohn)(neen-gyōh)* ... Japanese dolls
Nihongo *(nee-hohn-goh)* .... Japanese language
Nihonjin *(nee-hohn-jeen)* .... Japanese (people)
nijū *(nee-jōō)* .... twenty
nijuppun *(nee-joop-poon)* .... twenty minutes
niku *(nee-koo)* .... meat
nikuya *(nee-koo-yah)* .... butcher shop
nishi *(nee-shee)* .... west

nita *(nee-tah)* . . . . boiled in sauce
niwa *(nee-wah)* . . . . garden
nizukuri shimasu *(nee-zoo-koo-ree)(shee-mahss)* . . pack
no *(noh)* . . . . particle (P) word, indicates possesion
nomimasu *(noh-mee-mahss)* . . . . drink
nomimono *(noh-mee-moh-noh)* . . . . beverage
noriba *(noh-ree-bah)* . . . . stand (taxi)
norikaemasu *(noh-ree-kah-eh-mahss)* . . . . transfer
norimasu *(noh-ree-mahss)* . . . . ride
nōto *(nōh-toh)* . . . . note
nozomi *(noh-zoh-mee)* . . . . . . super express bullet train
Nyūjīrando *(nyōō-jēē-rahn-doh)* . . . . New Zealand
nyūsu *(nyōō-soo)* . . . . news

O

o *(oh)* . . . . particle (P) word
o *(oh)* . . . . . honorable (added to the beginning of the word)
oba *(oh-bah)* . . . . aunt
ōbā *(ōh-bāh)* . . . . overcoat
obāsan *(oh-bāh-sahn)* . . . . grandmother
ōbāshūzu *(ōh-bāh-shōō-zoo)* . . . . overshoes
ocha *(oh-chah)* . . . . green tea
ōdā *(ōh-dāh)* . . . . order
ofisu *(oh-fee-soo)* . . . . office
ōfuku *(ōh-foo-koo)* . . . . round-trip
ofuro *(oh-foo-roh)* . . . . bath
Ogenki desu ka? *(oh-gen-kee)(dess)(kah)* . . How are you?
ohashi *(oh-hah-shee)* . . . . chopsticks
ohayō gozaimasu *(oh-hah-yōh)(goh-zye-mahss)* . . . . good morning
oji *(oh-jee)* . . . . uncle
ojiisan *(oh-jēē-sahn)* . . . . grandfather
okane *(oh-kah-neh)* . . . . money
okāsan *(oh-kāh-sahn)* . . . . mother
ōkē *(ōh-kēh)* . . . . okay, all right
ōkesutora *(ōh-keh-soo-toh-rah)* . . . . orchestra
ōkii *(ōh-kēē)* . . . . big
okurimasu *(oh-koo-ree-mahss)* . . . . send
omen *(oh-men)* . . . . masks
omiyage *(oh-mee-yah-geh)* . . . . souvenir
omoshiroi *(oh-moh-shee-roy)* . . . . interesting
omuretsu *(oh-moo-reh-tsoo)* . . . . omelet
ōnā *(ōh-nāh)* . . . . owner
onamae *(oh-nah-mah-eh)* . . . . your name
onna no hito *(ohn-nah)(noh)(hee-toh)* . . . . woman
onna no kyōdai *(ohn-nah)(noh)(kyōh-dye)* . . . . . sister
onsu *(ohn-soo)* . . . . ounce
opera *(oh-peh-rah)* . . . . opera
ōpun *(ōh-poon)* . . . . open
orenji *(oh-ren-jee)* . . . . orange
origami *(oh-ree-gah-mee)* . . . . . . origami, folding paper
orugan *(oh-roo-gahn)* . . . . organ
osake *(oh-sah-keh)* . . . . rice wine
osara *(oh-sah-rah)* . . . . plate
Oshokuji o dōzo! *(oh-shoh-koo-jee)(oh)(dōh-zoh)* . . . . Enjoy your meal!
osoi *(oh-soy)* . . . . slow
osu *(oh-soo)* . . . . push
Ōsutoraria *(ōh-soo-toh-rah-ree-ah)* . . . . Australia
otera *(oh-teh-rah)* . . . . temple
ōtobai *(ōh-toh-by)* . . . . motorcycle
otoko no hito *(oh-toh-koh)(noh)(hee-toh)* . . . . man
otoko no kyōdai *(oh-toh-koh)(noh)(kyōh-dye)* . . . brother
ōtomīru *(ōh-toh-mēē-roo)* . . . . oatmeal
otomodachi *(oh-toh-moh-dah-chee)* . . . . friend
otōsan *(oh-tōh-sahn)* . . . . father
oyasumi nasai *(oh-yah-soo-mee)(nah-sigh)* . . good night

P

pai *(pie)* . . . . pie
painappuru *(pie-nahp-poo-roo)* . . . . pineapple
paipu *(pie-poo)* . . . . pipe
pajama *(pah-jah-mah)* . . . . pajamas
pakkingu *(pahk-keen-goo)* . . . . packing
pan *(pahn)* . . . . bread
pankēki *(pahn-kēh-kee)* . . . . pancake
panku *(pahn-koo)* . . . . puncture
panorama *(pah-noh-rah-mah)* . . . . panorama
pantī *(pahn-tēē)* . . . . underpants for women
pantī sutokkingu *(pahn-tēē)(soo-tohk-keen-goo)* . . . . pantyhose
pantsu *(pahn-tsoo)* . . . . pants, underpants for men
panya *(pahn-yah)* . . . . bakery
papaia *(pah-pie-ah)* . . . . papaya
pārā *(pāh-rāh)* . . . . parlor
parashūto *(pah-rah-shōō-toh)* . . . . parachute
parasoru *(pah-rah-soh-roo)* . . . . parasol
pāsento *(pāh-sen-toh)* . . . . percent
paseri *(pah-seh-ree)* . . . . parsley
pasu *(pah-soo)* . . . . pass, free ticket
pasupōto *(pah-soo-pōh-toh)* . . . . passport
pasuteru *(pah-so-teh-roo)* . . . . pastel
pātī *(pāh-tēē)* . . . . party
pedaru *(peh-dah-roo)* . . . . pedal
pējento *(pēh-jen-toh)* . . . . pageant
pēji *(pēh-jee)* . . . . page
pen *(pen)* . . . . pen
penī *(peh-nēē)* . . . . penny
piano *(pee-ah-noh)* . . . . piano
pikunikku *(pee-koo-neek-koo)* . . . . picnic
pin *(peen)* . . . . pin
pinku *(peen-koo)* . . . . pink
poketto *(poh-ket-toh)* . . . . pocket
pondo *(pohn-doh)* . . . . pound
ponpu *(pohn-poo)* . . . . pump
posutā *(poh-soo-tāh)* . . . . poster
posuto *(pohss-toh)* . . . . mailbox
pōtā *(pōh-tāh)* . . . . porter
pudingu *(poo-deen-goo)* . . . . pudding
purasu *(poo-rah-soo)* . . . . plus
pūru *(pōō-roo)* . . . . pool, swimming pool

R

rajio *(rah-jee-oh)* . . . . radio
raketto *(rah-ket-toh)* . . . . racket
ranpu *(rahn-poo)* . . . . lamp
rasshuawā *(rahs-shoo-ah-wāh)* . . . . rush hour
raudosupīkā *(rah-oo-doh-soo-pēē-kāh)* . . . loudspeaker
referī *(reh-feh-rēē)* . . . . referee
reinkōto *(rain-kōh-toh)* . . . . raincoat
reizōko *(ray-zōh-koh)* . . . . refrigerator
reji *(reh-jee)* . . . . counter
rekōdo *(reh-kōh-doh)* . . . . record
remon *(reh-mohn)* . . . . lemon
renshū *(ren-shōō)* . . . . practice
renta kā *(ren-tah)(kāh)* . . . . rental car
ressha *(res-shah)* . . . . train (long-distance)
resutoran *(ress-toh-rahn)* . . . . restaurant
ribon *(ree-bohn)* . . . . ribbon
ringo *(reen-goh)* . . . . apple
rittoru *(reet-toh-roo)* . . . . liter
robī *(roh-bēē)* . . . . lobby
roku *(roh-koo)* . . . . six
Rokugatsu *(roh-koo-gah-tsoo)* . . . . June
rokujū *(roh-koo-jōō)* . . . . sixty

rōru pan *(rōh-roo)(pahn)* . . . . bread roll
Roshiago *(roh-shee-ah-goh)* . . . . Russian language
rubī *(roo-bēē)* . . . . ruby
ryōgaejo *(ryōh-gah-eh-joh)* . . . . money-exchange office
ryokan *(ryoh-kahn)* . . . . inn
ryōkin *(ryōh-keen)* . . . . fare
ryokō *(ryoh-kōh)* . . . . journey, trip
ryokō shimasu *(ryoh-kōh)(shee-mahss)* . . . . travel
ryokōgaisha *(ryoh-kōh-guy-shah)* . . . . . . travel agency
ryokōsha *(ryoh-kōh-shah)* . . . . traveler
ryōri *(ryōh-ree)* . . . . dish, meal
ryōriya *(ryōh-ree-yah)* . . . . restaurant
ryōshin *(ryōh-sheen)* . . . . parents
ryōshūsho *(ryōh-shōō-shoh)* . . . . receipt
ryōtei *(ryōh-tay)* . . . . restaurant serving Japanese food

S

sābisu *(sāh-bee-soo)* . . . . service
saidā *(sigh-dāh)* . . . . cider
saifu *(sigh-foo)* . . . . wallet
sain *(sign)* . . . . sign
sairen *(sigh-ren)* . . . . siren
saizu *(sigh-zoo)* . . . . size
sakana *(sah-kah-nah)* . . . . fish
sakanaya *(sah-kah-nah-yah)* . . . . fish market
sakazuki *(sah-kah-zoo-kee)* . . . . sake cups
sake *(sah-keh)* . . . . rice wine
sakkarin *(sahk-kah-reen)* . . . . saccharin
samui *(sah-moo-ee)* . . . . cold
san *(sahn)* . . . . three
san *(sahn)* . . . . used as a term of respect
san gai *(sahn)(guy)* . . . . third floor
sanbanme *(sahn-bahn-meh)* . . . . third (rank)
sandaru *(sahn-dah-roo)* . . . . sandal
sandoitchi *(sahn-doh-eet-chee)* . . . . sandwich
Sangatsu *(sahn-gah-tsoo)* . . . . March
sangurasu *(sahn-goo-rah-soo)* . . . . sunglasses
sanjippun *(sahn-jeep-poon)* . . . . . . 30 minutes, half hour
sanjū *(sahn-jōō)* . . . . thirty
sanjūnichi *(sahn-jōō-nee-chee)* . . . . thirty days
sara ni *(sah-rah)(nee)* . . . . more
sarada *(sah-rah-dah)* . . . . salad
sashimi *(sah-shee-mee)* . . . . raw fish
satsu *(sah-tsoo)* . . . . measure (M) word for bound items
satsu *(sah-tsoo)* . . . . bill, currency
sayōnara *(sah-yōh-nah-rah)* . . . . good-bye
seki *(seh-kee)* . . . . seat
sekken *(sek-ken)* . . . . soap
semento *(seh-men-toh)* . . . . cement
sen *(sen)* . . . . one thousand
sen *(sen)* . . . . line, track
senmendai *(sen-men-dye)* . . . . washstand
sētā *(sēh-tāh)* . . . . sweater
sesshi *(sehs-shee)* . . . . Centigrade
shako *(shah-koh)* . . . . garage
shanpen *(shahn-pen)* . . . . champagne
shatsu *(shah-tsoo)* . . . . shirt
shawā *(shah-wāh)* . . . . shower
shi *(shee)* . . . . four, city (address)
shichi *(shee-chee)* . . . . seven
Shichigatsu *(shee-chee-gah-tsoo)* . . . . July
Shigatsu *(shee-gah-tsoo)* . . . . April
shigoto *(shee-goh-toh)* . . . . work
shihei *(shee-hay)* . . . . bill
shimaguni *(shee-mah-goo-nee)* . . . . island country
shimasu *(shee-mahss)* . . . . do
shinai denwa *(shee-nye)(den-wah)* . . local telephone call
shinbun *(sheen-boon)* . . . . newspaper
shindaisha *(sheen-dye-shah)* . . . . sleeping car
Shingapōru *(sheen-gah-pōh-roo)* . . . . Singapore
shinhonī *(sheen-hoh-nēē)* . . . . symphony
shinkansen *(sheen-kahn-sen)* . . . . bullet train
Shinkyōto *(sheen-kyōh-toh)* . . . . Protestant
shinnyū kinshi *(sheen-nyōō)(keen-shee)* . . do not enter
shinshitsu *(sheen-shee-tsoo)* . . . . bedroom
Shintō *(sheen-tōh)* . . . . Shintoism
Shintōka *(sheen-tōh-kah)* . . . . Shintoist
shio *(shee-oh)* . . . . salt
shiroi *(shee-roy)* . . . . white
shirowain *(shee-roh-wine)* . . . . white wine
shirumono *(shee-roo-moh-noh)* . . Japanese-style soup
shita *(shtah)* . . . . under, below, low
shitai *(shee-tye)* . . . . would like, want to do
shitsumon *(sheet-soo-mohn)* . . . . question
shitte imasu *(sheet-teh)(ee-mahss)* . . . . know
shōgo *(shōh-goh)* . . . . noon
shokkidana *(shohk-kee-dah-nah)* . . . . cupboard
shokubutsuen *(shoh-koo-boo-tsoo-en)* . . . . botanical gardens
shokudōsha *(shoh-koo-dōh-shah)* . . . . dining car
shokuji *(shoh-koo-jee)* . . . . meal
shokuryōhinten *(shoh-koo-ryōh-heen-ten)* . . grocery store
shosai *(shoh-sigh)* . . . . study (room)
shotengai *(shoh-ten-guy)* . . . . shopping center
shōto pantsu *(shōh-toh)(pahn-tsoo)* . . . . shorts
shouuindō *(shoh-oo-een-dōh)* . . . . show window
shūkan *(shōō-kahn)* . . . . week
shūkan *(shōō-kahn)* . . . . tradition, custom
shukuhakudai *(shoo-koo-hah-koo-dye)* . . . . . bill (hotel)
shuppatsu *(shoop-pah-tsoo)* . . . . departure
shuyō *(shoo-yōh)* . . . . major
soba *(soh-bah)* . . . . noodles
sobaya *(soh-bah-yah)* . . . . noodle shop
sobo *(soh-boh)* . . . . grandmother
sōda *(sōh-dah)* . . . . soda
sofā *(soh-fāh)* . . . . sofa
sofu *(soh-foo)* . . . . grandfather
sofubo *(soh-foo-boh)* . . . . grandparent
soko *(soh-koh)* . . . . there, over there
sono *(soh-noh)* . . . . that, those
sore *(soh-reh)* . . . . that
sōsu *(sōh-soo)* . . . . sauce
subete *(soo-beh-teh)* . . . . everything
suchuwādesu *(soo-choo-wāh-deh-soo)* . . . . . stewardess
sugi *(soo-gee)* . . . . after
sugu *(soo-goo)* . . . . just
Suisu *(soo-ee-soo)* . . . . Switzerland
Suiyōbi *(soo-ee-yōh-bee)* . . . . Wednesday
sukāto *(soo-kāh-toh)* . . . . skirt
sukejūru *(soo-keh-jōō-roo)* . . . . schedule
sukī *(soo-kēē)* . . . . ski
sukoshi *(soo-koh-shee)* . . . . a little
sukurīn *(soo-koo-rēēn)* . . . . screen
sumimasen *(soo-mee-mah-sen)* . . . . . sorry, excuse me
sunakku *(soo-nahk-koo)* . . . . snacks
sunde imasu *(soon-deh)(ee-mahss)* . . . . live, reside
sūpā *(sōō-pāh)* . . . . supermarket
Supein *(soo-pain)* . . . . Spain
supōtsu *(soo-pōh-tsoo)* . . . . sports
sūpu *(sōō-poo)* . . . . Western-style soup
supūn *(soo-pōōn)* . . . . spoon
surippa *(soo-reep-pah)* . . . . slipper
surippu *(soo-reep-poo)* . . . . slip (clothing)
sushi *(soo-shee)* . . . . vinegared rice and raw fish
sushiya *(soo-shee-yah)* . . . . restaurant serving sashimi and sushi

sutēki *(soo-tēh-kee)* .... steak
sūtsu *(sōō-tsoo)* .... suit
sūtsukēsu *(sōō-tsoo-kēh-soo)* .... suitcase

T

tabako *(tah-bah-koh)* .... tobacco
tabakoya *(tah-bah-koh-yah)* .... tobacco store
tabemasu *(tah-beh-mahss)* .... eat
tadashii *(tah-dah-shēē)* .... correct
taipu *(tie-poo)* .... type
tairu *(tie-roo)* .... tile
taisetsu *(tye-seh-tsoo)* .... important
taiya *(tie-yah)* .... tire
taizai shimasu *(tye-zye)(shee-mahss)* .... stay, remain
taka sugi *(tah-kah)(soo-gee)* .... too expensive
takai *(tah-kye)* .... tall, high, expensive
takusan *(tah-koo-sahn)* .... a lot, many
takushī *(tah-koo-shēē)* .... taxi
takushī noriba *(tah-koo-shēē)(noh-ree-bah)* ... taxi stand
tamago *(tah-mah-goh)* .... egg
tango *(tahn-goh)* .... word
tanku *(tahn-koo)* .... tank
Tanoshinde kudasai! *(tah-noh-sheen-deh)(koo-dah-sigh)* .... Have fun!
taoru *(tah-oh-roo)* .... towel
tāru *(tāh-roo)* .... tar
tasai *(tah-sigh)* .... multi-colored
tatami *(tah-tah-mee)* .... straw mat
tatoeba *(tah-toh-eh-bah)* .... for example
tebukuro *(teh-boo-koo-roh)* .... glove
tēburu *(tēh-boo-roo)* .... table
tegami *(teh-gah-mee)* .... letter
teikoku *(tay-koh-koo)* .... imperial
tenisu *(teh-nee-soo)* .... tennis
tenisu shūzu *(teh-nee-soo)(shōō-zoo)* ..... tennis shoe
tenki *(ten-kee)* .... weather
tenpura *(ten-poo-rah)* ... deep-fried fish and vegetables
tenrankaijō *(ten-rahn-kye-jōh)* .... exhibition hall
tento *(ten-toh)* .... tent
tēpu *(tēh-poo)* .... tape
terebi *(teh-reh-bee)* .... TV
terehon kādo *(teh-reh-hohn)(kāh-doh)* ... telephone card
tī shatsu *(tēē)(shah-tsoo)* .... T-shirt
to *(toh)* .... and
to *(toh)* .... metropolitan area (address)
tobimasu *(toh-bee-mahss)* .... fly
tōchaku *(tōh-chah-koo)* .... arrival
toire *(toy-reh)* .... lavatory, toilet
tokei *(toh-kay)* .... clock
tokeiya *(toh-kay-yah)* .... watchmaker's shop
tokkuri *(tohk-koo-ree)* .... sake bottles
tomato *(toh-mah-toh)* .... tomato
tomodachi *(toh-moh-dah-chee)* .... friend
ton *(tohn)* .... ton
tonari *(toh-nah-ree)* .... next to
tonneru *(tohn-neh-roo)* .... tunnel
toraberāzu chekku *(toh-rah-beh-rāh-zoo)(chek-koo)* .. .. traveler's check
torakku *(toh-rahk-koo)* .... truck
toranku *(toh-rahn-koo)* .... trunk
tōri *(tōh-ree)* .... street
toriniku *(toh-ree-nee-koo)* .... poultry, chicken
torofī *(toh-roh-fēē)* .... trophy
toshi *(toh-shee)* .... year, city
toshiyori *(toh-shee-yoh-ree)* .... old
toshokan *(toh-shoh-kahn)* .... library
tōsuto *(tōh-soo-toh)* .... toast
tsugi *(tsoo-gee)* .... next, following
tsukatte imasu *(tsoo-kaht-teh)(ee-mahss)* ... occupied
tsukemono *(tsoo-keh-moh-noh)* .... pickled vegetables
tsukemono ni shita *(tsoo-keh-moh-noh)(nee)(shtah)* .. .. pickled
tsuki *(tsoo-kee)* .... month
tsukimasu *(tsoo-kee-mahss)* .... arrive
tsukue *(tsoo-koo-eh)* .... desk
tsukurikata *(tsoo-koo-ree-kah-tah)* .. ways of preparation
tsumetai *(tsoo-meh-tye)* .... cold

U

udon *(oo-dohn)* .... noodles
udonya *(oo-dohn-yah)* .... noodle shop
ue *(oo-eh)* .... over, above, on top
uētā *(oo-ēh-tāh)* .... waiter
uētoresu *(oo-ēh-toh-reh-soo)* .... waitress
unten shimasu *(oon-ten)(shee-mahss)* .... drive
urimasu *(oo-ree-mahss)* .... sell

W

wa *(wah)* .... particle (P) word
wagashi *(wah-gah-shee)* .... cake
wagaya *(wah-gah-yah)* .... our home
wain *(wine)* .... wine
wakai *(wah-kye)* .... young
wakari mashita *(wah-kah-ree)(mahsh-tah)* .... (I) understood
wakarimasu *(wah-kah-ree-mahss)* .... understand
wanpīsu *(wahn-pēē-soo)* .... dress
warui *(wah-roo-ee)* .... bad
watashi *(wah-tah-shee)* I
watashitachi *(wah-tah-shee-tah-chee)* .... we

Y

yaita *(yai-tah)* .... baked, grilled
yakkyoku *(yahk-kyoh-koo)* .... pharmacy
yaoya *(yah-oh-yah)* .... vegetable shop
yasai *(yah-sigh)* .... vegetable
yasui *(yah-soo-ee)* .... inexpensive
yobarete imasu *(yoh-bah-reh-teh)(ee-mahss)* ... be called
yōbi *(yōh-bee)* .... day of the week
yōfuku dansu *(yōh-foo-koo)(dahn-soo)* .. clothes closet
yoku *(yoh-koo)* .... well, thoroughly
yomimasu *(yoh-mee-mahss)* .... read
yon *(yohn)* .... four
yonjū *(yohn-jōō)* .... forty
Yōroppa *(yōh-rohp-pah)* .... Europe
yoru *(yoh-roo)* .... night
yoyaku *(yoh-yah-koo)* .... reservation
yoyaku shimasu *(yoh-yah-koo)(shee-mahss)* .... reserve, book, make reservations
yūbin *(yōō-bean)* .... mail
yūbinkyoku *(yōō-bean-kyoh-koo)* .... post office
yudeta *(yoo-deh-tah)* .... boiled in water
yukata *(yoo-kah-tah)* .... cotton robe
yuki *(yoo-kee)* .... snow
yukisaki *(yoo-kee-sah-kee)* .... destination
yukkuri *(yook-koo-ree)* .... slowly
yunomi jawan *(yoo-noh-mee)(jah-wahn)* ..... tea cups
yūshoku *(yōō-shoh-koo)* .... dinner

Z

zasshi *(zahsh-shee)* .... magazine
zeikin *(zay-keen)* .... tax
zenbu *(zen-boo)* .... everything
zensai *(zen-sigh)* .... appetizer
zero *(zeh-roh)* .... zero
zubon *(zoo-bohn)* .... trousers

25 Beverage and Menu Guides

This beverage guide is intended to explain the variety of beverages available to you in **Nihon.** It is by no means complete. Some of the experimenting has been left up to you, but this should get you started.

OCHA (Japanese tea)

hōjicha	roasted tea
gyokuro	green tea
kōcha	black tea
miruku tī	tea with milk
remon tī	tea with lemon
aisu tī	iced tea
ban cha	brown tea
genmai cha	popped-rice tea

WAIN (wine)

Wain can be purchased by the **gurasu** or by the **bin** (bottle). Most **wain** is imported from France and Italy.

Sake (rice wine) is a traditional **Nihon no** drink, brewed from rice. It is served in porcelain cups and goes well with **Nihon no** food.

atsukan	hot sake
reishu	chilled sake
umeshu	plum wine
shirowain	white wine
akawain	red wine
roze wain	rosé wine
shanpen	champagne

BĪRU (beer)

Bīru is available by the bottle or on draught. Both imported and domestic **bīru** are served in **Nihon. Nihon no bīru** has a distinctive taste, somewhat like English Lager.

ARUKŌRU INRYŌ (alcoholic beverages)

Both imported and domestic **arukōru inryō** are available in **Nihon.**

uisukī	whisky
uokka	vodka
ramu	rum
jin	gin
jin tonikku	gin and tonic
burandē	brandy
konyakku	cognac
sherī	sherry
berumotto	vermouth
aperitifu	aperitif

HOKA NO NOMINOMO (other beverages)

kōhī	coffee (strong)
Amerikan kōhī	American coffee
aisu kōhī	iced coffee
ekkusupuresso kōhī	espresso coffee
furūtsu jūsu	fruit juice
orenji jūsu	orange juice
painappuru jūsu	pineapple juice
gurēpu jūsu	grape juice
tomato jūsu	tomato juice
remonēdo	lemonade

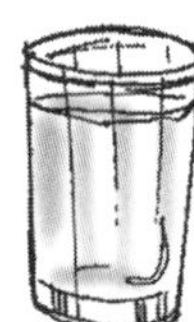

mizu	water
mineraru-uōtā	mineral water
tonikku-uōtā	tonic water
sōda	soda water
miruku	milk
miruku sēki	milk shake
hotto chokorēto	hot chocolate
kokoa	cocoa

Zensai (appetizers)

kani	crab
ika	cuttlefish / squid
ika no shiokara	salted cuttlefish guts
kanisu	vinegared crab
kaisō moriawase	selected seaweed
nishin	herring
kunsei no nishin	smoked herring
maguro	tuna
ebi	shrimp
hamaguri	clams

Shirumono (soup)

akadashi	red-bean paste soup
misoshiru	white-bean paste soup
suimono / sumashijiru	clear soup
oden	vegetable and fish-paste stew

Tamago Ryōri (egg dishes)

tamagoyaki / omuretsu	omelette
okonomiyaki	meat-and-vegetable omelette
tamagodōfu	egg custard
tamago sandoicchi	egg sandwich
medamayaki	sunny-side up
yude tamago	hard-boiled egg
hanju ku tamago	soft-boiled egg
iritamago	scrambled eggs
chawan mushi	cup-steamed egg custard

Sunakku (snacks)

kēki	cake
ita chokorēto	chocolate bar
aisu kurīmu	ice cream
okashi / yōgashi	sweets, pastry
pai	pie
wagashi	Japanese sweets / cake
mitsumame	boiled peas and gelatin
zenzai	sweet red-bean soup with pounded rice cakes
pīnattsu	peanuts
āmondo	almonds

FOLD HERE

Kudamono / Furūtsu (fruit)

nashi	pear
budō	grapes
mikan	tangerine
meron	melon
ringo	apple
remon	lemon
banana	banana
orenji	orange
painappuru	pineapple
suika	watermelon
momo	peach
gurēpu furūtsu	grapefruit
kaki	persimmon
ichigo	strawberries
puramu	plum
furūtsu sarada	fruit salad

Nomimono (beverages)

ocha	green tea
kōcha	black tea
kōhī	coffee
miruku	milk
jūsu	juice
mineraru-uōtā	mineral water
sake	rice wine
bīru	beer
wain	wine

(oh-shoh-koo-jee) *(oh)* *(dōh-zoh)*

Oshokuji o dōzo!

enjoy your meal

FOLD HERE

Menyū

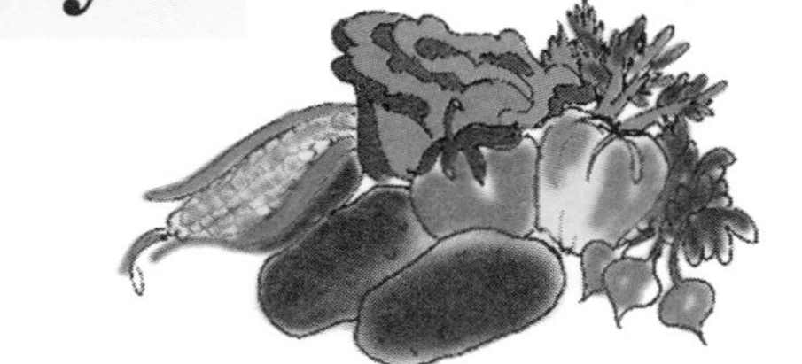

Tsukurikata (ways of preparation)

nama	raw
tsukemono ni shita	pickled
yudeta	boiled in water
mushita	steamed
yaita	baked / grilled
ageta	deep-fried
itameta	stir-fried
nita	boiled in sauce

Ippan (general)

tōfu	bean curd
shōyu	soy sauce
shio	salt
koshō	pepper
satō	sugar
abura	oil
su	vinegar
batā	butter
māgarin	margarine
gohan	rice
udon	noodles
soba	noodles
pan	bread
sandoitchi	sandwich
jamu	jam
jerī	jelly
chīzu	cheese
kechappu	ketchup
karashi	mustard
rāmen	Chinese noodles
nori	seaweed
senbei	rice crackers
takuan	pickled radish
tōgarashi	hot pepper
tsukemono	pickles
wasabi	horseradish

Yasai (vegetables)

tsukemono	pickled vegetables
renkon	lotus root
daikon	white radish
tororoimo	grated yam
shiso	beefsteak plant
moyashi	bean sprouts
kyabetsu	cabbage
hakusai	Chinese cabbage
tōmorokoshi	corn
hōrensō	spinach
ninjin	carrots
kyūri	cucumber
ninniku	garlic
negi	leeks / green onions
tamanegi	onion
retasu	lettuce
tomato	tomato
pīman	green pepper
shiitake	mushrooms
nasu	eggplant
asuparagasu	asparagus

Niku Ryōri (meat dishes)

Gyūniku (beef)

bīfu karē raisu	beef curry over rice
sukiyaki	beef and vegetables in soy sauce broth
shabu shabu	beef and vegetables in seasoned broth
teppan yaki	meat and vegetables cooked on iron grill
hanbāgā	hamburger
bīfusutēki	beefsteak
sāroin	sirloin
hireniku	filet mignon

Butaniku (pork)

tonkatsu	pork cutlet, breaded and fried
sōsēji	sausage
hamu	ham
buta no kakuni	stewed, cubed pork
hotto doggu	hot dog

FOLD HERE

Toriniku (chicken)

yakitori	grilled chicken on skewers
rōsuto chikin	roast chicken
tori no karaage	fried chicken

Sakana ryōri (fish and seafood dishes)

sashimi	sliced raw fish
maguro	tuna
katsuo	bonito
aji	horse mackerel
saba	mackerel
tako	octopus
awabi	abalone
ebi	shrimp
hirame	flat fish
tai	sea bream
ikura	salmon roe
hotategai / kaibashira	scallops
kani	crab
tarako	cod roe
kazunoko	herring roe
anago	conger eel
ika	cuttlefish / squid
kisu	smelt
uni	raw sea urchin
aoyagi	round clam
hamachi	young yellowtail
mirugai	surf clam
ise ebi	lobster
unagi	eel
iwashi	sardine
kaki	oyster
kamasu	pike
karei	turbot
sake	salmon
tara	cod
nishin	herring
masu	trout
koi no arai	sliced raw carp
fugusashi	sliced globefish
ebi furai	fried shrimp
wakasagi no furai	fried smelt
kabayaki	eel split and broiled
mushi awabi	steamed abalone
saba no misoni	stewed mackerel with soybean paste

FOLD HERE

yakizakana	broiled fish
sushi	vinegared fish and rice
nigirizushi	rice ball with seafood
chirashizushi	vinegared rice with egg and seafood topping
makizushi	egg and vegetables rolled in vinegared rice and seaweed
inarizushi	rice wrapped in bean curd
tekka maki	tuna rolled in vinegared rice and seaweed
kappa maki	cucumber wrapped in seaweed and rice
takuan maki	pickled white radish wrapped in seaweed and rice
norimaki	egg and vegetables rolled in vinegared rice and seaweed
tenpura	deep-fried prawns and vegetables

Udon / Soba (noodles)

tenpura udon	noodles with deep-fried prawns and vegetables
kitsune udon	noodles with fried bean curd
nabeyaki udon	noodles with fish cakes and vegetables
tsukimi udon	noodles with raw egg
tamago toji udon	noodles with egg
tanuki udon	noodles with **tenpura** batter crusts
yakisoba	sauced noodles tossed with cabbage and other vegetables
kake soba	noodles served with broth
tororo soba	noodles with yam paste
supagettī	spaghetti

Gohan (rice)

tendon	shrimp and vegetable **tenpura** over rice
unadon	eel over rice
katsudon	pork cutlet over rice
oyakodon	chicken and egg over rice
tamagodon	egg over rice
omu raisu	rice omelette
pirafu	rice pilaf
kome	uncooked rice

(wah-tah-shee)
watashi

(wah-tah-shee-tah-chee)
watashitachi

(kah-reh)
kare

(ah-nah-tah)
anata

(kah-noh-joh)
kanojo

(kah-reh-rah)
karera

(hah-nah-shee-mahss)
hanashimasu

(soon-deh) (ee-mahss)
sunde imasu

(kye-mahss)
kaimasu

(tye-zye) (shee-mahss)
taizai shimasu

(chōō-mohn) (shee-mahss)
chūmon shimasu

(yoh-bah-reh-teh) (ee-mahss)
yobarete imasu

we	I
you	he
they	she
live	speak
stay	buy
be called	order

(kee-mahss) **kimasu**	*(ee-kee-mahss)* **ikimasu**
(nah-rye-mahss) **naraimasu**	*(moht-teh) (ee-mahss)* **motte imasu**
(hoh-shēē) (dess) **hoshii desu**	*(ee-ree-mahss)* **irimasu**
(tah-beh-mahss) **tabemasu**	*(noh-mee-mahss)* **nomimasu**
(ēē-mahss) **iimasu**	*(oo-ree-mahss)* **urimasu**
(wah-kah-ree-mahss) **wakarimasu**	*(koo-ree-kah-eh-shee-mahss)* **kurikaeshimasu**

go

come

have

learn

need

would like

drink

eat

sell

say

repeat

understand

(mah-chee-mahss)
machimasu

(mee-mahss)
mimasu

(oh-koo-ree-mahss)
okurimasu

(neh-mahss)
nemasu

(shee-mahss)
shimasu

(hah-rye-mahss)
haraimasu

(mee-seh-mahss)
misemasu

(kah-kee-mahss)
kakimasu

(yoh-mee-mahss)
yomimasu

(dess)
desu

(ee-mahss)
imasu

(sheet-teh) (ee-mahss)
shitte imasu

see

wait for

sleep

send

pay

do

write

show

is, are, am

read

know

is, are
(with people and animals)

(deh-mahss)
demasu

(toh-bee-mahss)
tobimasu

(ryoh-kōh) (shee-mahss)
ryokō shimasu

(noh-ree-mahss)
norimasu

(tsoo-kee-mahss)
tsukimasu

(noh-ree-kah-eh-mahss)
norikaemasu

(nee-zoo-koo-ree) (shee-mahss)
nizukuri shimasu

(ah-rye-mahss)
araimasu

(ah-ree-mahss)
arimasu

(nah-koo-shee-mahss)
nakushimasu

(oon-ten) (shee-mahss)
unten shimasu

(yoh-yah-koo) (shee-mahss)
yoyaku shimasu

fly	leave
ride	travel
transfer (vehicles)	arrive
wash	pack
lose	is, are (with things)
reserve / book	drive

(kyōh) **kyō**	*(oh-gen-kee) (dess) (kah)* **Ogenki desu ka?**
(kee-nōh) **kinō**	*(koo-dah-sigh)* **kudasai**
(ahsh-tah) **ashita**	*(ah-ree-gah-tōh) (goh-zye-mahss)* **arigatō gozaimasu**
(sah-yōh-nah-rah) **sayōnara**	*(soo-mee-mah-sen)* **sumimasen**
(foo-roo-ee) (ah-tah-rah-shē̄) **furui - atarashii**	*(ee-koo-rah) (dess) (kah)* **Ikura desu ka?**
(ōh-kē̄) (chē̄-sigh) **ōkii - chiisai**	*(kye-ten) (hay-ten)* **kaiten - heiten**

How are you?

today

please

yesterday

thank you

tomorrow

excuse me

good-bye

How much does this cost?

old - new

open - closed

big - small

(ken-kōh) *(byōh-kee)* **kenkō - byōki**	*(ēē)* *(wah-roo-ee)* **ii - warui**
(ah-tsoo-ee) *(tsoo-meh-tye)* **atsui - tsumetai**	*(mee-jee-kye)* *(nah-guy)* **mijikai - nagai**
(tah-kye) *(hee-koo-ee)* **takai - hikui**	*(oo-eh)* *(shtah)* **ue - shita**
(hee-dah-ree) *(mee-gee)* **hidari - migi**	*(oh-soy)* *(hah-yai)* **osoi - hayai**
(toh-shee-yoh-ree) *(wah-kye)* **toshiyori - wakai**	*(tah-kye)* *(yah-soo-ee)* **takai - yasui**
(been-bōh) *(kah-neh-moh-chee)* **binbō - kanemochi**	*(tah-koo-sahn)* *(soo-koh-shee)* **takusan - sukoshi**

good - bad	healthy - sick
short - long	hot - cold
above - below	high - low
slow - fast	left - right
expensive- inexpensive	old - young
a lot - a little	poor - rich

Now that you've finished...

You've done it!

You've completed all the Steps, stuck your labels, flashed your cards and cut out your menu guide. Do you realize how far you've come and how much you've learned? You've accomplished what it could take years to achieve in a traditional language class.

You can now confidently

- ask questions,
- understand directions,
- make reservations,
- order food and
- shop anywhere.

And you can do it all in a foreign language! You can now go anywhere — from a large cosmopolitan restaurant to a small, out-of-the-way village where no one speaks English. Your experiences will be much more enjoyable and worry-free now that you speak the language and know something of the culture.

Yes, learning a foreign language can be fun. And no, not everyone abroad speaks English.

Kristine Kershul

* What about shipping costs?

STANDARD DELIVERY per address

If your items total	please add
up to $ 20.00	$5.00
$20.01 - $ 40.00	$6.00
$40.01 - $ 60.00	$7.00
$60.01 - $ 80.00	$8.00
$80.01 - $ 100.00	$9.00

If over $100, please call for charges.

For shipping outside the U.S., please call, fax or e-mail us at info@bbks.com for the best-possible shipping rates.

Chūmonsho

order form

10 minutes a day® Series	QTY.	PRICE	TOTAL
CHINESE *in 10 minutes a day®*		$17.95	
FRENCH *in 10 minutes a day®*		$17.95	
GERMAN *in 10 minutes a day®*		$17.95	
HEBREW *in 10 minutes a day®*		$17.95	
INGLÉS *en 10 minutos al día®*		$17.95	
ITALIAN *in 10 minutes a day®*		$17.95	
JAPANESE *in 10 minutes a day®*		$17.95	
NORWEGIAN *in 10 minutes a day®*		$17.95	
PORTUGUESE *in 10 minutes a day®*		$17.95	
RUSSIAN *in 10 minutes a day®*		$19.95	
SPANISH *in 10 minutes a day®*		$17.95	

Language Map™ Series	QTY.	PRICE	TOTAL
CHINESE *a language map™*		$7.95	
FRENCH *a language map™*		$7.95	
GERMAN *a language map™*		$7.95	
GREEK *a language map™*		$7.95	
HAWAIIAN *a language map™*		$7.95	
HEBREW *a language map™*		$7.95	
INGLÉS *un mapa del lenguaje™*		$7.95	
ITALIAN *a language map™*		$7.95	
JAPANESE *a language map™*		$7.95	
NORWEGIAN *a language map™*		$7.95	
POLISH *a language map™*		$7.95	
PORTUGUESE *a language map™*		$7.95	
RUSSIAN *a language map™*		$7.95	
SPANISH *a language map™*		$7.95	
VIETNAMESE *a language map™*		$7.95	

† For delivery to individuals in Washington State, you must add 8.8% sales tax on the item total and the shipping costs combined. If your order is being delivered outside Washington State, you do not need to add sales tax.

Item Total	
* Shipping	+
Total	
† Sales Tax	+
ORDER TOTAL	

Name ______________________________

Address ______________________________

____

City ____________ State ______ Zip ________

Day Phone (________)______________________

❑ My check or money order for $______________ is enclosed.

Please make checks and money orders payable to Bilingual Books, Inc.

❑ Bill my credit card ❑ VISA ❑ MC ❑ AMEX

No. ______________________ Exp. date ____/____

Signature ______________________________

Send us this order form with your check, money order or credit card details. If paying by credit card, you may fax your order to **(206) 284-3660** or call us toll-free at **(800) 488-5068**. All prices are in US dollars and are subject to change without notice.

Bilingual Books, Inc. • 1719 West Nickerson Street
Seattle, WA 98119 USA

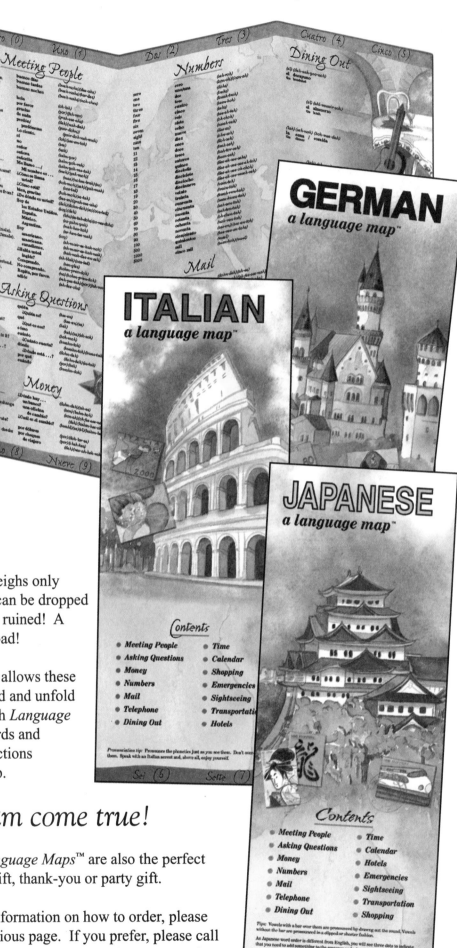

Language Maps™

by Kristine K. Kershul

Finally a phrasebook which weighs only ounces, doesn't fall apart and can be dropped in a mud puddle without being ruined! A must for anyone traveling abroad!

A patented lamination process allows these handy *Language Maps*™ to fold and unfold in a snap without tearing. Each *Language Map*™ contains over 1,000 words and phrases split into important sections covering the basics for any trip.

A traveler's dream come true!

These attractive, flip-style *Language Maps*™ are also the perfect stocking stuffer, bon voyage gift, thank-you or party gift.

For languages available and information on how to order, please see our order form on the previous page. If you prefer, please call us at (206) 284-4211 or toll free at (800) 488-5068. You may also fax us at (206) 284-3660. E-mail: info@bbks.com